An Introduction to

VAX
Assembly Language
Programming

An Introduction to

VAX
Assembly Language
Programming

Nonna Kliss Lehmkuhl
Northeastern University

West Publishing Company
St. Paul   New York   Los Angeles   San Francisco

Copyeditor: Hazel Blumberg-McKee
Composition and Artwork: Carlisle Graphics
Cover Design: Theresa Jensen
Cover Research: Kirk Gilmore
Cover image courtesy of the Smithsonian Astrophysical Observatory,
created by Rudolph Schild.

About the cover: The cover is an "Elliptical Galaxy Brightness Profile" provided by the Smithsonian Astrophysical Observatory. To emphasize how strongly the brightness is concentrated in the center of this relatively formless galaxy, a plot of the brightness (white line) has been measured along the line cutting through the center of the galaxy (yellow line).

This image was stored on a VAX 11/750 computer and then displayed and manipulated on a high resolution color monitor. Attached to the computer is an electronic drawing board that allows a scientist to write directly on the screen . . . a feature particularly useful for drawing intensity curves as illustrated on this slide.

COPYRIGHT © 1987 By WEST PUBLISHING COMPANY
50 W. Kellogg Boulevard
P.O. Box 64526
St. Paul, MN 55164-1003

Library of Congress Cataloging-in-Publication Data

Lehmkuhl, Nonna Kliss.
    An introduction to Vax assembly language programming.

    Includes index.
    1. VAX-11 (Computer)—Programming. 2. Assembler
language (Computer program language) I. Title.
QA76.8.V37L44 1987   005.2'45   86-24708
ISBN 0-314-93194-5

To my children
Kathryn, Natalie, Robert, and Elizabeth Kliss

Contents

Preface

This textbook is intended to be used as the first book in an assembly language course for computer science or computer engineering curricula taught on the VAX. It is suitable for a one-semester, two-semester, or graduate level course and generally follows the guidelines outlined in the ACM Curriculum '78. It begins with an elementary overview of the MACRO language and progresses through a detailed discussion of the various fundamental aspects. Several specialized and advanced topics concerning assembly language are also presented.

Flexibility is built into the text as much as possible. It will satisfy an assembly language requirement with a prerequisite of at least one higher level language. It is also intended for those students who need to learn assembly language as a prerequisite for more advanced courses such as compiler design and computer architecture.

In each chapter, the student is led step by step, from the understanding of the primitive actions performed by a computer, to the ability to write nontrivial assembly language programs. The top-down design and modular construction of programs, both of which indicate good programming techniques, are emphasized throughout the textbook. Every effort is made to supply the student with an adequate opportunity to practice the writing and running of various types of assembly language programs. A small subset of integer instructions is presented in Chapter 3, along with the symbolic addressing mode, to allow the student to gain hands-on experience with some simple assembly language programming as quickly as possible. This experience is designed to stimulate the student's interest in and understanding of this complicated yet powerful language. Additionally, the end of each chapter contains a set of exercises and problems from a variety of disciplines, which were developed to aid the student.

The exercises provide drill and testing practice while the problems provide actual opportunity to write programs. The abundance of example programs, which have been machine-tested and are included directly from computer printouts, provide added demonstration for student comprehension.

The modular feature of this text, the Core and Enrichment sections, allows for the selection of topics according to the instructor's needs. Core topics have been carefully organized and separated from the more advanced topics so that instructors can easily select the amount of depth and breadth they wish to cover. For example, a one-semester course could cover all of Chapters 1, 2, 3, 5, and part 1 of Chapters 4, 6, 7, 8. A two-semester or graduate-level course should also include the second half of Chapters 4, 6, 7, 8.

Chapters 1 and 2 contain a portion of the essentials needed for learning assembly language, as well as the basis for the more advanced topics in latter chapters.

Chapter 3 introduces hands-on computer activitiy by presenting a subset of the integer instruction set, basic branch instructions, and input/output operations through the use of FORTRAN or Pascal procedures. These input/output procedures are not part of the main body of the text. They are contained in Appendix C. Therefore, if an instructor wishes to use another method to perform the input/output operations, it may be done without disturbing the contents of the text. In addition, debugging is introduced through the use of the symbolic debugger. A more comprehensive explanation of the debugger, including the screen mode and keypad, is found in Appendix A.

Chapter 4 describes various register addressing techniques. Since addressing can be a difficult topic, several detailed illustrations on each addressing mode are included. Each example presents what happens when the addressing mode is used in an instruction.

Chapter 5 contains various topics dealing with assembly language and the processes performed by the assembler during assembly. The topics covered in this chapter can be covered in any order, and may be referenced in either Chapter 3 or delayed until Chapter 6.

Chapter 6 is a long and detailed chapter and must be presented after Chapter 4 because of the addressing techniques used. The procedures contained in this chapter are applied to the programs of latter chapters.

Chapter 7 is an extension of Chapter 3. The topics presented here may either be covered after the completion of Chapter 3 or delayed until Chapter 7.

Chapter 8 describes the construction and expansion of macros in detail. This information may be used to teach the functionality of a macro facility. The material in this chapter was previously used in a Systems course as the basis for a project on the development of an assembly macro facility.

Chapter 9 contains a detailed presentation of an assembly language input and output facility. Also, system I/O macro and the concept that input data is converted from ASCII to binary code and that output data is converted from binary code to ASCII are covered.

Chapter 10 presents the entire set of character instructions. The information contained here may be used as a basis to develop a project that simulates an editor.

Chapters 11 through 13 are highly specialized. Each deals with a specific data type. Chapter 11 introduces instructions which manipulate real numbers. Chapter 12 covers the decimal instruction set that is the basis of the Cobol language. Finally, Chapter 13 discusses bit string and logical manipulation which are mostly used in system programming.

Features

The back matter has been carefully designed to provide the most complete reference possible. The extensive debugger appendixes include the latest release including screen mode and keypad mode.

An I/O appendix which explains procedures allows the instructor the flexibility to adapt the material to suit personal teaching tastes.

A reference card, which can be removed, is bound into each text giving students a quick reference to the main features and instructions of VAX assembly language. The student can take the card into a lab situation and avoid carrying the entire text.

Supplements

An instructor's manual which includes a test bank and answers to exercises is also available.

Special Acknowledgments

Special thanks are in order for several professors who provided me with helpful reviews of the manuscript as it was being developed:

Paul Jackowitz, University of Scranton
Ryan Popken, University of Nebraska
Howard Evans, University of New Orleans
Joan Calvert, Central Connecticut State
Paul Gormley, Villanova University
Barbara Kersham, Hollins College
Conrad Russo, Lynchberg College
Gary Greenfield, University of Richmond
Bernard Lovell, University of Connecticut
Jack Kester, University of Dayton
Gerald Gordon, DePaul University
Bruce Wampler, University of New Mexico
James McKim, University of Hartford
Wayne Cardoza, Digital

To my youngest daughter Elizabeth, a Bio-medical Engineering student and my student reader, I express deep gratitude for her patience and understanding throughout the writing of this text. Her recommendations and/or critiques were extremely helpful in arriving at the final version. I would also like to thank my husband, Dr. Carlton B. Lehmkuhl, for without his and my daughter's support I would not have been able to write this text.

N.K.L.

An Introduction to

VAX

Assembly Language
Programming

CHAPTER

Computer Organization

Computers have many uses. Bank tellers use computers to deposit and withdraw money; laboratory technicians use them to interpret experimental results, and military personnel use computers to track satellites. Computers control activities as diverse as factory operations and the timing of traffic lights. These are but a few of the many computer applications.

What is a computer? It is an electronic machine that transforms incoming data (input) into outgoing data (output) by following a set of instructions (a *stored program*) given to it ahead of time. Computers, totally electronic machines, have no moving parts; therefore, any movement or manipulation of *data* is carried out by electronic signals moving at tremendous speeds.

The ability to follow a set of *instructions* (program) makes computers powerful. If the program is changed, the computer will change what it is doing. Thus computers can perform an unlimited number of jobs, since there is no limit to the number of programs that can be written. Computers have no "intelligence"; therefore, they have no ability to think for themselves. Their greatness lies in the following:

1. Repetitive operations. Computers can perform similar operations thousands of times without becoming bored, tired, or careless.
2. Speed. Computers process data at high speeds. Modern computers can solve certain classes of problems millions of times faster than a skilled mathematician.
3. Flexibility. Computers can be programmed to carry out many types of jobs.

3

   4. Accuracy. Computers can be programmed to calculate answers with an accuracy level that the programmer specifies.

Each computer must include a set of instructions that, when used as a group, will allow the user to formulate any conceivable data-processing task. Computers must therefore include a sufficient number of instructions in each of the following categories:

   1. Instructions for moving data to and from memory.
   2. *Arithmetic* and *logic* instructions.
   3. Instructions for checking *status information*, which enables the computer to provide decision-making capabilities.
   4. Input and output instructions.

Instructions for moving data to and from memory are essential because most information in a computer is stored in memory; all computations, however, are done in the part of the computer called *processor registers*. Therefore the computer must have the capability of moving data between these two. Arithmetic and logic instructions provide computational-processing capabilities.

Instructions that check status information enable the computer to carry out its decision-making capabilities. For example, in a program that calculates a company's payroll, it may be necessary to determine an employee's overtime wages when the employee works more than 40 hours a week. Because of this the total number of hours worked per week must be compared to the value of 40. The result from this comparison is reflected in the status information. The status information is checked by a *branch instruction* after which it directs the computer where to continue program execution. Input and output instructions make communication between the computer and the user possible. Programs and data must be placed in memory, and results of computations must be displayed in readable form. Finally, there must be an instruction that will halt further computer operations when necessary. The following sections describe (1) general computer organization and (2) VAX computer organization.

1.1   *General Computer Architecture*

Most general-purpose computers have the same basic architecture consisting of high-speed *primary memory, auxiliary memory,* and the *central processing unit* (CPU). Some of the devices found in the CPU are the *arithmetic and logical unit* (ALU), *control unit* (CU), *general-purpose register, program counter* (PC), *instruction register* (IR), *memory address register* (MAR), *memory buffer register* (MBR), and *program status register* (PSR). In addition, each computer system must have some *input* and *output devices,* which are typically called the I/O system. One or more *buses* move data between these devices. Although computers contain other de-

Figure 1.1

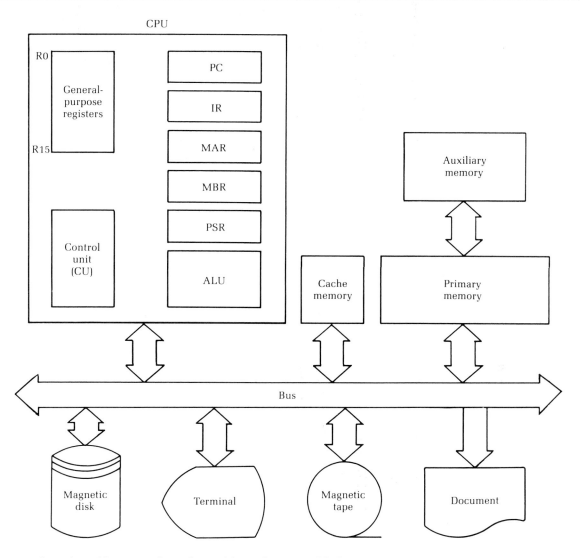

vices, those listed here are directly visible to the assembly language programmer and are part of user architecture. Figure 1.1 illustrates this basic computer's organization.

Primary Memory   *1.2*

Primary memory (also called *main memory*) is made up of *two-state components*. A two-state component is a constituent that can represent two measurable, distinct states. For example, assume that a light bulb is a two-state device. Therefore, the light bulb represents one state when it is on, and another state when it is off.

Figure 1.2

Cell size (8 Bits)

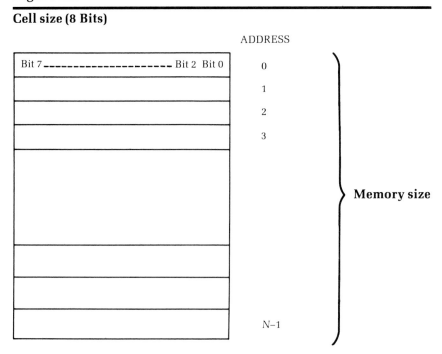

Of course, primary memory is not made up of light bulbs, but rather of semiconductor circuits capable of representing two states. This type of primary memory is very fast; the time required to either place information into memory or obtain information from memory is only a fraction of microseconds (one-millionth of a second or one μs).

Because primary memory is made up of two-state components, the *binary numbering system* is used to represent its contents. The binary numbering system consists of two digit symbols, 0 and 1. The 0 is used to represent one state and the 1 is used to represent the other.

One of the two-state components is called a *bit*. Bits make up primary memory; in particular, the primary memory is grouped into eight bits. Each group of eight bits is called a *byte*.

Primary memory may be viewed as a linear array of bytes. Each byte can be referenced or addressed, and can represent one alphanumeric character or a small numeric value. Figure 1.2 illustrates primary memory as a linear array. Note that there are 8 bits in each memory cell and that there are N number of memory cells. The numbering of bits in each memory cell begins with 0 and continues through to seven. The following example illustrates the numbering of a cell.

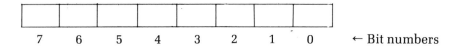

This same process applies to the numbering of memory cells. For example, N memory cells, are numbered from 0 to N-1.

All memories share two organizational features: (1) Each memory cell is the same size, and (2) each has associated with it a numeric address through which it can be uniquely referenced. Thus a memory cell has two characteristics:

1. An *address*, indicating the cell's relative position in reference to some known position.
2. The *contents*, representing a numeric value or an alphanumeric character contained (stored) in a particular memory cell. These contents may be changed or used in an operation.

Figure 1.3 illustrates the use of addresses to reference memory cells.

Figure 1.3

Memory represented by array M	Address of each cell equals the index of the cell	To obtain contents
M_0	0	M_0
M_1	1	M_1
M_2	2	M_2
M_i	i	M_i
M_{N-1}	$N-1$	M_{N-1}

In Figure 1.3 the memory is presented as a linear array M of size N. Each element in this array represents one memory cell. The index is used to address a memory cell in array M.

By changing the index value, any memory cell can be reached. In this way, new data can be placed into the memory cell, or existing data can be copied. When using memory, the address of a memory cell and the data found in the cell must be considered.

Computer designers choose memory cell size according to the applications for which the computer is intended. In many computers, each memory cell is known as a *word*. Word sizes typically range from 8 bits on *microprocessors* to 64 bits on large computers. When a memory cell contains 8 bits, the computer is referred to as a *byte machine*. When a memory cell contains a multiple of bytes, the computer is referred to as a *word machine*.

The key difference between byte and word machines is the size of the smallest addressable memory cell. In a byte machine, this cell contains one byte; that is, a cell of memory capable of representing a small numeric value or alphanumeric character. In a word machine, the smallest addressable memory cell is one word. Words can represent a large numeric value or several alphanumeric characters and often can be subdivided into a fixed number of bytes, where each byte contains either a character or a small numeric value. Even though words may have been subdivided, the data in them are referenced as whole collections of characters, rather than as individual characters.

Computers designed for business applications use a great deal of alphanumeric, rather than numeric, data. These computers are often *byte addressable*. In contrast, *word-addressable* computers are generally used for scientific calculations that process numeric data and require precise numerical results.

1.3   *Auxiliary Memory*

Lower-cost storage devices are economical backups for storing portions of a program and data that the CPU is not currently using. Devices that provide backup storage are called auxiliary memory. Auxiliary memory does not communicate directly with the CPU. Instead, information is moved to primary memory, from which the CPU obtains necessary instructions and data. Only programs and data that the processor currently uses reside in primary memory. All other information is stored in auxiliary memory and is then transferred to primary memory on demand. The most common auxiliary memory devices are *magnetic disks*, *magnetic drums*, and *magnetic tapes*.

1.4   *Virtual Memory*

In a computer memory hierarchy, programs and data are first stored in auxiliary memory. Portions of a program or data are brought into primary memory as they are needed for program execution. The idea of executing a program while only a portion of the program resides in the primary memory is referred to as *virtual memory*. Virtual memory thus permits the user to construct a program with memory space equal to the combined sizes of the auxiliary and primary memory.

The *virtual memory system* implements and manages virtual memory. A virtual memory system is made up of hardware and software. When a program is submitted for execution, the virtual system partitions the program into equal parts (*pages*). The virtual memory system also moves the pages between the primary and auxiliary memories. For example, consider a computer with 8K of memory (K = 1,024 cells) and 64K of auxiliary memory. Assume that the size of each page is 1K. Figure 1.4 illustrates the moving of pages between primary and auxiliary memory.

Figure 1.4

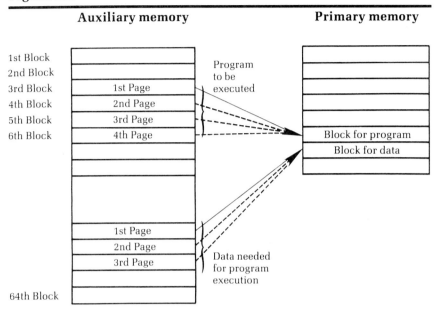

At the beginning of program execution, the first page of the program is placed into the first available primary memory *block*. A block of memory is a group of contiguous memory cells that is equal to the size of a page. As the program is executed and the next page of the program is needed, the virtual system moves the next page from the auxiliary memory to the same block of the primary memory. This process is also used for data that the program requires.

As the program is being executed, each address that the CPU references undergoes address mapping. This mapping transforms a *virtual address* into a *physical address*. The virtual address is only meaningful within the page's domain, whereas the physical address is the memory cell's actual address.

An address that a programmer uses represents a virtual address. The set of all virtual addresses is referred to as the *address space*. An address in primary memory is called a *location* or physical address. The set of such locations is called the *memory space*. Thus, the address space is the set of addresses that programs generate as they reference instructions and data. The memory space is the actual primary memory locations directly addressable for processing. In most computers, the address and memory spaces are identical. The address space may be larger than the memory space in computers with virtual memory.

1.5 *Cache Memory*

Locality of references means that references to memory at any given time interval tend to be confined within a few localized memory cells. Locality of reference occurs because a typical computer program flows sequentially from top to bottom, encountering frequent program loops and procedure calls. When a program loop is executed, the CPU repeatedly refers to the set of instructions that constitute the loop. Every time a procedure is called, its set of instructions must be fetched from memory. Thus, loops and procedures localize references to memory. To a lesser degree, reference to data stored in primary memory also tends to be localized.

All of these references cause locality of reference. Over a short time interval, a typical program generates addresses that repeatedly refer to a few localized memory cells. The program accesses the remainder of memory relatively infrequently. Therefore, it is economically advantageous to have another memory from which the required instructions and data can be obtained in less time than it takes to obtain them from primary memory.

If the active portions of the program and data are placed in a fast memory, the average memory access time can be reduced, thereby reducing the program's total execution time. Such memory is referred to as *cache memory*, (pronounced "cash," from the French verb *cacher* meaning "to hide"). Cache memory is placed between the CPU and the primary memory. Cache memory's access time is less than the primary memory access time by a factor of five to ten. Cache memory is the fastest memory device in the memory hierarchy and approaches the speed of CPU devices.

The fundamental idea of cache organization is to keep the most frequently accessed instructions and data in the fast cache memory. Although the cache is a small fraction of primary memory's size, many memory requests are to the fast cache memory because of locality of reference.

The cache's basic operation is as follows: When the CPU needs to access memory, it examines the cache. If the CPU finds the necessary instructions or data in the cache, the instructions or data are moved to the necessary device. However, if they are not found, primary memory will be accessed. A block of instructions or data containing the requested information is then moved to the cache memory. This process ensures that future references to memory will find the required information in the fast cache memory.

Whereas a virtual memory system moves data between auxiliary memory and primary memory, cache organization transfers data between primary memory and the CPU. Thus, each memory type involves a different level in the memory hierarchy system.

Although virtual memory and cache memory are similar in principle, they have different purposes. The cache holds those parts of the program and data that are most heavily used, while the auxiliary memory holds those parts that the CPU is not presently using. Moreover, the CPU has direct access to both cache and primary memory but not to auxiliary memory.

Arithmetic and Logical Unit (ALU)   *1.6*

The arithmetic and logical unit (ALU) consists of electronic circuits, which receive and operate on the data. The ALU performs the basic arithmetic operations of addition, subtraction, shift operation as well as logical operations such as AND, OR, and COMPLEMENT.

The ALU usually includes a *binary adder* and *binary shifter*. The adder accepts two binary numbers and produces a binary sum. The shifter moves bits to the left or right. The shifter, together with the adder, can perform multiplication. Subtraction is performed by complimentary addition. Repeated subtraction and shift can perform division. *Complementary addition* performs subtraction. These operations are called binary arithmetic and are covered in Chapter 2.

The adder and the shifter are not the only devices found in the ALU. Larger computers usually include hardware devices, such as hardware multipliers, to increase system performance. Some very high-performance computers include dedicated devices, which perform specific mathematical functions such as division or square roots.

General-Purpose Registers   *1.7*

In the CPU are a number of general-purpose registers that provide local, high-speed storage for the processors. Registers are discrete storage cells of fixed length; they are conceptually similar to, but physically separate from, primary memory. Registers receive, hold, and transfer data, but are typically used to hold data temporarily. For example, these registers are used to store intermediate results in a series of calculations. Registers are also used to store addresses. Some computers have different sets of registers that are used only in specific operations. For example, these computers may have registers that contain array addresses or hold floating-point numbers. Other computers have general-purpose registers that can be used for all operations. There are two advantages to using registers: Data contained in a register can be obtained more rapidly, and using a register in an instruction does not require as much memory space as does a memory address.

1.8   *Program Counter (PC)*

The program counter (PC) is a special register that holds the address of the next instruction to be executed. The PC is updated as the instruction is fetched from memory and placed in a special register in the CPU. The PC is increased by a number equal to the *length of the instruction*. The length of an instruction is equal to the number of bytes necessary to store it in memory.

Because memory is a linear array, the PC always contains the address of the next sequential instruction to be executed. The exception occurs when the current instruction is a transfer of control (branch) instruction. In this case, the CPU recognizes that the instruction to be executed is not the next sequential instruction. Therefore, the PC is updated, so that it will contain the address of the next instruction to be executed.

1.9   *Program Status Register (PSR)*

In the CPU are one or more program status registers (PSRs). These registers store status information, which describe the current state of the program in execution. One type of status information is the *condition code*, which provides information about the result obtained from instruction execution. Almost every instruction execution records some information in the condition code. On the basis of this information, the programmer decides which actions to take next. Condition codes provide the following information:

1. The result is zero.
2. The result is negative.
3. The result is positive.
4. The result is out-of-range (*overflow*).
5. The arithmetic operations using "carry-out-of" or "borrow-into."

The carry condition occurs when the sum of two single digits results in a two-digit rather than a one-digit answer. For example, representing the sum of 5 and 7 requires two digits. The borrow condition occurs in subtraction when a subtrahend (lower digit) is larger than a minuend (upper digit), and a positive result is desired.

1.10   *Control Unit (CU)*

The control unit (CU) manages the flow of data between all other devices. It also "understands" the operations represented by program instructions. Therefore, the CU sends signals to the devices that perform these operations.

The CU manages the flow of instructions and data to and from memory. The flow of both the instructions and data to memory is called the *store cycle*, and the flow of both from memory to various devices is called the *fetch cycle* or *read cycle*. Before program execution can begin, the PC must receive the memory address of the first instruction to be executed. The CU then begins program execution, which consists of *instruction execution cycles*. An instruction execution cycle begins with the read cycle of an instruction, one byte at a time. The cycle ends when a result is obtained. As the instruction is moved (copied) from primary memory, the CU interprets the instruction. During this interpretation, the CU sends the appropriate signals to the various devices necessary for processing the instruction. For example, if an arithmetic instruction is being interpreted, the CU sends signals to the ALU, indicating which arithmetic operation is to be carried out. In addition, the CU sends the necessary data to be used in the calculation to the ALU. Upon completion of the operation, the CU directs the answer from the ALU into the appropriate memory cell or register.

Instruction Execution Cycle   *1.11*

The instruction execution cycle is the amount of time the CU requires to obtain the address of an instruction and carry out the operation designated by the instruction. Figure 1.5 illustrates an instruction execution cycle.

An instruction execution cycle can be summarized as follows:

1. Place the address of the instruction to be executed into the memory address register (MAR).
2. Place the instruction to be executed into the memory buffer register (MBR).
3. Update the program counter (PC). (The PC contains the address of the next instruction to be executed.)
4. Move the contents (current instruction) of the MBR into the instruction register (IR).
5. Decode the instruction.
6. Check the instruction for operands.[1]
7. If the instruction contains operands, follow steps 7a through 7d. If the instruction does not contain operands, go to step 8.
   a. Move the address of the operand into the MAR.
   b. Move the data addressed by the operand into the MBR.

---

[1]The operand represents the data or the address of the data needed for the operation.

Figure 1.5

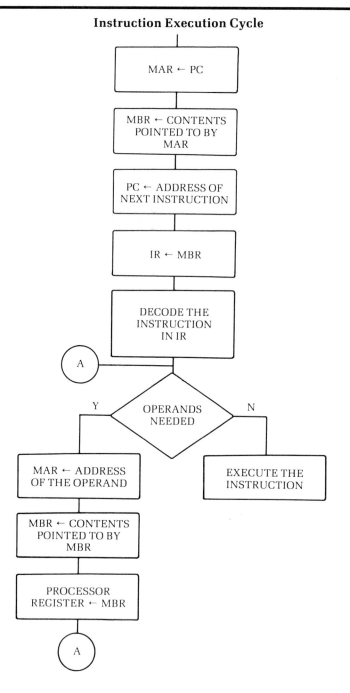

Instruction Execution Cycle

    c. Direct the contents of the MBR to an appropriate device
      (for example, an ALU or I/O device).
    d. Go to step 6.
8. Perform the designated operation.

Process

1.12

The *process* is the basic concept in computer organization. A process is a program in execution that changes the status of the computer system: For example, the position of the pen on a plotter as a flowchart is being drawn or to regulate a space shuttle's trajectory.

At any given time, a process is in a particular *state*. The state of a process describes the position at which the process is in its computation. It also describes all the necessary information needed to stop and then to restart the process. The process state must consist of at least the following information:

1. Program
2. Instruction to be executed next
3. Values of all the program's variables and constants
4. Status of all devices being used

As a process continues, its state changes. For example, the next instruction to be executed is not the same one that was previously executed, some variables are assigned new values, or different hardware devices are requested to perform an operation. In order to keep track of what constitutes a state, all the changeable parts of a state are grouped into a *state table*. A process is thought of as consisting of two parts: a program that does not change and a state table that keeps on changing. The instructions that make up a program change the state table. For an example, consider the Pascal program in Figure 1.6.

Figure 1.6

```
PROGRAM FIG16;
VAR I, SUM: INTEGER;
BEGIN
    I := 3;                (* INST 1 *)
    SUM := 0;              (* INST 2 *)
    SUM := SUM + I;        (* INST 3 *)
    SUM := SUM * I;        (* INST 4 *)
    SUM := SUM * SUM;      (* INST 5 *)
END.
```

This program's state table during its execution contains three entries: the variables I, SUM and the instruction to be executed next. Figure 1.7 illustrates the changes that occur in the state table as the process progresses from the beginning of the program execution to its completion.

Figure 1.7

Initial state	2nd state	3rd state	4th state	5th state	Final state
I = ?	I = 3	I = 3	I = 3	I = 3	I = 3
SUM = ?	SUM = ?	SUM = 0	SUM = 3	SUM = 9	SUM = 81
INST = 1	INST = 2	INST = 3	INST = 4	INST = 5	INST = done

For a program to be able to execute and become a process, it must have a computer or *processor* on which to execute a program. The processor moves the process from one state to the next by making changes in the process's state table.

1.13   *Introduction to VAX Architecture*

The VAX is a general-purpose digital computer, which extends the addressing capabilities of the PDP-11 (hence the name VAX, which stands for Virtual Address eXtension). Although some VAX instructions resemble those of the PDP-11, the VAX has an entirely new system architecture.

VAX architecture contains many high-level features that support operating systems and compilers. The VAX instruction set currently includes over 240 instructions and over 20 formats for operand specifiers, called *addressing modes*. This flexibility enables the programmer to select space-and-time-efficient instructions and addressing combinations. Thus an algorithm translated into MACRO language instructions usually produce a more compact program than if the same algorithm was to be translated into some other assembly language instruction. Figure 1.8 illustrates the VAX computer system's organizational structure.

Although it resembles a general computer, the VAX is somewhat "richer" in that additional devices increase its capabilities and speed. Some of these devices, such as the *floating-point accelerator*, increase the speed of some VAX instructions without affecting computer programming. Such devices are said to be *transparent* to the programs executed on the machine.

The VAX CPU shown in the center of Figure 1.8 is the master controller of the VAX system. The following sections describe some of the devices that constitute VAX architecture.

Figure 1.8

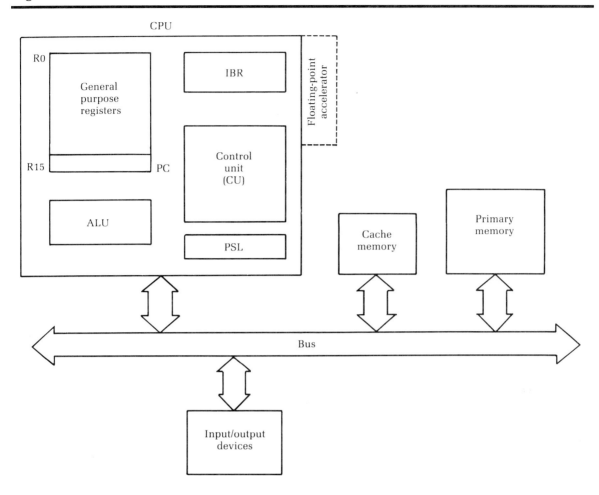

Address Space

Address space is the set of all addresses, or the number of distinct memory cells, that a program can reference. The number of bits representing an address determine the size of the address space. Address size is usually less than, or equal to, the word size for a given machine. Minicomputers have typically used 16-bit addresses, yielding 2^{16} or 65,536 unique memory cells (locations) that an address can reference. However, programmers quickly discovered that a 16-bit address is insufficient to represent large data structures or solve complex problems. The VAX, with a 32-bit address size, allows for a memory address space of 2^{32} or 4,294,967,296 unique addresses. This type of computer can therefore execute (run) very long programs.

You will recall that memory is represented by a large linear array of memory cells. In the VAX, each memory cell is represented by 8 bits, which is equal to 1 byte. Each byte must be accessible to use the data contained in the byte or to place new data into the byte. Accessing (referencing) a byte involves specifying that byte's address. The address for each byte is a 32-bit virtual address. This is called a virtual address because it does not specify the physical memory cell location. Rather, the CPU, under the control of the virtual system, translates a virtual address into a physical address.

Virtual addresses are divided into two sets, each designating a different user. The users are the processes (*user programs*) and the operating system. The part of memory containing the operating system is protected from the user's programs: If a user's program develops an address that accesses the memory cells containing the operating system, an error message will be displayed, thus indicating that protected memory is being accessed, and program execution will then stop.

General-Purpose Registers

VAX contains sixteen 32-bit registers called R0, R1, . . . R15. Not all sixteen registers are general purpose: Four have special uses and should not be used for general programming. These four registers also have special names:

1. R12, the *argument pointer* (AP), which is used in the procedure-calling facility described in Chapter 6.
2. R13, the *frame pointer* (FP), which is also used in the procedure-calling facility.
3. R14, the *stack pointer* (SP), which is used in accessing the program's stack, a data structure, described in Chapter 6.
4. R15, the program counter (PC), which is described in the following section.

Some assembly language instructions use registers R0 through R5 as work registers. These instructions use the registers to store intermediate results as the instruction is being executed. Therefore, these registers cannot be use indiscriminately.

Program Counter (PC)

The PC in the VAX system is the sixteenth general-purpose register. It receives the address of the first instruction at the start of program execution. To start program execution, the CU obtains the first instruction from memory location stored at the address contained in the PC. As an instruction's first byte is moved, the PC is increased by one. After all an instruction's bytes have been moved, the PC will be increased by a number equal to the number of bytes used to store an instruction. The PC now contains the address of the first byte of next instruction to be executed.

The first byte of each instruction is the opcode. The opcode contains the information that the CU requires to execute an instruction. Information contained in the opcode includes the operation to be carried out, the number of data items required by the operation, and the *data type* upon which to be operated, among others.

Program Status Longword (PSL)

In addition to the sixteen general-purpose registers, the VAX contains a register called the *program status longword* (PSL). The PSL register is a 32-bit register that reflects the *state of the process* at any time. The PSL's low-order 16 bits (numbered 0–15) are called the *program status word* (PSW). These 16 bits contain information about the user program and are accessible to the user. The PSW will be discussed in greater detail in Chapter 5. The PSL's high-order 16 bits (numbered 16–31) contain privileged processor information and can be modified only by the operating system. Thus, the user program can examine and change the contents of the PSW, but the upper 16 bits of the PSL are protected from user modification.

Local Memory (cache)

The VAX computer contains a cache memory that is transparent to the user. The cache memory substantially increases execution speed.

Buses

Various devices are connected to the common data bus, which is a collection of wires that carry information by signals between these devices. The information may be an address, data needed for calculation, or another signal. The common data bus may be compared to a highway for computer data flow. Information can be placed onto or taken from this highway by any of the input devices, output devices, or the CPU. The common bus thus provides an efficient and effective means for passing information between the units connected to the bus.

In the VAX, the common bus connecting the CPU, memory, and the I/O buses is called the *synchronous backplane interconnect* (SBI). All input and output devices are connected through this bus, so that they can communicate with each other, as well as with the CPU and memory. I/O devices can send data to and receive data from memory without processor intervention.

VAX Memory Cells

The VAX's basic memory cell is the 8-bit byte. However, the VAX's instruction set can also operate on a group of memory cells. These multiple-byte cells are the 16-bit word (2 bytes), 32-bit *longword* (4 bytes), 64-bit *quadword* (8 bytes) and 128-bit *octaword* (16 bytes). Figure 1.9 illustrates a byte, word, longword, and quadword.

Figure 1.9

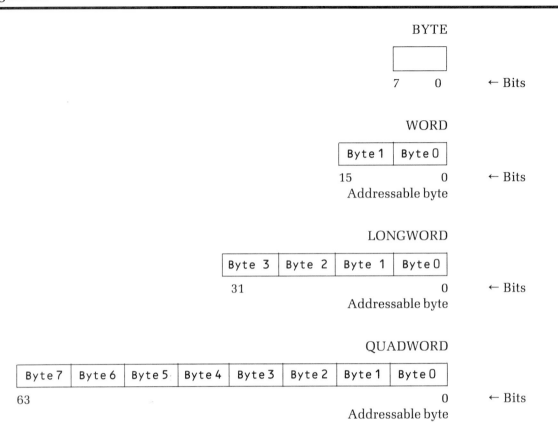

A sequence of contiguous bytes forms each group of memory cells. Each group is always addressed by the *low-order byte* of the group; the low-order byte of any data type is the zero byte in that group. You will recall that the numbering of bytes in a group begins with zero. Note that the bits within any memory cell are numbered from the *least significant bit* (bit 0, on the right), to the most significant bit (bit 7, 15, 31, 63, or 127, on the left, for the byte, word, longword, quadword, or octaword, respectively).

The byte, word, longword, quadword, and octaword are the VAX's fundamental memory cells. Built on these memory cells are various data types, which are interpretations of the bits contained in a group of cells. Each memory cell contains a string of binary digits that represent such data types as an integer, a real number, or a letter of the alphabet. The VAX processor is capable of operating on a number of different data types. Because of this wide choice of data types, programmers or compilers can produce very compact programs using the data types most closely tailored to their needs. A full set of instructions enables programmers or compilers to convert easily from one data type to another, thereby reducing the complexity of many programs.

Summary

A computer comprises various devices, each of which performs a specific task. Some of these tasks and the devices performing them are computation (arithmetic logical unit [ALU]); data storage (primary, auxiliary, and cache memories); status of program execution (PSW); address of next instruction to be executed (PC); and movement of data between devices (buses). The control unit (CU) coordinates all these tasks.

The computer is most inefficient in moving data between various devices. However, various memory devices increase computer efficiency. Design engineers must create primary and cache memories of the proper size to obtain ultimate performance. Although small auxiliary memory size does not make the computer inefficient, lack of large auxiliary memory does prevent the execution of large programs. In order for the programmer to use these devices efficiently, software must be developed.

VAX primary memory is divided into equal parts (bytes). Each byte is 8 bits long and has its own address. Each address is represented by 32 bits. The address size determines the maximum number of bytes that can be addressed during program execution.

The 16 general-purpose registers may be thought of as another type of memory, which is the VAX's fastest because it is part of the CPU. These registers are addressed by their number. Not all the registers are available to the user. Some have special uses and should never be used for storage, while others are used by some instructions for temporary storage during execution of the instruction.

Program execution is carried out sequentially, one instruction at a time. At the start of program execution, the PC receives the address of the first executable instruction. Then, the CU takes over, moving one byte of an instruction at a time. At the same time, the PC is increased by one. At the end of instruction execution, the PC contains the address of the next instruction to be executed. This cycle is called the instruction execution cycle.

New Terms

addressing modes	buses
address space	byte
argument pointer (AP)	byte addressable
arithmetic and logical unit (ALU)	byte machine
arithmetic instruction	cache memory
auxiliary memory	central processing unit (CPU)
binary adder	complementary addition
binary numbering system	condition code
binary shifter	control unit (CU)
bit	data
block	data type
branch instruction	fetch cycle

floating-point accelerator
frame pointer (FR)
general-purpose registers
input devices
input instructions
instruction
instruction execution cycle
instruction register (IR)
least significant bit
locality of reference
logic instruction
longword
low-order byte
output devices
output instruction
pages
physical address
primary memory
process
processor
processor registers
program counter (PC)

program status longword (PSL)
program status register (PSR)
program status word (PSW)
quadword
read cycle
stack pointer (SP)
state of the process
state vector
status information
store cycle
stored program
synchronous backplane
    interconnect (SBI)
transparent
two-state component
virtual address
virtual address space
virtual memory
virtual memory system
word
word addressable
word machine

Exercises

1. Are the following statements true or false? Correct any that are false.
   a. The PSW holds the address of the next instruction to be executed.
   b. The PC holds the next instruction to be executed by the processor.
   c. The most significant bit of a longword is bit 31.
   d. A word has 15 bits.

2. What is a bit?

3. Why is it necessary to group bits into bytes?

4. Why is the binary number system used to represent the contents of memory?

5. What are the disadvantages of assembly language as compared to a higher-level language?

6. Why should large computer systems have auxiliary memory?

7. What is the difference between auxiliary and primary memory?

8. Why is the general-purpose register included in computer architecture?

9. What is virtual memory?

10. How is cache memory used to shorten program execution time?

11. What is the difference between cache memory and auxiliary memory?

12. How does the computer perform decisions?

13. List all the registers in the VAX's CPU. Explain each register's function.

14. How does the CU know what is contained in a memory cell?

15. What is meant by an instruction cycle?

16. What does an operand represent in an instruction?

17. Assume that a computer has a 16-bit virtual address. How many possible addresses are in its virtual address space?

18. How would the VAX system differ if each of its memory cells consisted of 4 bits?

19. How does a programmer obtain information stored in a memory cell?

20. Why is it advantageous to connect all input/output, memories, and CPU devices to the same bus?

21. What does the length of an instruction indicate?

22. Why is it necessary in computer architecture to contain a program counter (PC)?

23. Why does the CU need to know the length of each instruction?

24. When is a PC used?

25. How does the computer execute branch instruction?

26. Which byte in a longword is addressed by its given address?

27. If the address size for the VAX is 16 bits, how many memory locations (units) will this address be able to address?

CHAPTER

Numbering Systems

Outline

Data are entered into a computer in alphanumeric form as letters, digits, and special characters. Similarly, data produced as output are in the same readable alphanumeric form. Internally, however, a computer code (the *ASCII code*) represents data. The ASCII code is a unique arrangement of bits within a byte; it represents a letter, number, or special character.

Numeric data represented in ASCII code cannot be used in arithmetic computations. Instead numeric data must be converted to an appropriate format, which is determined by the instruction being used. Most numeric data used for computation is represented in the binary numbering system for two reasons: (1) the ALU device works only with binary numbers; therefore, binary representation is a necessity. (2) Memory is made up of two-state devices (bits). You will recall that memory is divided into bytes, and each byte is made up of eight bits. Each bit can only represent two states. Therefore, binary digit 0 represents one state, and binary digit 1 represents the other.

When an assembly language program is being debugged, it is sometimes necessary to examine the contents of memory locations. However, it can be very tedious to interpret a long string of zeros and ones. Design engineers have therefore developed a new numbering system called the *hexadecimal number system*, which represents binary numbers in a condensed form. This number system allows for a fast conversion from binary to hexadecimal; therefore, the contents of memory locations are frequently displayed in hexadecimal.

2.1 *Positional Notation*

The *decimal number system* has ten digits or ten unique symbols or characters that represent a quantity. Each numeric symbol has a fixed value that is one higher than that of the symbol before it in a progression from smallest to largest: 0, 1, 2, 3, 4, 5, 6, 7, 8, 9. When several symbols (or digits) are combined, the value of the number depends upon the relative positions of the individual digits as well as upon their values. In the system of *positional notation* with which we are concerned, the digit on the extreme right has the lowest value called the *least significant digit* (LSD). The digit on the extreme left has the highest value and is called the *most significant digit* (MSD). Therefore, the value of each digit depends on its position in the number and its number system's *base* (radix). The base represents the number of unique digit symbols that the system uses. For example, in the decimal system, which has a base of 10, the value of the digit positioned to the left of the least significant (unit) digit increases by a power of 10 for each position. The decimal system has a base or radix of 10 because it has ten discrete number symbols (zero through nine) available for counting.

A decimal quantity may be represented by positional notation. For example, consider the decimal number 6,504. Although its value is immediately apparent, the notation 6,504 actually signifies the following:

$$6 \text{ thousands} + 5 \text{ hundreds} + 0 \text{ tens} + 4 \text{ ones}$$

or

$$6{,}000 \quad + \quad 500 \quad + \quad 0 \quad + \quad 4$$

Each digit's positional value is made even clearer when the number is expressed in powers of 10:

$$6{,}504 = 6 \times 10^3 \quad + 5 \times 10^2 + 0 \times 10^1 + 4 \times 10^0$$
$$= 6 \times 1{,}000 + 5 \times 100 + 0 \times 10 + 4 \times 1$$

These rules of positional notation are generally applicable to all number systems.

2.2 *Binary Number System*

The binary (base 2) number system uses only two distinct digit symbols, 0 and 1, in contrast to the decimal system, which uses ten digit symbols. Therefore, the value of the digit positioned to the left of the least significant digit increases by a power of 2 each time, rather than by a power of 10. For example, the binary number 101101 signifies

$$101101 = 1 \times 2^5 + 0 \times 2^4 + 1 \times 2^3 + 1 \times 2^2 + 0 \times 2^1 + 1 \times 2^0$$
$$= 1 \times 32 + 0 \times 16 + 1 \times 8 + 1 \times 4 + 0 \times 2 + 1 \times 1$$
$$= \quad 32 \quad + \quad 0 \quad + \quad 8 \quad + \quad 4 \quad + \quad 0 \quad + \quad 1$$
$$= 45 \text{ (in the decimal system)}$$

Expressing a binary number by its positional notation is one way of finding its decimal equivalent. To avoid confusion when several number systems are employed, it is customary to subscript each number with its base value. The subscript is represented in decimal notation, as in

$$101101_2 = 45_{10}.$$

Hexadecimal Number System

2.3

Large binary numbers consist of long strings of 0s and 1s, which are frequently awkward to interpret and handle. The hexadecimal (base 16) number system is a convenient way to represent such large binary numbers. Each hexadecimal digit stands for four binary digits.

Hexadecimal notation uses sixteen symbols to represent sixteen number values. Since the decimal system provides only ten digit symbols (0 through 9), six additional symbols are needed to represent the remaining six values. The letters A, B, C, D, E, and F have been adopted for this purpose. The entire list of hexadecimal symbols, therefore, consists of 0, 1, 2, 3, 4, 5, 6, 7, 8, 9, A, B, C, D, E, and F in an ascending sequence of value. Table 2.1 lists equivalent decimal, hexadecimal, and binary numbers from decimal 0 through decimal 20.

Table 2.1

Decimal	Hexadecimal	Binary
0	0	0
1	1	1
2	2	10 ←
3	3	11
4	4	100 ←
5	5	101
6	6	110
7	7	111
8	8	1000 ←
9	9	1001
10 ←	A	1010
11	B	1011
12	C	1100
13	D	1101
14	E	1110
15	F	1111
16	10 ←	10000
17	11	10001
18	12	10010
19	13	10011
20	14	10100

In the table the arrows to the right of several values indicate that an additional digit symbol is required to represent the next quantity. Therefore, additional digit symbols must be used to represent the quantity.

2.4   *Conversion of Decimal to Binary*

A number in base 10 can be converted to a number in base 2 in two ways. The first is the multiple-division method.[1] The number to be converted is divided repeatedly by the value of the base of the number system to which the conversion is being made. The division operation is repeated on the quotient until the quotient finally reaches zero. The remainder from the first division operation is used as the digit in the position farthest to the right in the resultant binary number; the remainder from the second division operation becomes the next digit; the process continues until the quotient equals zero. For example, converting the decimal number 44 to binary requires the following division operation:

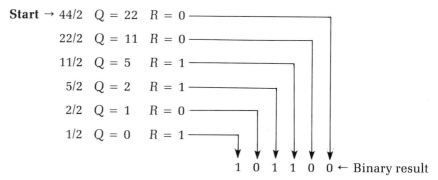

Thus, decimal number 44 equals binary number 101100.

A second method for converting decimal numbers to binary utilizes a table of the powers of 2 and the expanded form of the binary number (see Table 2.2).

Table 2.2

Powers of 2	Quantity
2^0	1
2^1	2
2^2	4
2^3	8
2^4	16
2^5	32
2^6	64
2^7	128
2^8	256
2^9	512
2^{10}	1024

---

1. The explanation that follows applies only to the integer portion of the numbers.

The following steps illustrate how Table 2.2 is used in converting the decimal value 74 to binary.

1. Locate the position of the desired value in the quantity column. In this case the value of 74 falls between 64 and 128.
2. Read the corresponding lower power of 2; this power represents the number of binary digits. For the example of 74, the lower power expression is 6; however, since numbering in computers begins with zero, there will be 7 binary digits.
3. Subtract the value from the lower quantity value. In this example $74 - 64 = 10$.
4. Repeat steps 1 to 3 with the new value of 10. Continue this repetition until the difference in step 3 is zero.

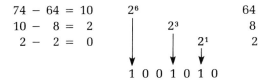

$$74 - 64 = 10 \qquad 2^6 \qquad\qquad 64$$
$$10 - 8 = 2 \qquad\qquad 2^3 \qquad\qquad 8$$
$$2 - 2 = 0 \qquad\qquad\qquad 2^1 \qquad 2$$

$$1\ 0\ 0\ 1\ 0\ 1\ 0$$

In the above example the power of 2 indicates each position of the binary digit 1, and 0s are inserted into the remaining positions.

Conversion of Decimal Fractions to Binary Fractions   *2.5*

The fractional part of a number must be converted separately from its integer part, since the process of conversion is different for each. Frequently, the conversion of a fraction is the inverse of integer conversion. Where the integer part is converted by a process of repeated division, the fractional part is converted by repeated multiplication.

Decimal fractions are converted into binary fractions by successively multiplying the fraction by 2. The integer parts obtained from the multiplication are the successive binary digits, the first integer being the most significant digit of the binary fraction. The fraction obtained from each multiplication is the fraction that is used in the multiplication. The multiplication is continued until either the fraction has been reduced to zero or a sufficient number of binary digits have been generated, in the event of a nonterminating fraction. The following example presents the conversion of decimal fraction 0.828125 into binary fraction.

Fraction	Product	Binary digit
$0.828125 \times 2 = 1.65625$		1
$0.65625 \times 2 = 1.3125$		1
$0.3125 \times 2 = 0.625$		0
$0.625 \times 2 = 1.25$		1
$0.25 \times 2 = 0.50$		0
$0.50 \times 2 = 1.00$		1

Collecting the digits from top to bottom and placing them to the right of binary point, the answer is 0.110101.

2.6 *Conversion of Decimal to Hexadecimal*

The multiple-division method is also used to convert decimal numbers to hexadecimal numbers. In this method the integer portion of the decimal number to be converted is divided repeatedly by 16, the base. The remainder after each division is the next hexadecimal number to the left. In this case the remainders are the decimal values of 0 to 15, which must be converted to the equivalent hexadecimal digits of 0 to F. For example, the conversion of the decimal value 1,583 to hexadecimal is as follows:

$$
\begin{array}{llll}
1583/16 & Q = 98 & R = 15 & (F_{16}) \\
98/16 & Q = 6 & R = 2 & (2_{16}) \\
6/16 & Q = 0 & R = 6 & (6_{16}) \\
\end{array}
$$

$$6 \quad 2 \quad F$$

2.7 *Conversion of a Number from any Number System to a Decimal Number*

Section 2.2 shows that a binary number can be converted to its equivalent decimal number by using positional notation. Positional notation can also be used to convert a number in any number system to decimal. The only difference is that the powers used will be those of the number system being converted. In the following example the hexadecimal number A53B is converted to its equivalent decimal value:

$$
\begin{aligned}
A53B &= A \times 16^3 + 5 \times 16^2 + 3 \times 16^1 + B \times 16^0 \\
&= 10 \times 16^3 + 5 \times 16^2 + 3 \times 16^1 + 11 \times 16^0 \\
&= 10 \times 4096 + 5 \times 256 + 3 \times 16 + 11 \times 1 \\
&= 40960 + 1280 + 48 + 11 \\
A53B &= 42299
\end{aligned}
$$

2.8 *Arithmetic in Different Number Systems*

Arithmetic in number systems with bases other than 10 can always be carried out by converting all operands to the decimal system, doing the required arithmetic, and then reconverting the results back to the original number base. This procedure is not recommended for binary arithmetic, which is extremely simple, but may be advisable for complicated hexadecimal arithmetic. Nevertheless, the programmer should at least be familiar with simple addition and subtraction in binary and hexadecimal notations.

The rules of arithmetic are the same in all positional number systems. Thus, it only is necessary to recall the corresponding rules of decimal arithmetic to be able to do arithmetic with any other number base.

Binary Addition and Subtraction

The binary system has only two digit symbols, 0 and 1. Hence, adding two binary 1s requires two binary digits to represent the quantity of 2. The same process is used to add the decimal digits 1 and 9. The decimal number system does not have a single digit symbol that represents the quantity of 10. The complete rules of binary addition are as follows:

Binary addition

```
    0 + 0 = 0
    1 + 0 = 1
    0 + 1 = 1
    1 + 1 = 0  with a carry of 1
1 + 1 + 1 = 1  with a carry of 1
```

The following are three examples of binary addition. The example on the left is self-explanatory. The example in the middle develops a carry, which is indicated by 1 above the proper digit position. In the example on the right, two 8-bit numbers are added; this process involves several carries, which are indicated.

```
                1◄────── carries ──────►1    11
     1010          10101010                00111011
   + 0101        + 00001001              + 00100011
   ──────        ──────────              ──────────
     1111          10110011                01011110
```

During the debugging process of an assembly language program, familiarity with the conventional method of subtraction, (borrowing) can be useful. The rules of binary subtraction are as follows:

Binary subtraction

```
 0 - 0 = 0
 1 - 1 = 0
 1 - 0 = 1
 0 - 1 = 1  with a borrow of 1
10 - 1 = 1
```

Borrowing is necessary whenever the subtrahend (the number on the bottom) is larger than the minuend (the number on top). It consists of subtracting a 1 from the next-higher-order digit to the left in the minuend and placing it next to the lower-order digit in the minuend. For example,

```
               10
             0 Ø 10        }←Borrows
        1 0 X X Ø 1 1 ←Minuend
       -1 0 0 1  1 1 1 ←Subtrahend
        0 0 0 1  1 0 0
```

Note that many changes are necessary in the minuend to accommodate successive borrowing. These changes may become confusing at times, so it might be helpful to write down the minuend after each borrowing step is completed. The following are additional examples of binary subtraction:

```
 1000      10110001      11000011
 0001     -01010101     -01110001
 0111      01011100      01010010
```

Two's Complement

As discussed in Chapter 1, most computers perform subtraction by complementary addition. Complementary addition in binary involves converting the subtrahend into two's complement, and then carrying out addition.

The complement of a number is obtained by subtracting each digit of that number from the digit having the highest value in that number system (for a decimal number, this would be 9; and for a binary number, this would be 1). Then a value of 1 is added to the result in all cases. The resulting complement is sometimes referred to as the radix complement; the name refers to the base of the number system involved. For example, the ten's complement of the decimal number 756 would be calculated as follows:

```
    999  Subtract each digit from the
    756  highest value digit in that system.
    243
  +   1  Add 1 to the least significant digit.
    244  is the ten's complement of 756.
```

The same process is followed for a binary number. For example, the two's complement of 00101011 is 11010101.

```
    11111111   Subtract each digit from the
   -00101011   highest value digit in that system.
    11010100
  +        1   Add 1 to the least significant digit.
    11010101   is the two's complement.
```

Note that each digit in the result (11010100) is just the opposite of the digit in that position in the original number (00101011).

> 00101011   Original number
> 11010100   Result of the subtraction

This direct relationship between the digits in the original binary number and the result of the subtraction holds true, because the binary number system has only two digits. The subtraction of each digit position from the number can result in only one of two possibilities. Either you subtract a 1 from a 1 and the result is 0, or you subtract a 0 from a 1, and the result is 1. The result is always the opposite of the original digit.

Since each binary digit is equivalent to a bit, the two's complement of a binary number is calculated by first "flipping" the setting of each bit to its opposite state and then adding 1 to the result. The process of flipping each bit is called calculating the *one's complement*. Thus calculating the two's complement of any binary number involves two simple steps: (1) Flip all bits in the original number, and (2) add 1 to the result. The following example illustrates this process:

```
  1000110011    Given binary number
  0111001100    One's complement of the number
+          1
  ──────────
  0111001101    Two's complement of the number
```

Another way to perform subtraction in binary is to (1) find the two's complement of the subtrahend, and (2) add that to the minuend. The following example illustrates this process:

```
  0100001110
 -0010101010
  ──────────
  1101010101    One's complement of the subtrahend
+          1
  ──────────
  1101010110    Two's complement of the subtrahend
  0100001110    Minuend
  ──────────
 10001100100    Result of subtracting 001010101 from 0100001110
  ↑
```

The presence of 1 in the position pointed to by the arrow indicates to the CU that the result of subtraction is a positive value. If 0 occurs in this position, the result of subtraction is a negative value.

When subtraction is performed by complementary addition, both the subtrahend and the minuend must have the same number of binary digits as in the following example:

```
  1000100110
 -0010100001
```

When the subtrahend does not have as many binary digits as the minuend, the missing high-order positions in the subtrahend must be filled with 0s before it is converted to two's complement. If this is not done, the result will be incorrect as the following example illustrates:

Incorrect	Correct
1000100110	1000100110
− 10100001	−0010100001
01011110	1101011110
1	1
01011111	1101011111
1000100110	1000100110
1010000101	0110000101

Adding 0s is necessary because in the ALU the same number of bits represents both the subtrahend and minuend. The number of bits for each depends on the data type used.

Hexadecimal Addition and Subtraction

Addition in the hexadecimal system follows the same rules as decimal and binary addition. Working with alphanumeric symbols—numbers and letters—may appear strange at first, particularly since the results obtained from decimal addition have a different meaning in hexadecimal notation. Accordingly, a degree of reorientation and practice is required. For instance, $4 + 5 = 9$ in both the decimal and hexadecimal systems, but $7 + 8 = F$ (not 15) in hexadecimal notation. Whenever the sum of two digits exceeds F—the highest-value hexadecimal symbol—a carry of 1 to the next-higher-order digit position develops. Thus, $7 + 9 = 10$ (that is, 0 with a carry of 1), and $9 + 9 = 12$ (that is, 2 with a carry of 1). Table 2.3 makes the addition of two hexadecimal digits easier.

Using Table 2.3 is simple. To add two hexadecimal numbers, find the first number in the column farthest to the left; then find the second number in the top row. The sum of the two is found where the column and the row intersect. For example, the sum of 7 and 8 is 0F.

The notion of carry in hexadecimal is the same as in the decimal system. In the following examples, (a) is straightforward and does not involve any carries. Examples (b) and (c) develop a carry during the addition.

			11		1 1
(a)	9654	(b)	6AE	(c)	8F97
	+4528		+1FA		+D44C
	DB7C		8A8		163E3

Example (b) may be solved by using Table 2.3 as follows: A plus E equals 18; 8 is the low-order digit of the sum, and 1 is a carry to the next position. A plus F equals 19; adding the 1 carry equals 1A. A is the next

Table 2.3

+	1	2	3	4	5	6	7	8	9	A	B	C	D	E	F	10
1	02	03	04	05	06	07	08	09	0A	0B	0C	0D	0E	0F	10	11
2	03	04	05	06	07	08	09	0A	0B	0C	0D	0E	0F	10	11	12
3	04	05	06	07	08	09	0A	0B	0C	0D	0E	0F	10	11	12	13
4	05	06	07	08	09	0A	0B	0C	0D	0E	0F	10	11	12	13	14
5	06	07	08	09	0A	0B	0C	0D	0E	0F	10	11	12	13	14	15
6	07	08	09	0A	0B	0C	0D	0E	0F	10	11	12	13	14	15	16
7	08	09	0A	0B	0C	0D	0E	0F	10	11	12	13	14	15	16	17
8	09	0A	0B	0C	0D	0E	0F	10	11	12	13	14	15	16	17	18
9	0A	0B	0C	0D	0E	0F	10	11	12	13	14	15	16	17	18	19
A	0B	0C	0D	0E	0F	10	11	12	13	14	15	16	17	18	19	1A
B	0C	0D	0E	0F	10	11	12	13	14	15	16	17	18	19	1A	1B
C	0D	0E	0F	10	11	12	13	14	15	16	17	18	19	1A	1B	1C
D	0E	0F	10	11	12	13	14	15	16	17	18	19	1A	1B	1C	1D
E	0F	10	11	12	13	14	15	16	17	18	19	1A	1B	1C	1D	1E
F	10	11	12	13	14	15	16	17	18	19	1A	1B	1C	1D	1E	1F
10	11	12	13	14	15	16	17	18	19	1A	1B	1C	1D	1E	1F	20

(to the left) digit of the sum, and 1 is a carry to the next position. Then 6 plus 1 equals 7, plus the 1 carry equals 8. The last (high-order) digit is 8. Example (c) follows the same procedure as example (b).

Hexadecimal subtraction follows the same rules as decimal and binary subtraction. To obtain the difference between two hexadecimal digits, refer to Table 2.3. Locate the column heading that represents the digit to be subtracted (subtrahend); then go down the column to the digit(s) that represents the minuend. The heading of the row horizontally across from the minuend represents the difference between the two digits. When the subtrahend digit is greater than the minuend digit, it is necessary, of course, to add a borrow of 1 to the minuend digit before looking up the difference in the table. The following example illustrates this process:

```
    1B
   7 B 18
   8̸ ¢̸  8  ←  Minuend
  −1 F  A  ←  Subtrahend
   6 C  E
```

Start with the lowest-order digits at the right; A cannot be subtracted from 8 because it exceeds 8. Hence, a 1 is borrowed from C, the next-higher-order digit to the left, thereby reducing the symbol C to B (since C − 1 = B) and increasing the minuend digit to 18. To carry out the subtraction 18 − A, consult Table 2.3. Under the A-column (the subtrahend), the minuend digits, 18, appear in the E-row. Hence, 18 minus A equals E. After writing down E, proceed to the next-higher-order digit position: F cannot be subtracted from B; hence a 1 is borrowed from the 8 at the left, reducing the digit to 7 and increasing the minuend to 1B. Go down the F-column (subtrahend) in the table; the minuend digits (1B) appear in the A-row. Therefore, 1B minus F equals C. Write down C. Finally, find the difference between the high-order digits to the left; there 7 minus 1 equals 6. Write down 6, which completes the subtraction.

To perform hexadecimal subtraction without using Table 2.3, it is easier to carry out the subtraction by decimal notation. In that case, the borrow is not 1 but 16 as in the following example.

```
     25
  7 9 24
  8 A  8  ←  Minuend
 -1 F  A  ←  Subtrahend
  6 A  E
```

A cannot be subtracted from 8; therefore 16 + 8 = 24, and 24 − A = 14, which is a hexadecimal value of E. F cannot be subtracted from 9; therefore 9 + 16 = 25, and 25 − F = 10, which is the next hexadecimal value of A. Finally, 1 is subtracted from 7, yielding 6, which is the high-order digit of the answer. The following examples provide additional illustrations of hexadecimal subtraction.

```
   F9D5        D935F        FDE74B
  -EB63       -8E7C2       -7B3AF4
   E72         4AB9D        82AC57
```

Summary

As Chapter 1 explained, before a program can be executed, it must be entered into (stored in) primary memory. The instructions and data in memory are represented by 0s and 1s. Each letter, digit, and special character is represented by a unique arrangement of 0s and 1s within a byte. This arrangement is called the ASCII code.

Numeric data are represented by binary numbers, which are also 0s and 1s. The difference is that those 0s and 1s represent a quantity rather than a code for a digit, letter, or special character. Binary numbers are used in arithmetic calculations.

Table 2.4

Powers of 2		Powers of 16	
2^n	n	16^n	n
256	8	1	0
512	9	16	1
1024	10	256	2
2048	11	4096	3
4096	12	65536	4
8192	13	1048576	5
16384	14	16777216	6
32768	15	268435456	7
65536	16	4294967296	8
131072	17	68719476736	9
262144	18	1099511627776	10
524288	19	17592186044416	11
1048576	20	281474976710656	12
2097152	21	4503599627370496	13
4194304	22	72057594037927936	14
8388608	23	1152921504606846976	15
16777216	24		

Periodically, the programmer must examine the contents of certain memory locations. The contents are displayed in hexadecimal rather than binary, because information displayed in binary takes up too much space and is more difficult to interpret. Converting binary to hexadecimal is easy because four binary digits equal one of the sixteen hexadecimal digits. Because information is displayed in hexadecimal, the programmer needs to know how to convert from hexadecimal to binary or decimal and vice versa. Using Table 2.4 will speed up the conversion process.

Addition and subtraction with binary numbers or hexadecimal numbers follow the same rules as in decimal arithmetic. Subtraction in the ALU is performed by the complementary addition of binary numbers. In complementary addition, the subtrahend (bottom number) is converted to two's complement, and the result is added to the minuend (top number). The sum obtained is the result of subtraction. Two's complement of a binary number is obtained by changing every 0 to 1 and every 1 to 0, and then adding a 1.

New Terms

ASCII code
base
complementary addition
decimal number system
hexadecimal number system
least significant digit (LSD)

most significant digit (MSD)
one's complement
positional notation
radix
two's complement

Exercises

1. List two reasons why the binary number system is used by a computer.

2. Why is the hexadecimal number system used by a computer?

3. Define positional notation in number systems.

4. For what purpose is the complementary addition used by a computer?

5. Why is complementary addition of binary numbers easy to carry out?

6. What is ASCII code and what is it used for?

7. Convert the following numbers to their binary equivalents:

   a. 16_{10} e. $3AFC_{16}$
   b. 8_{16} f. 216_{16}
   c. $2C_{16}$ g. 79_{10}
   d. 234_{10} h. 111_{10}

8. Convert the following numbers to their hexadecimal equivalents:

   a. 01110101_2 d. 11110110_2
   b. 5826_{10} e. 30651_{10}
   c. 87643_{10} f. 111000001001_2

9. Convert the following numbers to their decimal equivalents:

   a. $AC7B_{16}$ e. $87F_{16}$
   b. 1111_2 f. 010111000011_2
   c. 0110101100_2 g. $F26C_{16}$
   d. $3607B3_{16}$ h. $380C_{16}$

10. What are the two's complements of the following numbers?

    a. 01011011_2 c. 00000000_2
    b. 01100110_2 d. 11111111_2

11. Perform the following addition operations:

    a. 10010110_2 c. 01100101_2
      $+01001001_2$ $+00110011_2$

    b. $6AC2_{16}$ d. $56B3_{16}$
      4237_{16} $15C7_{16}$

12. Perform the following subtraction operations:

    a. 10110111_2 c. $A682B_{16}$
      -00101011_2 $-92C6_{16}$

    b. 10110001_2 d. $F3123_{16}$
      -11000000_2 $-ABCDE_{16}$

13. Since only practice will help you master arithmetic operations in various number systems, try the following problems:

a. 01101001_2
     00111000_2
   $+10001110_2$

b. $38C72_{16}$
    $-1A26B_{16}$

c. $39B8_{16}$
    $-38C0_{16}$

d. $2C76_{16}$
     $3A42_{16}$
   $+13F8_{16}$

e. 10111001101_2
    -01001101010_2

f. $A67F26_{16}$
    $-87C29A_{16}$

14. Convert the following decimal fractions to binary fractions:

a. 0.111011 b. 0.00110111

Getting Started

Outline

The first step in solving a problem through the use of a computer is to develop an *algorithm* for the problem. The next step is to convert the algorithm into a *structured flowchart*, which is a blueprint of the problem. Then the program can be constructed by translating one block of the flowchart at a time in a top-down fashion. Each block is translated into one or more assembly language instructions.

The result of translating a flowchart is an assembly *source program*, which is a problem represented by assembly language instructions. This source program must be translated into *machine language* (0s and 1s) so that the CU can interpret each instruction. The program (software) that translates the source program into machine language is called the *assembler*; the process is called the *assembly*. A program presented in machine language is called an *object program*.

Assembly Language Instructions   3.1

Each assembly language instruction contains all of the information required for its execution. This information consists of (1) the operation to be performed, (2) the data or the location of the data needed for the operation, and (3) the location where the result will be stored. Not every instruction needs all three. For example, some branch instructions contain only one item, the address where to branch.

Each assembly language instruction is usually represented on one line, which ordinarily does not exceed eighty characters. The following is the general format for MACRO assembly instructions:

LABEL:	OPCODE	OPERANDS or ARGUMENTS	;COMMENT

The first field in an instruction may be a *label*. A label represents an address that refers to an assembly language instruction. Although a label must begin with a character, the entries that follow the first character can be alphanumeric. A label cannot have more than thirty-one alphanumeric characters. The assembler recognizes that a group of alphanumeric characters is a label by the colon (:) found at the end of the group. If a label is not required, the first field is left blank.

The second field is the *opcode*. An opcode informs the CU what operation is to be carried out. For example, addition (**ADDL2**), comparison (**CMPL**), or branch (**BLSS**). Unlike labels that you create yourself, opcodes are provided by the MACRO assembly language.

The third field may be an operand or an argument. When the third field is one or more *operands*, the operands designate the data to be used in the operation. The most common way to represent the data is by a label or constant. Most assembly language instructions contain a group of operands; some, however, have one; others, none. The opcode of each instruction indicates the number of operands required by the instruction.

If the third field is an *argument*, the instruction is a command to the assembler rather than to the CU. The argument can be a constant that is to be stored. It can also represent the size of a memory block that is to be set aside. These constants and memory blocks are to be used during program execution, and are referred to by labels.

The fourth field is a *comment*, which is a description in English of the operation that the instruction is going to accomplish. For example, in a payroll program a comment could be ADD OVERTIME HOURS TO REGULAR HOURS. The comment field must always be preceded by a semicolon (;).

Figure 3.1 presents the flowchart for the program that appears in Figure 3.2. The program illustrates the four fields that make up an instruction; all possible combinations of the four fields are included. This program calculates pay by multiplying the hours worked by the hourly rate.

To enhance the readability of the program, each field of an instruction should be placed in a specific position on a line. An accepted instruction format for VAX MACRO language follows:

```
LABEL        1 -  7
OPCODE       9 - 15
OPERANDS    17 - 40
COMMENTS    41 - 80 or 1 - 80
```

Figure 3.1

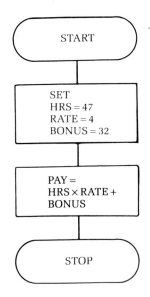

Figure 3.2

```
        .TITLE    FIG32

; THIS PROGRAM CALCULATES SIMPLE PAY WHICH IS BASED ON THE
; NUMBER OF HOURS WORKED TIMES RATE PER HOUR PLUS BONUS

HRS:        .LONG    47          ; NUMBER OF HOURS WORKED
RATE:       .LONG    4           ; RATE PER HOUR
BONUS:      .LONG    32          ; FLAT BONUS FOR EACH PAY PERIOD
TEMP:       .BLKL    1           ; MEMORY CELL TO CONTAIN INTERMEDIATE RESULTS
PAY:        .BLKL    1           ; DEFINE MEMORY CELL TO RECEIVE THE ANSWER

; BEGINNING OF THE EXECUTABLE PORTION OF THE PROGRAM

        .ENTRY   START,0         ; ENTRY POINT OF THE PROGRAM
        MULL3    HRS,RATE,TEMP   ; HOURS TIMES RATE PER HOUR
        ADDL3    TEMP,BONUS,PAY  ;
        $EXIT_S
        .END     START
```

The assembler translates an assembly language instruction into machine language from left to right. The first field encountered is interpreted as a label if it ends with a colon (:). Then the opcode is translated according to a table of opcodes found in the assembler; the operands are translated next. As the assembler translates, it may encounter a semicolon (;). If so, it interprets the remaining portion of the line as a comment. Good programming style includes adding entire lines of comments in addition to the comments contained at the end of an instruction. These additional lines of comments are designated by a semicolon at the beginning of the line. Groups of lines of comments are used to document a program, whereas the comments found at the end of each instruction are used to walk the reader through the logic of the program.

3.2 *Organization of Instructions in a MACRO Program*

Computer programs written in higher-level languages usually have a unique statement, which is physically the first statement of the program, but this is not the case in VAX assembly language programs. Each VAX MACRO program, however, must contain a unique instruction that indicates the beginning of *executable instructions.*

An executable instruction is an instruction that requests the CU to perform an operation. For example, an executable operation might be add two numbers, compare two numbers, or read a number. In Figure 3.2 the beginning of the executable portion of the program is indicated by the

```
.ENTRY START,0
```

instruction. **.ENTRY** is an *assembler directive instruction.* These provide information to the assembler to enable it to perform additional tasks besides translation. START is the first operand and the label of the instruction, and the 0 (zero) is the second operand. The assembler directive instruction .ENTRY will be covered in more detail in Chapter 6.

In addition to executable instructions, an assembly language program contains *nonexecutable instructions.* A nonexecutable instruction provides the assembler with information that is used during the assembly process. An example of this occurs when a program being assembled contains an instruction that directs the assembler to store a constant. A constant is stored so that when a program is being executed it is available for calculation. This type of nonexecutable instruction is called *data storage directive.* Another example of a nonexecutable instruction occurs when a program must set aside a block of memory which will be used to store an array. In this case the assembler does not store values that constitute the array, it only reserves a block of memory which is equal in size to the number of elements in the array. This type of nonexecutable instruction is called *storage directive.*

Each program must have a unique instruction that the CU will interpret as the last executable instruction. This instruction is **$EXIT__S.** In addition, each program should have an instruction to inform the assembler that there are no more assembly instructions to be translated; the **.END** assembler instruction indicates the end of an assembly program. The .END instruction contains one operand, which is the first operand used in the .ENTRY instruction.

Figure 3.3

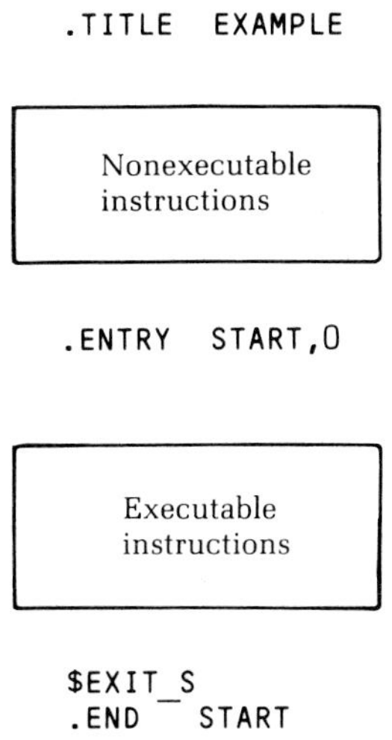

```
.TITLE  EXAMPLE
```

```
┌─────────────────────┐
│  Nonexecutable      │
│  instructions       │
└─────────────────────┘
```

```
.ENTRY  START,0
```

```
┌─────────────────────┐
│    Executable       │
│    instructions     │
└─────────────────────┘
```

```
$EXIT_S
.END    START
```

Another useful but not essential nonexecutable instruction is **.TITLE.** This assembler directive instruction provides a means to assign a title to a program. The assigned title is placed in the operand position of the .TITLE instruction and is developed according to the rules used for labels. The program in Figure 3.2 uses a figure number for the title.

Figure 3.3 uses a block diagram to illustrate instruction organization in a program. START, the .ENTRY instruction's label, occupies the first operand field rather than the label field. Even though this label does not occupy the first field, it does identify the first executable instruction of the program.

.LONG Data-Storage Directive Instruction　　　3.3

Data-storage directive instructions are used to store constants. **.LONG** is one of many data-storage directive instructions. This instruction stores a constant in a longword of memory. The constant is stored as an integer-type constant, which in memory is stored as binary number. The general format for the .LONG instruction is as follows:

LABEL:	.LONG	ARGUMENT	;COMMENT

Most data-storage directive instructions contain LABEL, which is used as an operand in an executable instruction when it needs the data stored at that location for a calculation. The second field, .LONG, is the opcode of a data-storage directive that instructs the assembler to store a constant in a longword of memory. The third field, ARGUMENT, represents the constant to be stored. The constant is represented by a decimal number. The COMMENT describes the uses of the constants as in the following example.

```
HRS:    .LONG 47    ; NUMBER OF HOURS WORKED
RATE:   .LONG 4     ; RATE PER HOUR
BONUS:  .LONG 32    ; BONUS FOR EACH PAY PERIOD
```

Although everything in memory is in binary, the contents of memory are displayed in hexadecimal to make it easier to interpret them. Exhibit 3.1 shows how these constants are stored in memory.

Exhibit 3.1

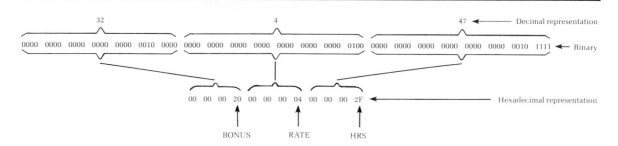

Exhibit 3.1 also illustrates the conversion of decimal numbers into binaries and hexadecimals. After a decimal number is converted into binary, the binary number is converted into hexadecimal by arranging the binary number in groups of four binary digits and then converting each group of four into a hexadecimal number. In addition, the grouping of two hexadecimal numbers together indicates the contents of a byte.

In Exhibit 3.1 the hexadecimal values 2F, 04, and 20 are equivalent to the decimal values 47, 4, and 32, respectively. These hexadecimal values are stored in a longword. The choice of the longword is indicated by the opcode .LONG.

Within a program, labels used as the first field in the data-storage directive instructions function as operands in the executable instructions. Note that in Figure 3.2 the label HRS is an address to the instruction .LONG, which stores the constant 47. The instruction **MULL3** uses the label HRS as an operand that is really an address to the memory location containing the value 47.

One data-storage directive may be used to store several constants. For example, the constants stored in Figure 3.2 may have been included in one instruction as the following example illustrates:

```
CON:    .LONG   47,4,32
NEG:    .LONG   -32
```

The following is the memory contents after the previous two data-storage directive instructions have been assembled.

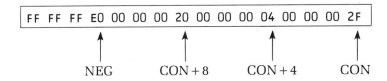

```
FF FF FF E0 00 00 00 20 00 00 00 04 00 00 00 2F
```

         NEG   CON+8   CON+4   CON

The first data-storage directive instruction stores three constants. Because the opcode .LONG is present, each constant is contained in a long-word. The first constant (47) is referenced by the label CON; the second constant (4) is referenced by CON+4; the third constant (32) is referenced by CON+8. The address of the label CON must be modified by 4 because the second constant is 4 bytes away from the first byte of the first constant. The third constant is accessed by CON+8 because the third constant is 8 bytes away from the first byte, which is addressed by the label CON. The second data-storage directive stores −32. Negative constants are stored in two's complement; therefore, the hexadecimal value of FF FF FF E0 represents −32 in two's complement. (Refer to the section on two's complement in Chapter 2.)

Defining a group of constants under the same label is not a recommended practice. In the first place, the label CON does not give any indication of the meaning of the constants. In addition, to use the second constant (4), the label CON must be modified, Therefore, care must be taken to ensure that the address modifier is correct. A group of constants can be defined under the same label, however, when they all represent the same type of information, such as a list of telephone numbers.

.BLKL Storage-Directive Instructions   *3.4*

Storage directive instructions set aside memory locations, but they do not store constants. Values are stored in these memory locations during program execution. The general format for storage directive instructions is the same as for data-storage directive instructions. However, the argument in storage directive instruction represents the block size to be set aside rather than the constant value to be stored, as does the data-storage directive.

```
TEMP:   .BLKL  1
PAY:    .BLKL  1
```

Each of these instructions set aside one block of memory which consists of a contiguous group of four bytes or a longword. The longword data type is used because the last letter of the opcode **.BLK***L* is L. The number of bytes contained in a block is the product of the size of the data type and the size of the block. In both instructions in the example the size of data type is four and the size of the block is one, therefore each instruction sets aside four bytes of memory.

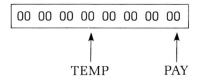

The assembler initializes the entire block of memory to 0.

A group of longwords that make up one block can be set aside as in the following instruction where the block consists of two longwords,

TEMP: .BLKL 2.

Therefore, eight bytes are set aside. The memory representation of the block set aside is as follows:

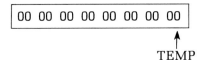

The difference between .BLKL and .LONG is the latter usually reserves one longword and stores a constant in it, whereas .BLKL may reserve one or any number of longwords and initialize the entire block to 0. You will recall that .LONG reserves and stores a constant in each longword if there are multiple arguments. Therefore, the following .LONG instruction can be used to initialize a group of longwords;

.LONG   0,0,0,0

The main purpose of .LONG is to store constants, and the main purpose of .BLKL is to set aside a group of longwords.

3.5   *Arithmetic Instructions*

Having learned how to store constants and set aside memory locations, we are ready to learn instructions that process the data stored in these longwords. The instructions discussed in this section deal with addition, multiplication, subtraction, and division, using the longword data type. These instructions contain either two or three operands. Their general format is as follows:

LABEL:	OPCODE	OPER1	,OPER2	;COMMENT

LABEL:	OPCODE	OPER1	,OPER2	,OPER3	;COMMENT

The first field, LABEL, is used only when the instructions need to be referenced. COMMENT should always be used to describe the operation; OPCODE indicates the operation. The different OPERs indicate the location of data used in the operation. In addition, one of the operands indicates where to store the result obtained from the operation.

The opcode of an executable instruction provides a great deal of information to the CU. To illustrate this, consider the two executable instructions used in Figure 3.2:

```
MULL3   HRS,RATE,TEMP
ADDL3   TEMP,BONUS,PAY
```

The first three letters of both opcodes inform the CU which operation is to be performed. MUL indicates multiplication and ADD indicates addition. In both opcodes, the fourth letter indicates the data type used in the operation. In each case the letter **L** indicates that a longword will be used. The digit at the end of each opcode indicates the number of operands included in the instruction. When no digit appears, it is assumed that the instruction has either two, one, or zero operands.

The difference between a two- and three-operand arithmetic instruction is the location of the result obtained from the operation. In a three-operand instruction, the first and second operands are used in the operation, and the result is stored at the third operand. In a two-operand instruction, the first and second operands are used in the operation, and the result replaces the second operand.

When using addition and, especially, multiplication instructions, the result may be too large to be represented by the data type indicated in the opcode. You will recall that the fourth letter of the opcode indicates the data type used in calculation. This letter also indicates the data type of the result. The operand in which the result is stored indicates the address where the result is placed; it does not indicate the type. When this is the case, a runtime overflow error occurs. This chapter will not be concerned with this type of error.

When divide instructions are used, only the quotient is retained from the division. The remainder is truncated. The *truncation* occurs because in integer division, only the whole value is retained. To retain the remainder, the EDIV instruction, which is covered in Section 7.7, must be used.

The information presented in the preceding sections of this chapter is sufficient to write an assembly language program. A program for the solution of the equation $y = 3x^2 + 5/x - 3$ appears in Figure 3.4.

It is not necessary to store constants by use of the data-storage directive. A constant may also be used to represent an operand. When a constant is used for an operand, the assembler must be informed of this, or it will interpret the constant value as a physical address. This is done by preceding the constant with a *number sign* (#). The assembler assumes that all constants used to represent operands are decimal values unless otherwise specified. The revised version of the program in Figure 3.4 appears in Figure 3.5.

Figure 3.4

```
             .TITLE    FIG34

; THE EQUATION Y=3X**2+5/X-3 IS SOLVED BY THIS PROGRAM

; NONEXECUTABLE INSTRUCTIONS

Y:           .BLKL     1              ; Y=ANSWER
X:           .BLKL     1              ; X=INPUT VALUE
CON3:        .LONG     3              ; DEFINES CONSTANT VALUE 3
CON5:        .LONG     5              ; DEFINES CONSTANT VALUE 5
TEMP:        .BLKL     1              ; TO HOLD INTERMEDIATE RESULTS

; EXECUTABLE INSTRUCTIONS

             .ENTRY    START,0        ; ENTRY POINT
             MULL3     X,X,Y          ; Y=X**2
             MULL3     CON3,Y,Y       ; Y=3X**2
             DIVL3     X,CON5,TEMP    ; TEMP=5/X
             ADDL3     TEMP,Y,Y       ; Y=3X**2+5/X
             SUBL3     CON3,Y,Y       ; Y=3X**2+5/X-3
             $EXIT_S
             .END      START
```

Figure 3.5

```
             .TITLE    FIG35

; THE EQUATION Y=3X**2+5/X-3 IS SOLVED BY THIS PROGRAM

; NONEXECUTABLE INSTRUCTIONS

Y:           .BLKL     1              ; Y=ANSWER
X:           .BLKL     1              ; X=INPUT VALUE
TEMP:        .BLKL     1              ; TO HOLD INTERMEDIATE RESULTS

; EXECUTABLE INSTRUCTIONS

             .ENTRY    START,0        ; ENTRY POINT
             MULL3     X,X,Y          ; Y=X**2
             MULL3     #3,Y,Y         ; Y=3X**2
             DIVL3     X,#5,TEMP      ; TEMP=5/X
             ADDL3     TEMP,Y,Y       ; Y=3X**2+5/X
             SUBL3     #3,Y,Y         ; Y=3X**2+5/X-3
             $EXIT_S
             .END      START
```

To execute the programs in Figure 3.4 and Figure 3.5, a value for X must be provided, and the contents of memory location Y must be displayed. The value of X is the data necessary for calculation, and the location Y contains the answer. In order to accomplish this task *input/output* operations must be performed.

Input/Output Performed by Higher-Level Languages   *3.6*

Performing input/output operations in assembly language requires many more instructions than the ones we have discussed thus far. As a result, the beginning assembly language programmer will find it easier to perform the I/O operations by using the higher-level language procedures discussed in this section.

Input and output procedures both need the addresses of memory locations, but for different reasons. A procedure that is used to perform an input operation must be informed of the address of the memory locations where the input data is to be stored, whereas an output procedure must be informed of the address of a memory location from which to copy the data that is to be printed. These memory location addresses make up an *argument list,* which in turn is used by the I/O procedures. The organization of an argument list is very specific. For example, if you are reading in two values, such as the name of an individual and his telephone number, the argument list contains one address for the name and another address for the telephone number. Every time a read operation is performed, the name is found in a specific memory location, and the telephone number is found in its own specific memory location. If, however, the addresses to the name and phone number were interchanged within the argument list, then the name is stored in the memory location that should hold the phone number and vice versa.

You will recall that each address is represented by 32 bits. Therefore the argument list consists of a group of longwords, with each longword containing an address. In addition to the list of addresses, the argument list must include the total number of arguments contained within the list, which is stored in the first longword of the list.

The program in Figure 3.6 uses the following two argument lists; the input procedure uses the first list, and output procedure uses the second.

```
ARG_IN:    .LONG      1
           .ADDRESS   X
ARG_OUT:   .LONG      2
           .ADDRESS   X
           .ADDRESS   Y
```

In both lists the first longword contains the number of arguments that make up the argument list. This longword is not counted as one of the arguments.

Figure 3.6

```
        .TITLE     FIG36

; THE EQUATION Y=3X**2+5/X-3 IS SOLVED FOR 10 VALUES OF X

; NONEXECUTABLE INSTRUCTIONS

Y:        .BLKL     1              ; Y=ANSWER
X:        .BLKL     1              ; X=INPUT VALUE
TEMP:     .BLKL     1              ; TO HOLD INTERMEDIATE RESULTS

; ARGUMENT LISTS

ARG_IN:   .LONG     1              ; NUMBER OF ARGUMENTS IN THE LIST
          .ADDRESS  X              ;     ADDRESS OF THE MEMORY LOCATION WHERE
                                   ;     THE INPUT VALUE IS PLACED

ARG_OUT:  .LONG     2              ; NUMBER OF ARGUMENTS IN THE LIST
          .ADDRESS  X              ;     ADDRESS OF THE INPUT VALUE
          .ADDRESS  Y              ;     ADDRESS OF THE RESULT

; EXECUTABLE INSTRUCTIONS

          .ENTRY    START,0        ; ENTRY POINT
          CALLG     ARG_IN,RDINPUT ; CALLS INPUT PROCEDURE
          MULL3     X,X,Y          ; Y=X**2
          MULL3     #3,Y,Y         ; Y=3X**2
          DIVL3     X,#5,TEMP      ; TEMP=5/X
          ADDL3     TEMP,Y,Y       ; Y=3X**2+5/X
          SUBL3     #3,Y,Y         ; Y=3X**2+5/X-3
          CALLG     ARG_OUT,WROUTPUT ; CALLS OUTPUT PROCEDURE
          $EXIT_S
          .END      START
```

The arguments in the argument list are entered by the use of the
.ADDRESS instruction, which is another data-storage directive instruction. This instruction stores an address rather than a constant. The address stored is the address of the label that is used as its argument. For
example, in the first argument list in Figure 3.6, the data-storage directive instruction .ADDRESS X stores the address that the label X represents, rather than the value stored at memory location X.

The program in Figure 3.6 uses two **CALLG** instructions, which call
the input and output procedures. CALLG instructions provide the CU
with the address of the beginning of the called procedure; then after the
procedure is executed they provide the CU with the address of the instruction that immediately follows the CALLG. Following are two

CALLG instructions; the first calls the input procedure, and the second calls the output procedure.

```
CALLG  ARG_IN,RDINPUT
CALLG  ARG_OUT,WROUTPUT
```

The second entry for both instructions (ARG__IN and ARG__OUT) is the label to the respective argument list. The third entry is the name of the procedure being called. The first instruction calls the input procedure (named RDINPUT), and the second instruction calls the output procedure (named WROUTPUT). The input and output procedures can be written in any language. See Appendix C for a sample of the FORTRAN and Pascal procedures that are used to perform the I/O operations under the VMS operating system.

Compare and Branch Instructions   3.7

The information presented thus far does not allow us to write many programs; moreover, the programs that we can write can be executed only once. For example, the program in Figure 3.6 executes its instructions once. Thus, only one value of Y is calculated. To calculate another value for Y, the program must be rerun. To repeat this program without rerunning it, the instruction that follows CALLG ARG__OUT,WROUTPUT must be an instruction that will direct the computer to go back to CALLG ARG__IN,RDINPUT instruction rather than to $EXIT__S instruction. In addition, the program must contain an instruction that will stop this repetition. In other words, the program must have a *finite loop.* This loop will be repeated again and again until a certain condition is reached. The flowchart in Figure 3.7 illustrates the use of a loop that will repeat the program in Figure 3.6 until the value of X equals 99.

A decision block is translated into assembly language by two instructions, the compare and branch. The *compare instruction* sets a condition code, which in turn is used to determine the path of a program's execution. The branch instruction tests this condition code and directs the CU to one of its paths.

In the flowchart in Figure 3.7, the arrow points to a decision block. This block is translated into assembly language by a compare instruction, which compares two data items. Both data items may be the contents of memory locations or one of them can be a constant value. The two data items compared in the decision block in Figure 3.7 are the contents of memory location X and the constant value of 99. Based upon the result of the comparison of the two data items, one of the two paths in the flowchart is followed. If the contents of memory location X do not equal 99, the path that continues program execution is followed. If the value equals 99, the path that stops program execution is followed. A

Figure 3.7

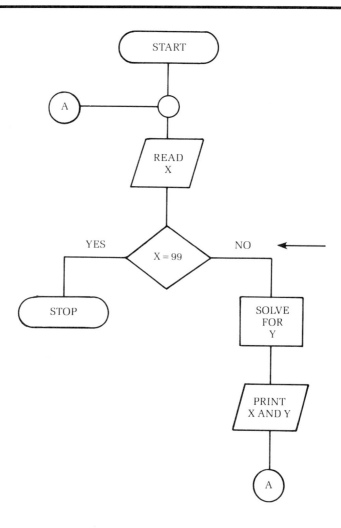

branch instruction translates the decision about which path to follow into assembly language.

The general format for the compare instruction is as follows:

LABEL:	CMPL	OPER1	,OPER2	;COMMENT

Every compare instruction has two operands, which represent the two data items to be compared. In this compare instruction, the two data items are *longword data type* because the opcode is CMPL. The **L** in the opcode indicates the longword. The two data items do not change during the compare operation. For example, in the following compare instruction the X is compared to the constant 99, but the contents of memory location X do not change during the operation of the compare instruction. For example, in the following compare instruction:

```
CMPL    X,#99
```

The result obtained from a compare instruction is the setting of the condition code or codes. You will recall that the PSL contains information about the current state of the program being executed. The current state of a program after executing a compare instruction is reflected in the condition codes, which are contained in the PSW, a part of the PSL. The state of the program recorded in these condition codes is determined by the following tests of the relationship between the contents of a memory location or a constant used as the first operand and the contents of a memory location or a constant used as the second operand.

1. The first is less than the second.
2. The first is greater than the second.
3. The first is equal to the second.
4. The first is less than or equal to the second.
5. The first is greater than or equal to the second.
6. The first is unequal to the second.

Branch instructions test for each of the preceding conditions. The general format for branch instructions follows:

| LABEL: | OPCODE | DESTINATION ADDRESS | ;COMMENT |

In this instruction LABEL, OPCODE, and COMMENT have the same meaning as in the compare instructions. The only operand in this instruction is an address that indicates the path to be followed if the condition tested for exists. If the tested condition does not exist, the next sequential instruction is executed. The condition to be tested for is indicated by the opcode of the branch instruction. The following opcodes for branch instructions test for the conditions in the preceding list.

```
BLSS  (Branch on less than)
BGTR  (Branch on greater than)
BEQL  (Branch on equal)
BLEQ  (Branch on less than or equal)
BGEQ  (Branch on greater than or equal)
BNEQ  (Branch on not equal)
```

The letters that follow the letter B indicate the condition to be tested. If the condition exists, the instruction to be executed is the one whose address appears as the operand of the branch instruction. This address is the address of the instruction that begins the proper path if the tested condition exists. The following compare instruction illustrates which branch instruction should be used to test the necessary condition.

```
CMPL    X,#99
```

The second column indicates the value of X to be tested.

Instruction	Condition it tests for
BLSS	X < 99
BGTR	X > 99
BEQL	X = 99
BLEQ	X ≤ 99
BGEQ	X ≥ 99
BNEQ	X ≠ 99

When compare and branch instructions are used in a program, the branch instruction should immediately follow the compare instruction. If it does not, the instruction(s) that separate them might change the condition code. Figure 3.8, which translates the flowchart in Figure 3.7, illustrates the use of the compare and branch instructions.

VAX provides three additional branch instructions, called *unconditional branch instructions*. Unlike the *conditional branch instructions* discussed above, these instructions do not test any condition codes. The general format for unconditional branch instructions is the same as for conditional branch instructions. The three unconditional branch instructions are:

```
JMP    (Jump)
BRB    (Branch with byte displacement)
BRW    (Branch with word displacement)
```

The three unconditional branch instructions each have a different number of bytes that the assembler uses to represent the *branch* (destination) *address.*

The destination address in VAX is represented by an *offset.* This means that the address is not the address of the instruction; rather, it is the *distance* between the destination instruction and the branch instruction. For example, in Figure 3.8 the destination address LOOP is represented by a value equal to the number of bytes that separate the instruction BRB from the instruction CALLG   ARG__IN,RDINPUT. The distance is contained in a byte, word, or longword. The number of bytes used to represent the distance depends on the branch instruction.

The JMP instruction directs the CU to any instruction in the program because the destination address is contained in a longword. You will recall that every virtual address is represented by 32 bits (longword); therefore, the distance cannot exceed the value that can be represented by 32 bits.

Figure 3.8

```
            .TITLE    FIG38

; THE EQUATION Y=3X**2+5/X-3 IS SOLVED FOR 10 VALUES OF X

; NONEXECUTABLE INSTRUCTIONS

Y:          .BLKL     1            ; Y=ANSWER
X:          .BLKL     1            ; X=INPUT 'VALUE
TEMP:       .BLKL     1            ; TO HOLD INTERMEDIATE RESULTS
ARG_IN:     .LONG     1            ; NUMBER OF ARGUMENTS IN THE LIST
            .ADDRESS  X            ;    ADDRESS OF MEMORY LOCATION WHERE
                                   ;    INPUT VALUE IS PLACED


ARG_OUT:    .LONG     2            ; NUMBER OF ARGUMENTS IN THE LIST
            .ADDRESS  X            ;    ADDRESS OF THE INPUT VALUE
            .ADDRESS  Y            ;    ADDRESS OF THE RESULT

; EXECUTABLE INSTRUCTIONS

            .ENTRY    START,0          ; ENTRY POINT
LOOP:       CALLG     ARG_IN,RDINPUT   ; CALL INPUT PROCEDURE
            CMPL      X,#99            ; IF X = 99 STOP PROGRAM EXECUTION
            BEQL      STOP             ;    ELSE CONTINUE PROGRAM EXECUTION
            MULL3     X,X,Y            ; Y=X**2
            MULL3     #3,Y,Y           ; Y=3X**2
            DIVL3     X,#5,TEMP        ; TEMP=5/X
            ADDL3     TEMP,Y,Y         ; Y=3X**2+5/X
            SUBL3     #3,Y,Y           ; Y=3X**2+5/X-3
            CALLG     ARG_OUT,WROUTPUT ; CALL OUTPUT PROCEDURE
            BRB       LOOP             ; REPEAT THE PROGRAM
STOP:       $EXIT_S
            .END      START
```

The BRB instruction can only be used when the next instruction to be executed is within ± 127 bytes. This is because the distance is contained in a byte. The BRW instruction will allow the program to continue with its execution if the next instruction is within ± 32,767 bytes. This is because the distance is contained in a word.

Another example of a loop in programs is the counting loop, which repeats a group of instructions a known number of times. Compare and branch instructions can be used to implement counting loops. Assume that the program in Figure 3.8 is to read 10 values of X. Therefore, the counting loop in this program should count the number of times the read operation is repeated. The flowchart for this problem appears in Figure 3.9.

The program in Figure 3.10 translates the flowchart in Figure 3.9.

Figure 3.9

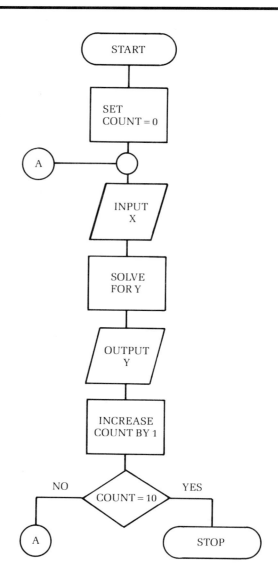

3.8 Implementing a Loop with the AOBx or SOBx Instructions

A loop can be implemented by a single instruction rather than by a group of instructions as in Figure 3.10. The loop in Figure 3.10 was accomplished by the following three instructions:

```
ADDL    #1,COUNT
CMPL    COUNT,#10
BLSS    LOOP
```

Figure 3.10

```
        .TITLE    FIG310

; THE EQUATION Y=3X**2+5/X-3 IS SOLVED FOR 10 VALUES OF X


; NONEXECUTABLE INSTRUCTIONS

Y:          .BLKL     1              ; Y=ANSWER
X:          .BLKL     1              ; X=INPUT VALUE
TEMP:       .BLKL     1              ; TO HOLD INTERMEDIATE RESULTS
COUNT:      .LONG     0
ARG_IN:     .LONG     1              ; THE NUMBER OF ARGUMENTS IN THE LIST
            .ADDRESS  X              ; ADDRESS OF THE MEMORY LOCATION WHERE
                                     ;   INPUT VALUE IS PLACED


ARG_OUT:    .LONG     2              ; THE NUMBER OF ARGUMENTS IN THE LIST
            .ADDRESS  X              ;   ADDRESS OF THE INPUT VALUE
            .ADDRESS  Y              ;   ADDRESS OF THE RESULT


; EXECUTABLE INSTRUCTIONS

            .ENTRY    START,0        ; ENTRY POINT
LOOP:       CALLG     ARG_IN,RDINPUT ; CALL INPUT PROCEDURE
            MULL3     X,X,Y          ; Y=X**2
            MULL3     #3,Y,Y         ; Y=3X**2
            DIVL3     X,#5,TEMP      ; TEMP=5/X
            ADDL3     TEMP,Y,Y       ; Y=3X**2+5/X
            SUBL3     #3,Y,Y         ; Y=3X**2+5/X-3
            CALLG     ARG_OUT,WROUTPUT ; CALL OUTPUT PROCEDURE
            ADDL      #1,COUNT       ; INCREASE COUNT BY 1
            CMPL      COUNT,#10      ; IF COUNT < 10 CONTINUE PROGRAM EXECUTION
            BLSS      LOOP           ;     ELSE STOP PROGRAM EXECUTION
STOP:       $EXIT_S
            .END      START
```

In this case, the instruction ADDL increases COUNT by 1; CMPL compares COUNT to 10; and BLSS branches to LOOP if COUNT is less than 10. These instructions can be condensed so that the ingredients needed to implement a loop are contained in one instruction, **AOBx** (add one, test, and branch). The AOBx instruction can only test for less than (**LSS**) or less than or equal (**LEQ**) conditions. The condition to be tested is included in the opcode of the instruction; therefore the x in AOBx is replaced by either LSS or LEQ. The AOBx instruction adds one to the counter, compares the counter to a given value, and finally determines whether to continue program execution with the next sequential instruction or to branch. The three data items used in this instruction (the counter, the given value and the branch address) are all part of the instruction. The general format for the AOBx instruction follows:

LABEL:	AOBx	LIMIT	,COUNTER	,DESTINATION ADDRESS	;COMMENT

The following AOBx instruction can be used to replace the three instructions used in Figure 3.10.

          AOBLSS   #10,COUNT,LOOP

The choice of LSS for x in the AOBx instruction is made because the test to determine whether to continue with the loop is made after the instructions that make up the loop have been executed. Therefore, when COUNT contains zero, the loop is executed once; and when COUNT equals nine, the loop has been repeated ten times. If the test were made for less than or equal to ten, the loop would have been repeated eleven times. If COUNT were initialized to one, however, you would choose LEQ for x.

VAX assembly language also supplies the **SOBx** (subtract one and branch) instruction, which decreases a counter by one, tests, and then branches. The value against which a counter is tested is always zero. The x of the instruction is represented by either **GTR** (greater than zero) or **GEQ** (greater than or equal to zero). The general format for this instruction is as follows:

LABEL:	SOBx	COUNTER	,DESTINATION ADDRESS	;COMMENT

The loop in Figure 3.10 could also be represented by the SOBx instruction. In that case COUNT must be initialized to ten, and the following SOBx instruction must be used:

          SOBGTR   COUNT,LOOP

Note that SOBx has two operands. This is because one of the two values used in the comparison is always a zero; therefore, in the SOBGRT instruction, COUNT is compared to zero. On the other hand, the AOBx instruction contains three operands because the two values, which are represented by the first two operands, are compared.

3.9 *Debugger*

The *Debugger* is a software package that can be used as a tool in debugging a program. Because each assembly language instruction contains many fields and a program written in assembly language contains many instructions, finding errors is time-consuming. During the process of locating errors, it would be helpful if specific memory locations could be examined at the end of an instruction's execution. To do this, the program must halt its execution at the end of an instruction's execution. These and many other situations are possible when the debugger is engaged during program execution. This section provides an introduction to the debugger commands, and a more detailed description appears in Appendix A.

To use the debugger in debugging a program, it must first be engaged by the following DCL commands:

```
MACRO/DEBUG FIG35
LINK/DEBUG FIG35
RUN FIG35
```

The last entry (FIG35) in all three commands indicates the file name of the program to be debugged. When the command RUN is executed, the debugger is engaged. The /DEBUG qualifier in both the MACRO and LINK commands is needed to set up tables used by the debugger during the debugging session.

Once the debugger is engaged, the program execution begins at the rate of one instruction or one group of instructions at a time. To execute one instruction at a time, the debugger command **STEP** is used. To execute a group of instruction at a time, the group must first be identified, and then be executed. Group execution is covered in the latter part of this section.

Using the STEP command makes it possible for the programmer to examine memory locations after the execution of each instruction, and therefore to follow the progress of the program's execution.

To examine memory location while the debugger is engaged, the **EXAMINE** command must be used. The general format of the EXAMINE command is as follows:

```
EXAMINE   LABEL
```

or

```
E    LABEL
```

Here LABEL is an address to a memory location. This address is defined by the program being debugged. For example, assume that the memory location X contains the value 6 and the instruction MULL3   X,X,Y is executed. Upon the completion of the instruction's execution, the following debugger command is issued:

```
E   Y
```

This debugger command displays the contents of memory location Y in hexadecimal and also as a longword data type. This occurs because the debugger is programmed to display everything in hexadecimal and as a longword data type. This is referred to as the *default conditions* of the debugger. Thus the contents of memory location Y would be displayed as follows:

```
00 00 00 24
```

This longword is interpreted from right to left. The hexadecimal value of 24 converted to decimal value equals 36, which is the correct result.

The displayed values are easier to interpret if they are in decimal. The debugger can be directed to change its default hexadecimal conditions to decimal condition by issuing the following command:

```
SET MODE DECIMAL
```

This command will cause all the memory locations to be displayed in decimal. When only one memory location needs to be examined, the EX-AMINE command should contain the qualifier /DEC. For example, if only the Y memory location in the program in Figure 3.5 is to be examined in decimal, the EXAMINE command would be as follows:

```
E/DEC Y
```

When a qualifier is used in a debugger command, it must be preceded by a slash and must be placed immediately after the command. This qualifier only affects the command with which it is used.

During the initial stages of a program's development, it is convenient not to include the input instructions. Some data items, however, must be supplied to the program so that it can be tested. This can be accomplished by using the debugger command DEPOSIT, which specifies the memory location and the data to be stored in that memory location. The general format of the DEPOSIT command is as follows:

```
DEPOSIT    LABEL=DATA
```

or

```
D   LABEL=DATA
```

LABEL is a label defined by the program, and DATA is the data to be stored in the memory location LABEL. An equal sign (=) must separate LABEL and DATA. To enter a value of 6 for X, the following command is issued:

```
D X=6
```

As a result of this debugger command, the value 6 is placed into memory location X. Figure 3.11 illustrates a debugging session of the program in Figure 3.5. This debugging session uses the debugger commands presented thus far.

Figure 3.11

```
            VAX DEBUG Version V4.4-4

%DEBUG-I-INITIAL, language is MACRO, module set to 'FIG35'
DBG>  D  X=6
DBG>  S
stepped to FIG35\START+9: MULL3          S^#03,B^FIG35\Y,B^FIG35\Y
DBG>  S
stepped to FIG35\START+0F: DIVL3         B^FIG35\X,S^#05,B^FIG35\TEMP
DBG>  E  Y
FIG35\Y:            0000006C
DBG>  SET MODE DECIMAL
DBG>  E  Y
FIG35\Y:             108
DBG>  S
stepped to FIG35\START+21: ADDL3         B^FIG35\TEMP,B^FIG35\Y,B^FIG35\Y
DBG>  S
stepped to FIG35\START+28: SUBL3         S^#3,B^FIG35\Y,B^FIG35\Y
DBG>  S
stepped to FIG35\START+34: PUSHL         S^#1
DBG>  S
stepped to FIG35\START+36: CALLS         S^#1,@#SYS$EXIT
DBG>  S
%DEBUG I-EXITSTATUS, is '%SYSTEM S-NORMAL, normal successful completion'
DBG>  E  Y
FIG35\Y:             105
DBG>  EXIT
```

The first line of output from the debugger informs the programmer of the debugger's version. The second line states both the language in which the program being debugged was written and the title of the program. The debugger prompt is indicated by DBG>. When DBG> is displayed, the debugger is waiting for a command. Each debugger command is terminated by using the <RET> key. In this example the underlined information is entered by the programmer; the remaining information is the output from the debugger.

Another debugger command that might be useful is the GO command, which instructs the debugger to execute a group of instructions. When a group is not defined, the debugger assumes that the program is to be executed to its completion.

The execution of instruction $EXIT__S indicates to the CU that the end of the program execution has been reached, and the debugger displays the following message if no error was detected:

```
%DEBUG-I-EXITSTATUS, is '%SYSTEM-S-NORMAL, normal successful completion'
```

In order to exit the debugging session, the debugger command EXIT must be entered. This command returns the control of the computer from the debugger to the operating system.

The debugging session can be stored, either entirely or in part, by informing the debugger that every line displayed on the screen is to be included in a log file. Both of the following debugger commands are needed to create a log file:

1. The first command informs the debugger to create a log file of the debugging session. This command is as follows:

   `SET OUTPUT LOG`

2. The second command provides the debugger with the name of the log file. This second command is as follows:

   `SET LOG FIG35.LOG`

The debugger session of the program in Figure 3.5 appears in Figure 3.12, and the log file of that session appears in Figure 3.13.

Note that no DBG> prompts appear in the hard copy. In addition, each output line produced by the debugger is treated as a comment line. Comment lines may be entered during a debugging session by preceding the line with an exclamation mark (!). The two debugger commands SET OUTPUT LOG and SET LOG FIG35.LOG are not displayed be-

Figure 3.12

```
        VAX DEBUG Version V4.4-4

%DEBUG-I-INITIAL, language is MACRO, module set to 'FIG35'
DBG> SET OUTPUT LOG
DBG> SET LOG FIG35.LOG
DBG> D X=6
DBG> S
stepped to FIG35\START+9: MULL3        S^#03,B^FIG35\Y,B^FIG35\Y
DBG> S
stepped to FIG35\START+0F: DIVL3       B^FIG35\X,S^#05,B^FIG35\TEMP
DBG> E Y
FIG35\Y:           0000006C
DBG> E/DEC Y
FIG35\Y:              108
DBG> S
stepped to FIG35\START+15: ADDL3       B^FIG35\TEMP,B^FIG35\Y,B^FIG35\Y
DBG> S
stepped to FIG35\START+1C: SUBL3       S^#03,B^FIG35\Y,B^FIG35\Y
DBG> S
stepped to FIG35\START+22: PUSHL       S^#01
DBG> S
stepped to FIG35\START+24: CALLS       S^#01,@#SYS$EXIT
DBG> S
%DEBUG-I-EXITSTATUS, is '%SYSTEM-S--NORMAL, normal successful completion'
DBG> E/DEC Y
FIG35\Y:              105
DBG> EXIT
```

cause they set the necessary conditions to begin generating the log file of the debugging session.

The SET BREAK command is also helpful in debugging. This command will execute a program by groups of instructions rather than by one instruction. The SET BREAK command's general format is as follows:

```
DBG>SET BREAK LOOP
```

Here LOOP is a label assigned to the instruction where a break is to occur during the program execution. Refer to the program in Figure 3.9, which contains a loop. Debugging this program by using the STEP command could be time-consuming, if, for example, only the result obtained at the end of each loop cycle needs to be examined. The SET BREAK LOOP command speeds up the debugging process by stopping program execution only at the end of each loop cycle.

To use the BREAK command, first enter the command and then follow it with the GO command. The debugger will allow the instructions to be executed, starting with the instruction at which it stopped and proceeding up to the instruction whose label appears in the SET BREAK command. When program execution stops, continue with the debugging session by using any of the debugging commands. Of course, if the loop is to be repeated, just enter the GO command. In this manner the loop execution can be monitored.

Figure 3.13

```
D  X=6
S
!stepped to FIG35\START+9: MULL3        S^#03,B^FIG35\Y,B^FIG35\Y
S
!stepped to FIG35\START+0F: DIVL3       B^FIG35\X,S^#05,B^FIG35\TEMP
E Y
!FIG35\Y:           0000006C
E/DEC Y
!FIG35\Y:           108
S
!stepped to FIG35\START+15: ADDL3       B^FIG35\TEMP,B^FIG35\Y,B^FIG35\Y
S
!stepped to FIG35\START+1C: SUBL3       S^#03,B^FIG35\Y,B^FIG35\Y
S
!stepped to FIG35\START+22: PUSHL       S^#01
S
!stepped to FIG35\START+24: CALLS       S^#01,@#SYS$EXIT
S
!%DEBUG-I-EXITSTATUS, is '%SYSTEM-S-NORMAL, normal successful completion'
E/DEC Y
!FIG35\Y:           105
EXIT
```

Summary

This chapter introduces the user to the basics of elementary programming on the VAX using assembly language. Assembly language consists of instructions that direct the computer to carry out given operations. Operations discussed in this chapter were addition, subtraction, multiplication, division, comparison, and branch.

The simplest programs require decision-making capabilities, reading of values, and the display of answers produced by executing the program. The decision-making capabilities in assembly language are frequently implemented in two steps: (1) comparing two data items and (2) making a decision on whether to branch.

Input and output operations in assembly language can be performed by the use of higher-level language procedures. This chapter introduced the procedure calling standards used in assembly language. The procedures are called by the use of CALLG instruction.

Debugging programs in assembly language is very time-consuming. The software package Debugger speeds up the process. The debugger makes it possible to execute a program one instruction at a time, which allows the programmer to examine memory locations after executing each instruction.

New Instructions

ADDL2	BRB	SOBGTR
ADDL3	BRW	SUBL2
AOBLEQ	CALLG	SUBL3
AOBLSS	CMPL	.ADDRESS
BEQL	DIVL2	.BLKL
BGTR	DIVL3	.END
BGEQ	JMP	.ENTRY
BLEQ	MULL2	.LONG
BLSS	MULL3	.TITLE
BNEQ	SOBGEQ	$EXIT_S

New Terms

algorithm	debugger
argument	debugging
argument list	default condition
array size	entry point
assembler	executable instruction
assembler directive instructions	finite loop
assembly	input/output
branch address	integer value
comments	label
compare instruction	longword data type
conditional branch	machine language
data-storage directive	nonexecutable instructions

number sign
object program
offset
opcode
operand
overflow

source program
storage directive
structured flowchart
truncation
unconditional branch

Exercises

1. What information do all executable instructions provide the CU?

2. What do the arguments in data-storage and storage directives represent?

3. Why should programs written in assembly language contain comments?

4. What is the difference between executable and non-executable instructions?

5. Why should programmers use labels in every data-storage or storage directive instruction?

6. What instructions should be used to translate a decision block of a flowchart into assembly language?

7. What is the order of the instructions used to translate a decision block in a flowchart? Why?

8. Write the necessary assembly language instructions that will solve the following equation.

$$v = 3x + 4x - 5$$

9. What will the memory contents be after the following data storage directives are assembled?

```
CON1:    .LONG    13
CON2:    .LONG    25,19
CON3:    .LONG    -15,-1,1
```

10. Given the following group of data-storage directives,

```
X:    .LONG       7
Y:    .LONG      -7
Z:    .ADDRESS    X
```

What is stored in longword addressed by Z? Assume that value 7 is stored in memory location 2000.

11. Translate the following statements by using compare and branch assembly language instructions.

    a. If HRS < 40, go to the instruction labeled CALPAY.
    b. If HRS > 40, go to the instruction labeled OVERTIME.

  c. If HRS = 0, go to instruction labeled ERROR.
  d. If HRS > 40 and the employee DEPENDENT = 0, go to
   VALIDATE

12. How many bytes of memory would each of the following storage directives set aside?

```
LISTA:    .BLKL 5
LISTB:    .BLKL 1
LISTC:    .BLKL 0
```

13. In Figure 3.2 could the data-storage directive PAY: .LONG 0 be used in place of the storage directive PAY: .BLKL 1? Explain your answer.

14. Rewrite the program presented in Figure 3.2 so that it will read HRS, RATE, BONUS and print HRS, RATE, BONUS, and PAY. The input and output should be done by high-level input/output procedure, but don't write out the I/O procedures.

15. Can giving the SOBx instruction replace the following instructions? If it can, write the necessary instruction(s).

```
COUNT: .LONG 0

       ADDL    #1,COUNT
       CMPL    COUNT,#10
       BLSS    LOOP
```

16. Indicate whether the following instructions are correct or incorrect, and explain what is wrong with any that are incorrect.

  a. AOBLSS VAL,COUNT,LOOP
  b. CMPL   #99,X
  c. ADDL   #15,#20,SUM
  d. SUBL   SUM,#5

Problems

1. In the near future all our measurements may be metric. Write a program that converts weight in pounds to kilograms. The answers will be whole numbers, because the instructions presented in this chapter can handle only whole integers. The input file contains 10 records and each record contains one weight to be converted. Print the weight in pounds and its equivalent weight in kilograms.

2. Modify the program in problem 1 such that each input record contains two weights rather than one.

3. Write a program that will square numbers 1 through 20. Use the debugger for output. Create a hard copy of the debugging session that would contain the answers.

4. Write a program that reads an unknown number of test grades, calculates their average, and prints all the input grades and the average. A negative value of 99 will indicate the end of the input file.

5. Expand the problem in question 4 by printing the highest and lowest grades received on the test.

6. Write a program that reads a value for x; then compute the square, cube, and fourth power of x. Read 10 values for x, starting with 1 and proceding through 10. The output should consist of x, x^2, x^3, and x^4.

7. Write a program that calculates and prints the average temperature for the month of January. The total number of readings is unknown. Each input record contains a morning and evening reading.

8. Write a program that reads three values (x, y, and z), determines the largest of the three, and prints the three values followed by the largest.

9. Write a program that reads a number, and then continuously reads more numbers until the sum of the second number and subsequent numbers equals the first number. After each number is read, print the quantity needed to halt the program's execution.

10. Assume that your computer does not have the divide instruction. Write a program that will perform division using add and subtract instructions. The values to be divided are obtained from an input file that contains n records. Each record contains two numbers; the first number is divided by the second. The output of the program should contain the two values used in division, the quotient and the remainder.

11. Write a program that converts a given date in the form DD/MM/YY to the number of days. For example in the date

2/3/86

all entries except the slashes are numeric. The output should be as follows:

THE DATE 2/3/86 IS 34 DAYS FROM JANUARY 1

The input file contains n records, and each record contains one date. Assume that February has 28 days.

12. Write a program that will dump itself; that is, print the program. Print every byte of the program along with its location.

CHAPTER

Addressing
Techniques

Outline

Part 1. Core Topics

Arrays represent a list of information that is used in solving many programming problems. Each entry in an array is the same type of information; for example, a list of grades, names, or telephone numbers. To work with an array in assembly language, a block of memory that will contain the array must first be set aside; second, each item of information (element) should be easily obtainable during program execution. This chapter will examine different addressing methods that are used to obtain elements in an array easily. Before, discussing the different addressing methods, a better understanding of an assembly language instruction is helpful.

Overview of Assembly Language Instructions   4.1

VAX assembly language instructions that are represented in *machine language* vary in length. An instruction may be as short as one byte or as long as several bytes, depending upon the method used to express the operands. Each instruction consists of an opcode (*mnemonic*) followed by zero to six operands. Each operand may be expressed as (1) a label, (2) a register number, (3) any type of constant, (4) an expression, or (5) the current location counter. (Chapter 5 discusses expressions and location counters.) Regardless of the way an operand is expressed, it has two properties with which the programmer must be concerned: (1) the data type and (2) the *access type*. Access type indicates how the memory location is to be used. First, it can be used as a receptacle from which the CU can obtain data that will be used during an operation; second, it can be used as a place to store a result obtained from an operation; and third, it can be used for both to obtain and to store data.

The data type informs the CU the number of bytes used to store the data. The data type is defined by a letter in the opcode of the instruction. For example, in the instruction ADD**L**2 (add longword), the letter **L** indicates that the operand represents a longword data type, whereas in the instruction **ADDW2** (add word), the letter **W** represents a word data type.

An opcode in the instruction indicates how an operand will be used in an operation. The operand is used to obtain the needed data for the operation, or it is used to store the result obtained from the operation. Sometimes the same operand is used for both, first obtaining the data and then storing the result of the operation. In this case the programmer must remember that the data used in the operation are no longer available for future use because the result replaces the previous contents of the memory location.

When an operand represents an address to a memory location, the operand represents a 32-bit virtual address. This 32-bit virtual address is calculated during the execution of an instruction from the data provided in the operand. After the address is calculated, the data located at that address are copied from memory and used in the operation. The following sections examine the various addressing techniques available in the VAX.

4.2   *Relative Addressing Mode*

The *relative addressing mode* occurs when an operand is a label and is used as an address. Using relative addressing mode while working with arrays makes a program very long and tedious to write. For example, adding an array of twenty test scores would require twenty ADD instructions, because each test score in the array has its own unique address. The program segment in Figure 4.1 illustrates this problem.

To add up the twenty scores, the address GRADE, which is assigned to the array, is contained in an *expression*. When the CU solves the expression (GRADE + 4), the address, GRADE, will be increased by 4 because each test score is stored in a longword (4 bytes). Therefore, to go from test score to test score, the address must be increased by a value that is multiples of 4. The first test score is added by using the address GRADE. To add the second test score, the address of the array must be increased by 4; to add the third test score, the address of the array must be increased by 8. Thus to add in the last test score, the address of the array must be increased by 76. To shorten the program, the programmer needs an addressing technique that will express the operand in such a way that each time the virtual address is calculated, it would be the address of the next test score. If this were possible, then the instruction

Figure 4.1

```
            .TITLE  FIG41
SUM:        .LONG   0           ;INITIALIZE THE ACCUMULATOR
GRADE:      .BLKL   20          ;A BLOCK OF 20 LONGWORDS
                                ;TO BE USED FOR THE ARRAY GRADE


            .ENTRY  START,0

; ASSUME THAT THE TEST SCORES ARE READ IN THIS PART OF THE PROGRAM

            ADDL2   GRADE,SUM       ;ADD IN THE FIRST TEST SCORE
            ADDL2   GRADE+4,SUM     ;ADD IN THE SECOND TEST SCORE
            ADDL2   GRADE+8,SUM     ;ADD IN THE THIRD TEST SCORE
            ADDL2   GRADE+12,SUM    ;ADD IN THE FOURTH TEST SCORE


            ADDL2   GRADE+76,SUM    ;ADD IN THE 20TH TEST SCORE
```

ADDL would be contained in a loop that would be repeated twenty times. This type of address change can be accomplished either by (1) changing the increment used in the calculation of the address before the execution of the instruction or (2) modifying the address before each execution of the ADDL instruction. The following sections examine these and other techniques.

Register Addressing Mode   *4.3*

An operand represented by a label informs the CU which memory locations to access to obtain the required data for an operation. This same data also can reside in a general-purpose register.[1] When the data are stored in a register, the operand that references this data is represented by the *register addressing mode*. The register addressing mode is represented by the register number in the form R*n*, where *n* is a number from 0 to 11. For example, R4 represents the use of register 4. Only registers 0 through 11 are used because registers 12 through 14 are used in procedure calls (discussed in Chapter 6), and register 15 is the PC, or program counter register (discussed in Chapter 1), which contains the address of the next instruction to be executed.

When an operand is represented by a register, the CU does not calculate the virtual address as in the relative addressing mode because registers are not part of primary memory. The register addressing mode has two advantages and one disadvantage compared with the relative ad-

---

1. From this point on, the word "register" means general-purpose register.

dressing mode. The advantages are that the access time is fast and that the instructions are shorter. Because the access time is short, the execution of an instruction is faster. Because the instructions are shorter, memory space is saved, and the instruction cycle is faster. The disadvantage, however, is that only twelve registers can be used for the register addressing mode. Since the access time (time required to obtain data) is faster when using the register addressing mode, registers should be used as accumulators, counters, and temporary storage locations. For example in Figure 4.1, the program segment adds twenty test scores; to speed up this process, the label SUM should be replaced by a register as in the following example:

```
GRADE:   .BLKL    20

         .ENTRY   START,0

         CLRL     R7
         ADDL2    GRADE,R7
         ADDL2    GRADE+4,R7
         ADDL2    GRADE+8,R7

         ADDL2    GRADE+76,R7
```

When a register is used as an accumulator, the register should be initially set to zero by using the **CLRL** (clear longword) instruction. In our example the longword that is set to zero is R7.

The general format of an instruction using the register addressing mode is as follows:[2]

```
                      First     Second
                      Operand   Operand

| LABEL: | OPCODE | Rn | , . . . . . | ;COMMENT |
```

Whenever the register addressing mode represents an operand, the operand occupies one byte of memory. The machine language format of this byte is as follows:

```
        | 5 | n |
        7  43 0   ← Bits
```

Only in the register addressing mode is the number 5 always contained in bits 7 through 4, which the CU interprets as the *address specifier*. This

---

2. In this chapter, the addresses are illustrated in the first operand, but this applies to all operands in any instruction.

specifier is used during the instruction execution. Bits 3 through 0 contain the number of the register used as an address. Whenever any type of register addressing mode is used, the high-order 4 bits (7 through 4) indicate the type of register addressing mode, and the low-order 4 bits (3 through 0) indicate the register being used as an address.

An example of an instruction using the register addressing mode follows, with the assembly language instruction on the right and its machine language instruction on the left.

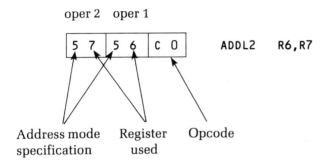

The following example illustrates R6 and R7 used as operands and shows the contents of these registers prior to and after the execution of the preceding instruction.

Before execution	After execution
R6	R6
14 A9 D1 07	14 A9 D1 07
R7	R7
13 21 13 A1	27 CA E4 A8

Note that the contents of R7 have changed while the contents of R6 remain the same. This happened because the instruction is a two-operand instruction. In a two-operand instruction, the first operand is used only to obtain data; the second operand is used first to obtain data and then to store the result.

Register addressing mode should be used to implement counters and accumulators. For example, in cases when the register is to be used as a counter, the instructions **DECL** (decrement longword) or **INCL** (increment longword) can be used. The instruction INCL adds one to the longword whose address is the first and only operand. The instruction DECL subtracts one from the longword whose address is the first and only operand. In the following example, where the register is used as a counter the INCL instruction uses R8 as its operand.

```
INCL    R8
```

Before execution	After execution
R8	R8
00 00 00 A5	00 00 00 A6

In the preceding instruction, the first and only operand is used first to obtain the data and then, after the operation is finished, to store the result in the same memory location. In the following example, a register is used as an accumulator.

```
ADDL2    GRADE+4,R7
```

Before execution	After execution
GRADE+4	GRADE+4
00 00 00 50	00 00 00 50
R7	R7
00 00 01 29	00 00 01 79

Registers can also be used to store intermediate results during calculations. For example, the program in Figure 3.5 uses TEMP as a memory location to store intermediate results during the calculation of the equation. TEMP can be replaced by a register as in the following example.

```
.ENTRY    START,0
MULL3     X,X,Y
MULL3     #3,Y,Y
DIVL3     X,#5,R8
ADDL3     R8,Y,Y
SUBL3     #3,Y,Y
$EXIT_S
.END      START
```

Here the program does not initialize R8 to zero because R8 is used as the third operand, whose only function is to receive the result of the operation.

Storing information in a register can be done in one of two ways: (1) the register is used as an operand, which receives the result from the operation, or (2) information is moved into the register. The instruction DIVL3 X,#5,R8 in the preceding program performs the first method.

The second method is performed by using the **MOVL** (move longword) instruction. To move information into a register means to copy some information from either a memory location or another register. For example, the following MOVL instruction copies data from R8 to R9:

```
MOVL    R8,R9
```

Before execution	After execution
R8	R8
00 A5 78 FF	00 A5 78 FF
R9	R9
00 A7 B3 CE	00 A5 78 FF

The register addressing mode does not help us process arrays. For that we need the deferred addressing mode and the index addressing mode.

Register Deferred Addressing Mode   4.4

The *register deferred addressing mode* uses a register to hold the address of the data rather than the data required in a calculation. Sometimes it is called an *indirect addressing* mode, because the operand indirectly specifies the address of the required data. The general format of an instruction using the register deferred addressing mode is as follows:

```
            First    Second
            Operand  Operand

  LABEL:  OPCODE  (Rn)  ,  .  .  .  .  .  ;COMMENT
```

The register used to represent the register deferred addressing mode must be enclosed by a set of parentheses; for example,

```
ADDL2    (R7),R8
```

Exhibit 4.1 illustrates the contents of registers R7 and R8, and the memory location addressed by the contents of register R7, both before and after execution of the preceding instruction. The contents of R7 (00 00 0A 18) are used as an address to a byte of memory. The opcode of the instruction specifies that the longword data type is used in the operation. The address A18 addresses the low-order byte of that longword.

Thus the value 78 CD 0A 05 is added to the contents of R8, which is 17. The result of this addition, 78 CD 0A 1C, is then stored in R8, and the original contents of R8 are destroyed.

Exhibit 4.1

Before execution	After execution
R7	R7
00 00 0A 18	00 00 0A 18
R8	R8
00 00 00 17	78 CD 0A 1C

Memory address	Memory contents	Memory address	Memory contents
A15	15	A15	15
A16	F5	A16	F5
A17	7B	A17	7B
A18 ⟶	05	A18	05
A19	0A	A19	0A
A1A	CD	A1A	CD
A1B	78	A1B	78

In Section 4.2, it was mentioned that better addressing methods for writing programs to process arrays do exist. One of these is the deferred addressing mode. To illustrate this method, we will use the problem in Figure 4.1, that calculates the sum of twenty test scores.

The following .BLKL storage directive allocates a block of memory consisting of twenty longwords in which the twenty test scores are to be stored.

```
GRADE:    .BLKL    20
```

Assume that the twenty test scores are read from an input file and stored in array GRADE. The following MOVAL instruction copies the address of array GRADE into register R8:

```
MOVAL    GRADE,R8
```

The ADDL2 instruction adds the first test score in the array to the contents of R7.

```
ADDL2    (R8),R7
```

The following instruction increases the contents of register R8 by 4:

```
ADDL2    #4,R8
```

After these instructions are executed, the contents of R8 are equivalent to the address of GRADE + 4. Repeated execution of the ADDL2 #4,R8 instruction changes the contents of R8 so that each new address makes it possible to obtain the next sequential test score in the array. The program segment in Exhibit 4.2 uses this method to add the twenty test scores. Here the instruction **CLRL** (clear longword) initializes the registers R10 and R7 to 0. The instruction AOBLSS causes the loop to repeat twenty times so that the twenty test scores are added.

Exhibit 4.2

```
GRADE:    .BLKL    20                ; ARRAY OF TEST SCORES


          MOVAL    GRADE,R8          ; COPY ADDRESS OF ARRAY GRADE INTO R8
          CLRL     R7                ; INITIALIZE R7 TO 0
          CLRL     R10               ; INITIALIZE R10 TO 0
LOOP:     ADDL2    (R8),R7           ; INCREASE R7 BY A TEST SCORE
          ADDL2    #4,R8             ; INCREASE R8 BY 4
          AOBLSS   #20,R10,LOOP      ; IF R10 < 20 CONTINUE WITH THE LOOP
                                     ;    ELSE CONTINUE WITH THE NEXT INSTRUCTION
```

Index Addressing Mode
4.5

One of the most powerful addressing techniques in the VAX is its ability to use a register as an *index register*. An index register is used to specify the index of an array entry; that is, the register contains the number of the element in the array required for the operation. The index addressing mode can be used *only* in combination with another addressing mode such as the register deferred mode; it *cannot* be used with the register addressing mode. The general format of an instruction using the index addressing mode is as follows:

First Operand		Second Operand	
LABEL:	OPCODE	BASE ADDRESS [Rx]	, ... ;COMMENT

Here BASE ADDRESS is the address of an array, and Rx is a register that contains the *index value*. Note that BASE ADDRESS is immediately followed by Rx, which must be enclosed by square brackets ([ ]). The square brackets inform the assembler that the register contained within them is to be translated as an index register. The CU calculates the address of the data by performing the following steps:

1. It calculates the base value by evaluating the addressing mode used for the base address.
2. It multiplies the contents of the index register by a value equal to the size of each element in the array. (The product does not replace the index value in the Rx.)
3. It calculates the virtual address by adding the base value obtained from Step 1 and the product obtained from Step 2.
4. It accesses the data.

When the index addressing mode is used, the first operand contains one byte for the index specifier [Rx] and *m* number of bytes for the base address. The value for *m* depends upon the type of addressing mode used in conjunction with the indexing. The following example illustrates the use of index addressing mode. The base address is represented by the deferred addressing mode, which is (R7); The indexing is represented by [R5]; for example,

```
ADDL2    (R7)[R5],R6
```

The first operand is represented by two bytes in machine language. One byte is used for the deferred addressing mode (base address), and the second is used to represent the index register. Exhibit 4.3 illustrates the contents of R5, R7, and R6 and the memory location addressed by the first operand, both before and after the execution of the preceding instruction.

F018 is the address obtained from evaluating the first operand of the instruction ADDL2 (R7)[R5],R6. The two values added by this instruction are

$$
\begin{array}{ll}
01\ 00\ 05\ 07\ \leftarrow & \text{First operand} \\
\underline{00\ 00\ 00\ B3}\ \leftarrow & \text{Second operand} \\
01\ 00\ 05\ BA\ \leftarrow & \text{Second operand (result)}
\end{array}
$$

Note that only the contents of R6 change; everything else remains the same. The only reason R6 changes is because it is used as the accumulator in the summation of the test scores. Figure 4.2 presents the same program as in Figure 4.1 except that now this program segment uses the index register addressing mode to sum the twenty test scores. The program segment presented in Figure 4.2 uses R10 as the counter and also as the index register. This is possible because the AOBLSS instruction increases R10 by one every time the loop is executed.

The important point to keep in mind when using the index register addressing mode is that the CU knows from the opcode of the instruction what factor to use to multiply the contents of the index register. So

Exhibit 4.3

Before execution	After execution
R5	R5
00 00 00 01	00 00 00 01
R7	R7
00 00 F0 14	00 00 F0 14
R6	R6
00 00 00 B3	01 00 05 BA

Memory address	Memory contents	Memory address	Memory contents
F014	15	F014	15
F015	10	F015	10
F016	07	F016	07
F017	05	F017	05
F018⟶	07	F018	07
F019	05	F019	05
F01A	00	F01A	00
F01B	01	F01B	01

Figure 4.2

```
        .TITLE   FIG42

GRADE:  .BLKL    20              ;ALLOCATE THE ARRAY

        .ENTRY   START,0

; ASSUME THAT THE TEST SCORES ARE READ IN THIS PART OF THE PROGRAM

        MOVAL    GRADE,R8        ;COPY ADDRESS OF ARRAY GRADE INTO R8
        CLRL     R7              ;INITIALIZE R7 TO 0
        CLRL     R10             ;INITIALIZE R10 TO 0
LOOP:   ADDL2    (R8)[R10],R7    ;INCREASE R7 BY A TEST SCORE
        AOBLSS   #20,R10,LOOP    ;IF R10 < 20 CONTINUE WITH THE LOOP
                                 ;   ELSE CONTINUE WITH THE NEXT INSTRUCTION
```

far, we have not studied instructions that operate on different data types. However, there are such instructions and, when these instructions use the index addressing mode, the CU chooses the correct factor to multiply the contents of the index register. In Chapter 1, it was stated that there are byte, word, longword, quadword and octaword data types; the correct factors that the CU would choose are 1, 2, 4, 8 and 16, respectively. Each of these data types is covered in later chapters.

Index addressing mode can be used in conjunction with the relative addressing mode. For example, the program segment in Figure 4.2 could have been written as follows:

```
GRADE:   .BLKL    20

         .ENTRY   START,0

         CLRL     R7
         CLRL     R10
LOOP:    ADDL2    GRADE[R10],R7
         AOBLSS   #20,R10,LOOP
```

The relative addressing mode should not be used in a loop because it slows down the loop processing. This is because the calculation of the virtual address represented by relative address mode is longer than when an operand is represented by register deferred addressing mode.

The index addressing mode can be used to sort the array of test scores. Figure 4.3 presents a flowchart for sorting the array of twenty test scores. The sorting technique used in the flowchart is commonly called the interchange sort.

The program in Figure 4.4 was coded from the flowchart presented in Figure 4.3. This program may either use a FORTRAN or a Pascal procedure to perform input and output operations. Sample FORTRAN and Pascal procedures can be found in Appendix C.

Figure 4.4 uses two index registers in the sorting procedure. The first register, R10, compares the same test score to every test score in the array. Using R8 makes all test scores sequentially available for the comparison to the same test score.

4.6 *Displacement Addressing Mode*

The addressing modes presented thus far assume that all elements in a list are the same length and that the list is processed sequentially. The *displacement addressing* mode makes it possible to access elements in a list that contains different-sized elements; in addition, this addressing mode makes it possible to process a list randomly. The displacement addressing mode informs the CU of the distance in bytes between the needed

Figure 4.3

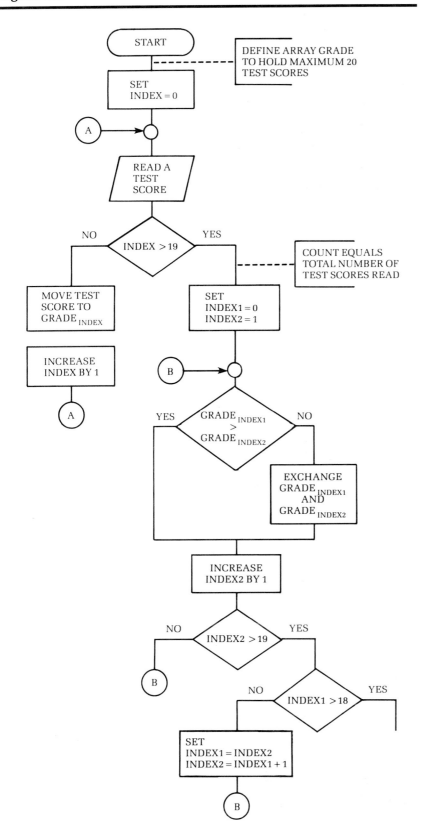

Figure 4.4

```
        .TITLE  FIG44

; THIS PROGRAM READS TEST SCORES,  ONE VALUE PER LINE.
; THE READING IS ACCOMPLISHED BY THE USE OF A HIGHER LEVEL
; LANGUAGE PROCEDURE. THE ARRAY OF TEST SCORES IS SORTED AND
; THIS SORTED ARRAY IS PRINTED, ONE VALUE PER LINE. THE OUTPUT
; IS ACCOMPLISHED BY THE USE OF A HIGHER LEVEL LANGUAGE PROCEDURE.

; THE SORTING METHOD USED IS THE INTERCHANGE SORT

GRADE:  .BLKL   20                      ;MAXIMUM NUMBER OF TEST SCORES THAT THIS
                                        ;PROGRAM CAN PROCESS
ADDRESS_GRADE:
        .ADDRESS GRADE
SCORE:  .LONG   0
INARG:  .LONG   1                       ;INFORMATION REQUIRED BY THE INPUT PROCEDURE
        .ADDRESS SCORE
OUTARG: .LONG   1                       ;INFORMATION REQUIRED BY THE OUTPUT PROCEDURE
        .ADDRESS SCORE

        .ENTRY  START,0
        MOVL    ADDRESS_GRADE,R7        ;MOVE ADDRESS OF ARRAY GRADE INTO R7
        CLRL    R9                      ;INITIALIZE REGISTER TO BE USED AS INDEX REGISTER
READLOOP:
        CALLG   INARG,RDINPUT           ;CALL A PROCEDURE TO READ A TEST SCORE
        MOVL    SCORE,(R7)[R9]          ;MOVE TEST SCORE INTO ARRAY GRADE
        AOBLEQ  #19,R9,READLOOP         ;IF R9 < OR = 19 GO TO READLOOP
                                        ;   ELSE CONTINUE WITH THE NEXT INSTRUCTION
START_SORT:
        CLRL    R10                     ;SET INDEX REGISTER TO ZERO
LOOP1:  ADDL3   #1,R10,R8
LOOP2:  CMPL    (R7)[R10],(R7)[R8]      ;COMPARE TWO CONSECUTIVE TEST SCORES
        BGTR    SKIP                    ;IF EQUAL DO NOT EXCHANGE
        MOVL    (R7)[R10],R6            ;IF NOT EQUAL, MOVE SMALLER TEST SCORE INTO R6
        MOVL    (R7)[R8],(R7)[R10]      ;MOVE THE LARGER TEST SCORE INTO LOCATION OF SMALLER SCORE
        MOVL    R6,(R7)[R8]             ;MOVE THE SMALLER TEST SCORE INTO WHERE THE LARGER WAS
SKIP:   AOBLEQ  #19,R8,LOOP2            ;IF R8 < OR = 19 GO TO LOOP2
        AOBLEQ  #18,R10,LOOP1           ;   ELSE IF R10 < OR = 18 GO TO LOOP1
                                        ;         ELSE CONTINUE WITH THE NEXT INSTRUCTION

; BEGIN PRINTING

        CLRL    R10                     ;SET THE INDEX REGISTER TO ZERO
        MOVL    ADDRESS_GRADE,R7        ;MOVE THE ADDRESS OF THE ARRAY GRADE INTO R7
PRINT:  MOVL    (R7)[R10],SCORE         ;MOVE A TEST SCORE INTO OUTPUT FIELD
        CALLG   OUTARG,WROUTPUT         ;CALL A PROCEDURE TO PRINT A TEST SCORE
        AOBLEQ  #19,R10,PRINT           ;IF R10 < OR = TO 19 GO TO PRINT
        $EXIT_S                         ;   ELSE STOP PROGRAM EXECUTION
        .END    START
```

element and the first element of the list. The general format of the instruction using the displacement addressing mode is as follows; note that the displacement value directly precedes (Rn).

	First Operand		Second Operand	
LABEL:	OPCODE	DISPLACEMENT (Rn)	, ...	;COMMENT

The CU calculates the virtual address represented by the displacement addressing mode in the following manner:

1. If the displacement value is contained in a byte or word, the displacement value is *sign-extended* to a 32-bit value by the CU.
2. Then the CU adds the displacement value and the value obtained from the Rn. The sum of the two is the virtual address.
3. Finally, the CU accesses the data.

The displacement can be represented by a constant or an expression. The expression can yield either a positive or negative value and can occupy a byte, word, or longword in the *instruction stream*. The ability to express the displacement value in three different sizes saves memory space; thus, if the needed data item is within $+127$ to -128 bytes from the base address, the displacement value can be contained in one byte. If, however, the needed data item is within $+32K-1$ to $-32K$ bytes from the base address, a word must be used to contain the displacement value.

The following instruction illustrates how the displacement addressing mode works.

```
ADDL2    4(R5),R6
```

The first operand uses the displacement addressing mode, which in machine language is represented by two bytes, with the first byte containing the displacement value of 4, and the second byte containing the deferred addressing mode. Note that the displacement value of 4 is not preceded by a number sign (#). The number sign is only used in front of a constant that represents the entire operand. Exhibit 4.4 illustrates the contents of R5 and R6, and the memory locations addressed to by the first operand, both before and after the execution of the preceding instruction.

The F018 is the address that the CU calculates from the data provided in the first operand of the instruction ADDL2   4(R5),R6. The two values added by this instruction are as follows:

```
01 00 05 07  ← First operand
00 00 00 B3  ← Second operand
01 00 05 BA  ← Second operand (result)
```

The program in Figure 4.5 sorts an array of test scores by using the displacement addressing mode. The sorting method used in this program is called the bubble sort.

Exhibit 4.4

Before execution	After execution
R5	R5
00 00 F0 14	00 00 F0 14
R6	R6
00 00 00 B3	01 00 05 BA

Memory address	Memory contents	Memory address	Memory contents
F014	15	F014	15
F015	10	F015	10
F016	07	F016	07
F017	05	F017	05
F018 ——→	07	F018	07
F019	05	F019	05
F01A	00	F01A	00
F01B	01	F01B	01

In the following instruction from the program in Figure 4.5,

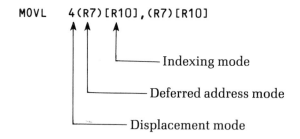

```
MOVL    4(R7)[R10],(R7)[R10]
```

both the displacement and the index addressing modes are used in one operand. In this case the virtual address is calculated by first adding the displacement value (4) to the address contained in R7. This sum is increased by the product obtained by multiplying the contents of R10 (the index register) and the factor of 4. A factor of 4 is used because the data type is longword.

Figure 4.5

```
        .TITLE   FIG45

; THIS PROGRAM READS TEST SCORES,  ONE VALUE PER LINE.
; THE READING IS ACCOMPLISHED BY THE USE OF A HIGHER LEVEL
; LANGUAGE PROCEDURE. THE ARRAY OF TEST SCORES IS SORTED AND
; IT IS PRINTED ONE VALUE PER LINE. THE OUTPUT IS
; ACCOMPLISHED BY THE USE OF A HIGHER LEVER LANGUAGE PROCEDURE.


; THE SORTING METHOD USED IS THE BUBBLE SORT

GRADE:  .BLKL    20               ;MAXIMUM NUMBER OF TEST SCORES THAT THIS
                                  ;PROGRAM CAN PROCESS
ADDRESS_GRADE:
        .ADDRESS GRADE
SCORE:  .LONG    0
INARG:  .LONG    1                ;INFORMATION REQUIRED BY THE INPUT PROCEDURE
        .ADDRESS SCORE
OUTARG: .LONG    1                ;INFORMATION REQUIRED BY THE OUTPUT PROCEDURE
        .ADDRESS SCORE

        .ENTRY   START,0
        MOVL     ADDRESS_GRADE,R7
        CLRL     R9               ;INITIALIZE REGISTER TO BE USED AS INDEX REGISTER
READLOOP:
        CALLG    INARG,RDINPUT    ;CALL AN INPUT PROCEDURE TO READ A TEST SCORE
        MOVL     SCORE,(R7)[R9]   ;MOVE TEST SCORE INTO ARRAY GRADE
        AOBLEQ   #19,R9,READLOOP  ;IF R9 < OR = 19 GO TO READLOOP
                                  ;   ELSE CONTINUE WITH THE NEXT INSTRUCTION

START_SORT:
        MOVL     ADDRESS_GRADE,R7 ;MOVE ADDRESS OF ARRAY GRADE INTO R7
        CLRL     R8               ;SET COUNTER FOR THE OUTSIDE LOOP EQUAL TO ZERO
LOOP1:  CLRL     R10              ;SET INDEX REGISTER TO ZERO
LOOP2:  CMPL     (R7)[R10],4(R7)[R10] ;COMPARE TWO CONSECUTIVE TEST SCORES
        BGTR     SKIP             ;IF EQUAL DO NOT EXCHANGE
        MOVL     (R7)[R10],R6     ;IF NOT EQUAL, MOVE SMALLER TEST SCORE INTO R9
        MOVL     4(R7)[R10],(R7)[R10] ;MOVE THE LARGER TEST SCORE INTO LOCATION OF SMALLER SCORE
        MOVL     R6,4(R7)[R10]    ;MOVE THE SMALLER TEST SCORE INTO WHERE THE LARGER WAS
SKIP:   AOBLEQ   #18,R10,LOOP2    ;IF R10 < OR = 18 GO TO LOOP2
        AOBLEQ   #19,R8,LOOP1     ;   ELSE IF R8 < OR = 19 GO TO LOOP1
                                  ;       ELSE CONTINUE WITH THE NEXT INSTRUCTION


; BEGIN PRINTING

        CLRL     R10              ;SET THE INDEX REGISTER TO ZERO
        MOVL     ADDRESS_GRADE,R7 ;MOVE THE ADDRESS OF THE ARRAY GRADE INTO R7
PRINT:  MOVL     (R7)[R10],SCORE  ;MOVE A TEST SCORE INTO OUTPUT FIELD
        CALLG    OUTARG,WROUTPUT  ;CALL SUBROUTINE TO PRINT A TEST SCORE
        AOBLEQ   #19,R10,PRINT    ;IF R10 < OR = 19 GO TO PRINT
        $EXIT_S                   ;   ELSE STOP PROGRAM EXECUTION
        .END     START
$
```

Part 2. Enrichment Topics

4.7 Autoincrement Addressing Mode

The *autoincrement addressing mode* is an addressing technique that can
be used to step through an array sequentially. This technique is similar
to the index addressing technique in that both permit the sequential processing of array elements without regard to the size of each element.
However, the manner in which the CU calculates the address of the next
sequential element is not the same for both the autoincrement and the
index addressing modes.

When an operand is represented by the autoincrement addressing
mode, the address contained in a register is automatically incremented
in such a way that the register contains the address of the next sequential element in the array. The value used to increase the contents of register equals the number of bytes used to represent an element in the array.
Every element in an array can be represented by either a byte, a word, a
longword, a quadword, or an octaword; the value for each, respectively,
is 1, 2, 4, 8, and 16. The CU interprets the opcode, which specifies the
size of an element to be operated on. Each time the virtual address is calculated for an operand represented by the autoincrement addressing
mode, the contents of a register are incremented by that value.

The autoincrement addressing mode is represented by (Rn)+. The
difference between the deferred addressing mode and the autoincrement addressing mode is the + (plus) sign that follows the right-hand
parenthesis. The general format of an instruction using the autoincrement addressing mode is as follows:

First   Second
Operand Operand

LABEL:	OPCODE	(Rn)1	, ...	;COMMENT

The CU performs the following operations when evaluating an oper-
and represented by the autoincrement addressing mode.

1. Obtains the data by using the contents of Rn as the virtual address
2. Increments Rn by a value equal to the size of each element in
   the array
3. Replaces the old value in Rn with the new value obtained in
   Step 2

The following instruction illustrates what happens to the contents of the
register that is used to represent the autoincrement addressing mode.

ADDL2   (R5)+,R4

Exhibit 4.5 illustrates the contents of R5 and R4, and the memory locations addressed by the first operand, both before and after the execution of the preceding instruction.

Exhibit 4.5

Before execution	After execution
R5	R5
00 00 0F 18	00 00 0F 1C
R4	R4
00 00 00 0F	00 F5 00 16

Memory address	Memory contents	Memory address	Memory contents
F17	AB	F17	AB
F18 ────→	07	F18	07
F19	00	F19	00
F1A	F5	F1A	F5
F1B	00	F1B	00

Note that the contents of the memory locations did not change, but that the contents of both registers did change. The autoincrement addressing mode can be thought of as post-increment, because the contents of the register containing the address change after the operand is evaluated.

The program segment presented in Figure 4.2 appears again in Figure 4.6 except that now the autoincrement addressing mode was used to add the twenty test scores.

Figure 4.6

```
        .TITLE   FIG46

; PROGRAM SEGMENT ADDS 20 TEST SCORES USING AUTOINCREMENT ADDRESSING MODE

GRADE:  .BLKL    20               ;ALLOCATE THE ARRAY

        .ENTRY   START,0

; ASSUME THAT THE TEST SCORES ARE READ IN THIS PART OF THE PROGRAM

        MOVAL    GRADE,R8         ;MOVE ADDRESS OF ARRAY GRADE INTO R8
        CLRL     R7               ;SET ACCUMULATOR TO 0
        CLRL     R10              ;SET R10 TO ZERO
LOOP:   ADDL2    (R8)+,R7         ;ADD A TEST SCORE TO SUM
        AOBLSS   #20,R10,LOOP     ;IF R10 < 20 CONTINUE WITH THE LOOP
                                  ;    ELSE CONTINUE WITH THE NEXT INSTRUCTION
```

In the instruction LOOP: ADDL2 (R8)+,R7, the first operand (R8)+ is represented by the autoincrement addressing mode. Initially, the contents of R8 are the address of the first element of the array GRADE. After this element is obtained for the operation, the CU increases R8 by 4; thus the contents of R8 are the address of the next element to be added. In this manner, each time the instruction LOOP: ADDL2 (R8)+,R7 is executed, the next sequential test score is added to R7. The difference between the index and the autoincrement addressing modes is that, when the index addressing mode is used, the contents of the register containing the address of the array (base address) do not change; when the autoincrement addressing mode is used, however, the contents of the register *do* change.

The autoincrement addressing mode can also be used to initialize an array. If we assume that the array GRADE must be initialized to 0 (zero), the program segment in Figure 4.7 will perform this task.

The contents of R8 are incremented by 4 each time the instruction CLRL is executed. Thus the next time the instruction CLRL is executed, R8 contains the address of the next sequential element. In this manner all twenty elements are set to zero. This procedure is used when an array must be reinitialized during the program execution. If, however, an array is to be initialized at the start of program execution, a data-storage directive can be used for its initialization. For example, the following data-storage directive will initialize the array GRADE to a -1.

```
GRADE:    .LONG    -1[20]
```

This data-storage directive will place a -1 in each longword of the array GRADE. The value used to initialize each element of the array is the value that directly precedes the square brackets. The value contained in the brackets is the size of the array.

The autoincrement addressing mode can also be used to search an array for specific value. For example, consider searching the array GRADE for the highest test score. The array, however, does not necessarily contain twenty test scores. Therefore the program's search ends when it encounters a value of -1, because the entire array was initialized to -1 prior to reading the test scores. The need for the AOBLSS instruction arises when the array GRADE does contain twenty test scores. If this is the case, there will be no -1 test score, and if the AOBLSS in-

Figure 4.7

```
        .TITLE   FIG47

GRADE:  .BLKL    20

        .ENTRY   START,0

        MOVAL    GRADE,R8
        CLRL     R10
LOOP:   CLRL     (R8)+            ;INITIALIZES AN ELEMENT OF THE ARRAY GRADE TO ZERO
        AOBLEQ   #20,R10,LOOP
```

Figure 4.8

```
        .TITLE     FIG48

;INITIALIZE EACH ELEMENT IN ARRAY GRADE TO -1

GRADE:  .LONG      -1[20]
MAX_GRADE:
        .BLKL      1

        .ENTRY     START,0

;ASSUME THE TEST SCORES ARE READ INTO ARRAY GRADE

        MOVAL      GRADE,R7         ;MOVE ADDRESS OF ARRAY GRADE INTO R7
        CLRL       R10              ;INITIALIZE R10 TO 0
        MOVL       (R7),MAX_GRADE   ;SET MAX_GRADE TO THE FIRST SCORE
LOOP:   CMPL       #-1,(R7)         ;IF SCORE = -1 THEN
        BEQL       FINISH           ;    STOP PROGRAM EXECUTION
                                    ;    ELSE CONTINUE WITH THE NEXT INSTRUCTION
        CMPL       (R7)+,MAX_GRADE  ;IF SCORE < OR = TO SCORE IN MAX_GRADE THEN
        BLEQ       NEXT             ;    CONTINUE WITH THE SEARCH
        MOVL       -4(R7),MAX_GRADE ;    ELSE COPY SCORE INTO MAX_GRADE
NEXT:   AOBLSS     #20,R10,LOOP     ;IF R10 < 20 GO TO LOOP
FINISH: $EXIT_S                     ;    ELSE STOP PROGRAM EXECUTION
        .END       START
```

struction had not been included, the program in Figure 4.8 would have
had an infinite loop.

Autodecrement Addressing Mode   *4.8*

The *autodecrement addressing mode* is another addressing technique
that allows sequential stepping through an array. The difference between the autoincrement and autodecrement addressing modes is that
in autodecrement, the stepping begins with the last element of the array
and moves toward the first element of the array; in autoincrement, it begins with the first and moves toward the last element. In the autodecrement addressing mode, the operand is a register whose contents are the
address of the required data, as was the case with the register deferred
addressing mode. The difference is that before the CU uses this address
to access the data, it automatically decreases the contents of Rn by a value
equal to the number of bytes indicated by the data type used in the operation. The data type is specified by the opcode of the instruction, which
also determines whether Rn is decremented by 1, 2, 4, 8, or 16 for a byte,
word, longword, quadword, or octaword operand, respectively. The
general format of an instruction using the autodecrement addressing
mode follows.

		First Operand	Second Operand	
LABEL:	OPCODE	-(Rn)	, ...	;COMMENT

Note that when the autodecrement addressing mode is used, not only is Rn enclosed in parentheses, but it is also immediately preceded by a minus sign (−).

The CU performs the following procedures when it evaluates an operand specified by the autodecrement addressing mode:

1. It decrements Rn by a value equal to the size of the data type of the instruction.
2. It replaces the old value in Rn with the new value obtained in Step 1. (The virtual address is the new contents of Rn.)
3. It accesses the data.

The following example illustrates what happens to a register when it is used to represent autodecrement addressing mode.

$$\text{ADDL2} \quad -(R8),R3$$

Exhibit 4.6 illustrates the contents of R8 and R3, and the memory locations addressed by the first operand of the preceding instruction, both before and after its execution.

Exhibit 4.6

Before execution	After execution
R8	R8
00 00 F0 18	00 00 F0 14
R3	R3
00 00 00 B6	01 00 15 C9

Memory address	Memory contents	Memory address	Memory contents
F013	11	F013	11
F014———————►13	13	F014	13
F015	15	F015	15
F016	00	F016	00
F017	01	F017	01

Figure 4.9

```
        .TITLE   FIG49

;PROGRAM SEGMENT ADDS 20 TEST SCORES USING AUTODECREMENT ADDRESSING MODE

GRADE:   .BLKL    20

         .ENTRY   START,0

; ASSUME THAT THE TEST SCORES ARE READ IN THIS PART OF THE PROGRAM

         MOVAL    GRADE+80,R7      ;MOVE ADDRESS OF THE BYTE WHICH IMMEDIATELY
                                   ;FOLLOWS THE LAST BYTE OF THE ARRAY GRADE
         CLRL     R10              ;SET LOOP COUNTER TO ZERO
         CLRL     R8               ;SET ACCUMULATOR (R8) TO 0
LOOP:    ADDL2    -(R7),R8         ;ADD A TEST SCORE TO SUM
         AOBLSS   #20,R10,LOOP     ;IF R10 < 20 CONTINUE WITH THE LOOP
                                   ;    ELSE CONTINUE WITH NEXT INSTRUCTION
```

The two values added as a result of executing the preceding instruction are as follows:

$$
\begin{array}{ll}
01\ 00\ 15\ 13 & \leftarrow \text{First operand} \\
\underline{00\ 00\ 00\ B6} & \leftarrow \text{Second operand} \\
01\ 00\ 15\ C9 & \leftarrow \text{Second operand}
\end{array}
$$

The program segment in Figure 4.9 performs the same job as the program in Figure 4.6, except that it uses the autodecrement addressing mode. When the autodecrement addressing mode is used, addition begins with the last test score in the array because the address value is decreased rather than increased.

The instruction MOVAL   GRADE + 80,R7 is used in the program in Figure 4.9. This instruction moves into R7, the address of the longword, which is located directly below the end of the array. This is necessary because the autodecrement addressing mode immediately decreases the address by a factor equal to the length of the data type. In this case it would decrease the contents of R7 by 4, producing the address of the last test score in the array. Autodecrement addressing mode can be thought of as pre-decrement, because the contents of the register containing the address change before the operand is evaluated.

Autoincrement Deferred Addressing Mode   4.9

The *autoincrement deferred addressing* mode is useful when the programmer needs to advance sequentially through a table of addresses instead of a table of values. In the autoincrement deferred addressing mode, Rn contains the address that points to a list of address. The general format of an instruction using the autoincrement addressing mode is as follows.

First   Second
Operand   Operand

LABEL:	OPCODE	@Rn+	, ...	;COMMENT

Note that the autoincrement deferred addressing mode is immediately preceded by the symbol @ and followed by a plus sign (+), and that Rn is enclosed in parentheses.

The CU performs the following procedures when it evaluates an operand specified by the autoincrement addressing mode.

1. Retrieves the contents of the memory longword that the contents of Rn point to.
2. Uses the value obtained from the longword as the physical address to access a longword containing an address.
3. Uses the address just retrieved as the physical address to access the needed data.
4. Increments the contents of Rn by a value of 4.
5. Replaces the old value in Rn with the new value obtained in Step 4.

The following example illustrates what happens to a register when it is used to represent the autoincrement addressing mode.

ADDW2   @(R7)+,R5

Exhibit 4.7 illustrates the contents of registers R7 and R5, and the memory locations addressed by the address contained in register R7, both before and after execution of the preceding instruction. The contents of register R7 are the address to the longword containing 00 00 24 0F, which is the address of the low-order byte of the word containing the needed data (A207).

Exhibit 4.7

Before execution	After execution
R7	R7
00 00 24 08	00 00 24 0A
R5	R5
00 00 00 0A	00 00 A2 11

Exhibit 4.7 (*continued*)

Memory address	Memory contents	Memory address	Memory contents
2406	00	2406	00
2407	00	2407	00
2408	0F	2408	0F
2409	24	2409	24
240A	00	240A	00
240B	00	240B	00
240C	00	240C	00
240D	AB	240D	AB
240E	67	240E	67
240F	07	240F	07
2410	A2	2410	A2
2411	05	2411	05

More on the Displacement Addressing Mode   **4.10**

During the assembly, the assembler places the *displacement value* into the smallest possible number of bytes. This process can be altered by instructing the assembler the specific number of bytes to be used to contain the displacement value. This is accomplished by preceding the displacement value with a length specifier. The length specifier is coded by one of the letters B, W, or L for byte, word, or longword, respectively; and the letter is followed by circumflex character (^). The length specifiers are as follows:

Displacement length specifier	Meaning
B^	Displacement contained in 1 byte
W^	Displacement contained in 1 word (2 bytes)
L^	Displacement contained in 1 longword (4 bytes)

When a displacement length specifier does not precede a displacement and the displacement is a constant, the assembler chooses the smallest number of bytes (1, 2, or 4) required to store the displacement. When the length specifier does not precede the displacement and the displacement is represented by an expression that cannot be evaluated at the time the instruction is being processed by the assembler, the assembler sets aside a word that ultimately will receive the displacement value. In a case where the word is too small to contain the displacement, the linker displays an error message. The machine language formats for an operand using byte, word, and longword for the displacement in the displacement addressing mode are displayed in Exhibit 4.8.

Exhibit 4.8

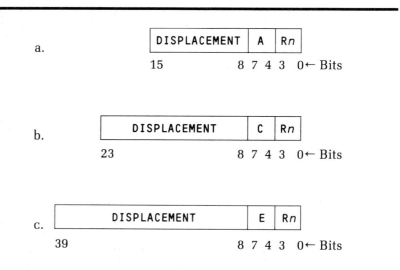

In Format a in Exhibit 4.8, bits 15 through 8 contain the displacement value; bits 7 through 4 contain the hexadecimal value A, denoting that the displacement will be contained in one byte; and bits 3 through 0 contain the register number used for the deferred addressing mode. In Format b, bits 23 through 8 contain the displacement value; bits 7 through 4 contain the hexadecimal value C, denoting that the displacement will be contained in one word; and bits 3 through 0 contain the register number used for the deferred addressing mode. In Format c, bits 39 through 8 contain the displacement value; bits 7 through 4 contain the hexadecimal value E, denoting that the displacement will be contained in one longword; and bits 3 through 0 contain the register number used for the deferred addressing mode.

By default, the assembler will represent the displacement value in the smallest possible data type. If the programmer wishes to override the default value, each displacement must be preceded by a B, W, or L, which informs the assembler that the displacement is to be represented in a byte, word, or longword, respectively. Each letter must be followed by a ^ (circumflex) to inform the assembler that the B, W or L does not begin a label. The following instructions illustrate how to override the default value:

```
MOVL    B^24(R8),R6             ;STORE DISPLACEMENT IN A BYTE
MOVL    W^386(R4),R5            ;STORE DISPLACEMENT IN A WORD
MOVL    L^75250(R3),R2          ;STORE DISPLACEMENT IN A LONGWORD
```

Summary

This chapter covers all possible register addressing modes. The register addressing modes discussed in Sections 4.0 through 4.4 are essential for writing programs in MACRO assembly language. Using the register addressing mode in place of the relative addressing mode increases the speed of program execution. Usually, the slowest part of program execution is the time required to obtain the data needed for an operation. To obtain the data, the address used to express an operand must be calculated. When an operand is expressed by a relative addressing mode, the CU requires more time to calculate the virtual address than when the operand is expressed by a register addressing mode.

The index addressing mode makes it convenient to work with sequential lists (arrays). It also makes it possible to work with two different data type arrays. This is possible because the index register is increased by one rather than by the size of an element in the array.

The addressing modes discussed in Sections 4.6 through 4.10 are supplementary to the addressing modes discussed in Sections 4.0 through 4.5. These additional addressing modes make certain applications easier to code. For example, processing of arrays is a frequent operation; therefore, in addition to the standard method of processing arrays by indexing, VAX MACRO assembly language provides two additional addressing modes to handle arrays: these are the autoincrement and autodecrement addressing modes.

New Instructions

ADDW2
CLRL
DECL
INCL
MOVAL
MOVL

New Terms

access type
address specifier
autodecrement addressing mode
autoincrement addressing mode
autoincrement deferred addressing
  mode
displacement addressing mode
displacement value
expression
index addressing mode
index value
index register

indirect addressing mode
instruction stream
length specifier
machine language format
mnemonic
post-increment
pre-decrement
register addressing mode
register deferred addressing mode
relative addressing mode
sign extended

Exercises

1. What makes MACRO language instructions vary in length?

2. Is there an advantage to having instructions of varying lengths? Why?

3. How does relative addressing mode differ from register addressing mode?

4. Why is it better to use register addressing mode when a data item must be referenced frequently?

5. What is the contents R5 after the following group of instructions are executed?

```
MOVL    #5,R7
MULL    R7,R7
MOVL    R7,R5
```

6. How does register addressing mode differ from register deferred addressing mode?

7. Given the following storage directive

```
INDEX:    .BLKL 20
```

Write the necessary instructions to initialize each element in the array INDEX to its index position.

   a. Use deferred addressing mode.
   b. Use index addressing mode.

8. Why should you not use displacement addressing mode when stepping through an array sequentially?

9. What is the difference between index and autoincrement addressing modes?

Use the following contents for both the registers and memory to answer Questions 10 and 11. Assume that each part of each question is executed independently.

Registers	Memory	
	Address	**Contents**
R1 00 00 01 09	00 00 01 04	00 00 01 0C
R2 00 00 01 08	00 00 01 08	00 00 01 0A
R3 00 00 01 00	00 00 01 0C	00 00 01 0B
R4 00 00 01 0C		
R5 00 00 01 04		
R6 00 00 00 01		
R7 00 A1 00 02		
R8 00 0F 08 9A		

10. Indicate the contents of the registers used and the contents of memory when they change for each of the following:

a.	ADDL2	R4,R6
b.	SUBL3	R3,R8,R1
c.	SUBL2	(R2),R8
d.	ADDL3	(R2),R3,(R2)
e.	SUBL2	R6,R1
	ADDL2	(R1),R3

11. Indicate the contents of the registers used for each of the following:

a.	ADDL2	(R5)+,(R5)+,R6
b.	ADDL3	(R5)+,-(R4),R6
c.	DIVW2	8(R3),R2
d.	MULL2	3(R1),R6

Use the following contents for both the registers and memory to answer Questions 12 through 14. Assume that each part of each question is executed independently.

Memory		Registers
Address	**Contents**	**before**
200	0000020C	R0 = 210
204	00000210	R1 = 1
208	00000214	R2 = 204
20C	00000208	R3 = 210
210	53778995	R4 = 208
214	00000208	R5 = 214
218	00000204	R6 = 218
		R7 = 200
		R8 = 204
		R9 = 20C
		R10 = 0
		R11 = 0

12. Indicate the contents of the registers used by each of the following, and indicate changes in memory, if any.

a.	MOVL	(R3)[R1],R7
b.	ADDL2	(R2)[R10],R8
c.	ADDL3	(R3)[R1],(R4)[R11],(R8)
d.	ADDL2	#2,R1
	SUBL2	(R7)[R1],(R5)
e.	SUBL3	R8,(R5),R5
	MOVL	(R7)[R5],R11

13. Indicate the contents of the registers used by each of the following:

```
a.    MOVL    4(R2),R7
b.    ADDL3   #4,8(R2),R5
      MOVL    4(R5),R8
c.    ADDL3   20(R7),R1,R10
d.    MOVL    4(R3)[R1],R7
```

14. Indicate the contents of the registers used by each of the following:

```
a.    MOVL    R5,R7
b.    MOVL    #9,R7
c.    MOVL    (R5),R7
d.    MOVL    (R5)[R1],R7
e.    MOVL    (R5)[R1],(R8)
f.    MOVL    (R8),(R9)[R1]
g.    MOVL    #524,R11
      MOVL    (R11),R6
```

15. What are the contents of A after the following program is executed?

```
ARRAY:  .LONG   1,2,3,4,5,6,7,8,9,10,11,12,13,14,15,16
A:      .LONG   0
        .ENTRY  START,0
        MOVAL   ARRAY,R5
        CLRL    R4
        ADDL    #3,R4
AGAIN:  ADDL2   (R5)[R4],A
        CMPL    #15,R4
        BEQL    DONE
        ADDL    #4,R4
        BRB     AGAIN       ;THIS BRANCH INSTRUCTION CONTINUES PROGRAM
                            ;EXECUTION STARTING WITH THE INSTRUCTION
                            ;WHOSE LABEL IS AGAIN
DONE:   $EXIT_S
        .END    START
```

16. Insert assembly instructions where necessary to complete the exercise.

```
GRADE:     .BLKL   50
SMALLEST:  .BLKL   1
POSITION:  .BLKL   1

;ENTER HERE ADDITIONAL STORAGE DIRECTIVES
;THAT MAY BE REQUIRED TO DO THE PROBLEM
```

```
      .ENTRY   START,0

;ASSUME THAT NECESSARY INSTRUCTIONS THAT READ THE
;TEST SCORES ARE INSERTED HERE

;WRITE THE NECESSARY INSTRUCTIONS THAT WILL FIND THE
;SMALLEST TEST SCORE AND ITS POSITION IN THE ARRAY GRADE



      .END    START
```

Problems

1. Write a program that reads three integer values from one input record. The program determines the largest value and prints only that value. The input file contains ten records.

2. Write a program that reads an input file where each record contains one value. Place the negative values into one array and the positive values into another array. Print both arrays in column order. Assume that the input file will not contain more than fifty records.

3. Expand the problem in Question 1 by finding the largest negative value and its position; print both the value and the position.

4. Write a program that reads a list of fifteen numbers and prints the list in reverse order; that is, the last value read in should be printed first.

5. Write a program that reads twenty grades. Each record of the input file contains two grades, and the input file consists of ten records. In addition to reading, the program must compute the number of grades that are below the average. The program must also print all grades in one column followed by the average and, finally, in another column the number of grades that are below the average.

6. Read in two numeric arrays, and then merge them into one array. The input file contains twenty-five input records, and each record contains two values. In addition, the records in the input file should be arranged in ascending order.

7. A teacher gave an exam to a class of thirty students. The exam consisted of one hundred true-and-false questions. Now the tests have been graded, and you must write a program that will assign a letter grade to each numeric grade. Use the following table in assigning the letter grades.

56 Below	F
61–57	D −
64–62	D
68–65	D +
71–69	C −
74–72	C
78–75	C +
81–79	B −
85–82	B
86–89	B +
90–93	A −
94–100	A

The letter grades can be assigned by moving a character constant; for example,

```
MOVW    #^A/B-/,(R6)[R7]
```

The character constant is represented by ASCII (^A) type data type. The MOVW is used because the character constant contains two characters, B − .

8. Write a program that will help Professor Lazy Goof score a test that he administers. The test consists of fifty multiple-choice questions. Each student enters a digit from 1 through 5 as an answer to each question. Immediately following the last answer is the student's ID number, which consists of the last five digits of the student's social security number. The first record in the input file is the key to the test. The remaining records are the students' answer records. The program should score each student's exam and print the ID number and the grade.

9. Write a program that will raise a real value having a format of xx.x to the *n*th power. This program should use the integer instruction set. Keep in mind that a real value of format xx.x in integer arithmetic is treated as xxx. Therefore the programmer must keep track of the position of the decimal point after each multiplication.

10. The following figure below illustrates a *linked list*, which is a form of an array. Each element (node) in this type of array holds data and the address of the next node. The first node holds the address of the next node, which contains the first data element of the linked list. If the linked list contains no data, it is called an "empty" list. In this case, the first node holds some value that indicates that the list is empty. The last node holds data, and the address of this node is some value that indicates that the end of the linked list has been reached.

Top

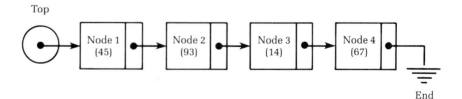

End

a. Write a program that builds the preceding illustrated linked list.

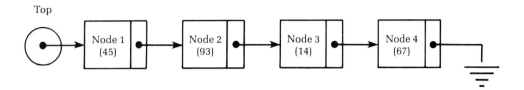

b. Write a program that will rearrange the nodes in the following linked list so that the data items of each node will be in ascending order. Note that the nodes do not move, and that only the addresses in the node are changed.

c. Write a program that updates the sorted linked list part a by inserting a node whose data item is 55.

C H A P T E R

Overview of MACRO Assembly Language and Assembler

A program written in an assembly language (source program) is translated into its machine language instructions by means of an *assembler*. Assembly language is readable, flexible, and versatile, and it provides complete access to all hardware facilities. A program written in assembly language often saves memory space and produces a much "tighter" object program than the same program written in a higher-level language. A compact object program saves memory and, more importantly, saves CPU time.

In addition to translating assembly language instructions into the appropriate machine language instructions, the assembler performs other important operations. These include providing for reserving and initializing blocks of memory for use by the program, expanding user-defined macros,[1] and evaluating certain expressions. The final result of the assembly process is an *object file* (also called an *object module*) and, possibly, an *assembly listing file*. An assembly listing is a printout of assembly language instructions, machine language instructions generated by the assembler and syntax errors (if any) of the machine code. The final version (called an *executable module*) is produced by the linker (via the LINK command). The following sections describe these assembler features in more detail.

---

1. Macro is a type of assembly language instruction that represents a
group of assembly language instructions.

5.1   *Types of Instructions*

Assembly language is made up of four types of instructions: executable, storage directive, assembler directive, and macro.

1. *Executable instructions* are operation oriented machine language instructions represented in symbolic form. They perform such operations as addition, data conversion, and transfer of control (branch). In addition to specifying the operation to be performed, executable instructions specify the memory location of the data or the data with which the instructions will work. Operands provide this information. In the case of transfer of control instructions, the operand indicates the address of the instruction that is to be executed next.

2. *Storage directive instructions* assign labels to memory locations and store constant values in them or assign labels to memory locations without storing anything. This information is provided by the arguments. Storage directive instructions begin with a period.

3. *Assembler directive instructions* guide the assembly process. Most of these instructions begin with a period. They can be used to perform the following tasks:
   a. Specify the entry point of the program
   b. Control the format and content of the listing file
   c. Display informational messages
   d. Specify the way in which symbols will be referenced
   e. Specify part of a program that is to be assembled only under certain conditions
   f. Control the assembler's options that are used to interpret the source program
   g. Define new opcodes
   h. Specify the methods of accessing the sections of memory in which the program will be stored
   i. Control the alignment in memory of parts of the program

4. *Macro instructions* are instructions that when translated into machine language, are replaced by equivalent groups of machine language instructions. Macro instructions may represent any part of the program. Macro instructions are discussed in Chapter 8.

Instruction Format

Any assembly language instruction can be written in *free format,* which means that each field of the instruction can appear anywhere on the line. The order, however, cannot be altered; that is, the label must be followed by the opcode, then by the operand(s) or argument(s), and finally,

by the comment. Whenever the optional entries are absent, the next sequential field in the instruction appears as the first entry. Each field of
the instruction is separated by at least one space. Each operand or argument is separated by a comma, which may be preceded by any number
of spaces and followed by any number of spaces. A label always ends
with a colon (:), and a comment always begins with a semicolon (;). Although the assembler allows free format, it is not recommended because
an assembly language program written in free format is more difficult to
read.

Each field of an instruction is made up of characters found in the
character set. The character set used by the VAX is found in Appendix
D. VAX MACRO language allows the use of lower and upper case letters
to express different fields of the source instruction. The assembler does
not differentiate between upper and lower case letters. The following
sections discuss each field of the instruction in more detail.

Label

A label is a symbol created by the programmer that is used to reference
an instruction or data in a program. The following rules and guidelines
should be followed when creating a label.

1. It can be made up of any alphanumeric characters and special characters, such as underline (_), dollar sign ($) and pe-
   riod (.).
2. It can be up to thirty-one characters long.
3. It begins with any alphabetic character or one of the three
   special characters specified in Rule one. A label, however,
   cannot begin with a digit.
4. It cannot contain embedded blanks.
5. It is ended by a colon (:) or a double colon (::). A single colon
   indicates that the label is defined only for the current module. A double colon indicates that the label is globally defined. Globably defined labels are accessible to all modules
   that are linked together.
6. It cannot be redefined in the same source program.
7. When a label is longer than seven characters, it is conventional to place the label on a line by itself and to place the opcode on the following line in position nine; for example,

```
LABEL:  OPCODE

SEARCH_LOOP:
        CMPL
```

Each label used in a program should be a meaningful abbreviation of
what the label represents. For example, a good label for maximum grade
would be MAX_GRADE or MAX_GR.

Opcode

The opcode follows the label if one is specified. The opcode represents symbolically the operation to be performed. In addition to specifying the operation to be performed, the opcode represents storage directives, assembler directives, and macros. Examples of storage directives are .LONG and .BLKL, which were discussed in Chapter 3. Examples of assembly directives are .ENTRY and .END, which were also discussed in Chapter 3. Other directives will be presented when appropriate. Macro instructions are covered in Chapter 8. A complete list of opcodes for the executable instruction set can be found in Appendix E.

Operand

The operand field follows the opcode and is separated from it by at least one blank or tab. Operands are defined labels, constants, or special symbols that represent an address. For example, R10 is a special symbol that informs the assembler that register 10 is used as a operand.

The number of operands to be contained in an instruction is indicated by the opcode of the instruction. Each operand must be separated by a comma (,). Although blanks or tabs may follow or precede the comma, the comma itself is mandatory and cannot be omitted.

Argument

An argument field follows the opcode and is separated from it by at least one blank or tab. Arguments represent information that the assembler must have when a storage or an assembly directive is being processed. The argument used by a storage directive instruction represents the constant value that is to be stored, or the size of a memory block that is to be allocated. The argument used by an assembler directive instruction represents information required by the assembler to carry out the task indicated by the opcode of the assembler directive.

Comments

Comments are short explanatory remarks that the programmer should add to explain the workings of the program. The comment itself does not affect program execution in any way because it is not translated into machine language and, therefore, is not in the object module. A comment can begin anywhere on a line; when a comment is an entire line, however, it usually begins in the first position of the line. When you enter a comment following an instruction, you can begin the comment in position forty-one, or you can choose a position and keep that position throughout the program. A convention such as this enhances the readability of a program. Keep in mind that each comment, regardless of where it begins, *must* be preceded by a semi-colon (;). Comments can contain any character found in Appendix B.

Function of the MACRO Assembler   *5.2*

The primary function that the VAX MACRO assembler performs is translation of each assembly language instruction into its equivalent machine language instruction. The translation process is accomplished by replacing each field of the instruction by its equivalent machine language code. Each field of the instruction is translated by the use of *table lookup.* If any field is not found in its equivalent table, a syntax error is displayed. Comments are not translated; they are retained so that they can be included in the listing.

The opcode portion of the instruction is translated according to a built-in table. Operands are translated according to either a built-in table (special symbols) or a user-defined table. The user-defined table is developed during the assembly process. As the program is translated, each label is entered into the user-defined table. When the operands of an instruction are translated and are user-defined labels, a table lookup is performed. When a label is defined after it is used as an operand, the assembler recognizes this and does not issue a syntax error. Exhibit 5.1 illustrates the assembly process.

In Exhibit 5.1 the opcode table and the *directive table* are built-in tables in the assembler. The location counter is established by the assembler and used solely for development of the user-defined symbol table. The object program is produced if the source program contains no syntax errors. The listing is produced only if it is specifically requested by a qualifier in the MACRO DCL command.

The following sections describe the assembly process in more detail. This description is by no means complete because the actual workings of the MACRO assembler are rather complex. Nevertheless, this introduction should give a good insight into the assembly process and should

Exhibit 5.1

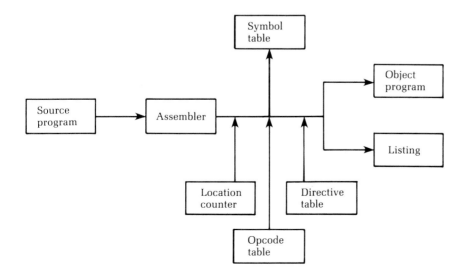

enable the programmer to read the object code of a VAX assembly program. In addition, this knowledge is very helpful in debugging.

Opcode Table

Each opcode is represented by a mnemonic and is translated by searching an internal (predefined) table called the *opcode table*. This table contains every mnemonic and its equivalent opcode. The assembler also uses the opcode table to determine whether the source program contains any illegal instructions. The assembler makes this determination when it does not find the mnemonic of an instruction in the opcode table. In this case, the assembler issues a syntax error.

Each opcode in the opcode table may contain other information, such as the length of the instruction or the number of operands the instruction requires. For example, the length of the instruction can be used for updating the location counter (discussed below), and the number of operands can be used to determine whether an instruction has too few or too many operands.

Symbol Table

The assembler must record every user-defined symbol (label) and its associated address. To do this, the assembler scans the source program and enters every label it encounters into a table along with that label's address. Such a table is called a *symbol table*. It is used by the assembler to create the machine language instructions and by the linker during the linking process.

The address with which the label is associated is referred to as its *value*. Note that *value* here is not the same as in in higher-level languages, where it refers to the contents of the memory location whose symbolic address is the label. The address assigned to the label during the assembly process is not the same as the physical address of that label used during the execution time.

In order to understand fully how labels, along with their associated addresses, are placed into the symbol table, we need to examine the location counter, which is discussed in the following section.

Location Counter

The assembler uses the location counter (LC) to assign an address to each label that is placed into the symbol table. The location counter holds the address of the byte of the instruction that is being translated. This address is calculated in the following manner.

At the beginning of the assembly process, the location counter is initialized to zero, which means that the first byte of the first instruction is assigned the address zero. If this first instruction has a label, then this label will have an associated address of zero. This address is known as the *relative address,* which means that this address has a reference point in the program. The reference point is the first byte of the program, which has been arbitrarily assigned a zero address. The relative address may be thought of as a value representing the number of bytes that separate the current byte from the first byte of the program.

To illustrate how the LC works, assume that the following instructions are the first instructions of a program.

```
RATE:    .LONG    5
HRS:     .LONG    45
PAY:     .BLKL    1
```

In this example, the label RATE is associated with the address 00 00, because the LC is initialized to 00 00. After the label RATE is defined, the LC is increased by a value of 4. This value is obtained from the opcode of the instruction (.LONG), which informs the assembler to store the constant, 5, in 4 bytes of memory. Accordingly, before the next instruction is translated, the LC contains the value 00 04. The current contents of LC are assigned as the address of the next label, which in this example is HRS. After this label is defined, the LC is increased to 00 08. The reason the LC increased by 4 again is that the second instruction's opcode informs the assembler to store the constant, 45, in 4 bytes of memory. The new contents of LC (8) are assigned as the address to label PAY. When the assembler encounters a storage directive instruction without a label, it updates the LC by the data type number that is indicated in an opcode and moves on to the next instruction. In this manner all storage directive instructions are translated, and user-defined labels along with their relative addresses are entered into the symbol table.

Eventually, the assembler finishes translating the storage directives and begins to translate the executable instructions. The executable instructions are translated one field at a time; for example,

```
MULL3    HRS,RATE,PAY
```

In this case the assembler looks up the mnemonic MULL3 in the opcode table. If it does not find the mnemonic in the table, the assembler inserts a syntax error. If the mnemonic is found, its equivalent machine language code is placed into a byte. As a result of this procedure, the LC is increased by 1. When the opcode is a macro instruction, a different procedure, which is discussed in Chapter 8, is used.

Next, the assembler translates the first operand by searching the user symbol table and the special symbol table. If the assembler does not find the operand in either table, it inserts a syntax error. If the operand is found, the next sequential group of bytes will receive its equivalent machine language code. The number of bytes used to store an instruction depends upon the method used to represent each operand. Assume that in this example, the assembler requires 2 bytes to represent each operand. Therefore, when the label HRS is translated into machine language, the LC will be increased by 2. In this same manner, the remaining operands are translated. The translation of the this instruction would require 7 bytes, 1 for the opcode and 6 for the three operands. At the end of the translation of this instruction, the LC is increased by 7.

Assembler Directive Table

The assembler *directive table* is a built-in table that contains the name of every assembler directive. The assembler searches this table to determine the legality of a directive. For every directive in the table, the table may also contain the name (location) of a routine to be used for processing that directive.

5.3 Ordering of Assembly Language Instructions

Programs are generally written on the assumption that successive instructions are stored in successive memory locations. Although decision instructions that alter the sequential flow are common, programmers normally write blocks of instructions in which the implicit flow of control is sequential. Consequently, most instructions do not include the address of the next instruction to be executed. Because instructions are executed sequentially, the CU can easily obtain the next instruction by using the address contained in the PC (program counter).

5.4 Program Counter

Because instructions are executed sequentially, the CU can keep track of the location of the next instruction to be executed by using the contents of the PC. When the execution of a program commences, the PC receives the physical address of the first byte of the first instruction. As each instruction is executed, the PC is incremented by a number equal to the number of bytes required to store the instruction in memory.

The operation of the LC and the program counter (PC) are very similar. When program execution begins, the PC points to the first byte of the first instruction of the program. When the assembly process begins, the LC contains a zero, which is the address assigned to the first byte of the first instruction to be translated. When the program is assembled or executed, the LC or PC, respectively, is incremented by a value equal to the size of the instruction being processed.

5.5 Assembly Instruction Continuation

One assembly instruction should be represented on multiple lines when it cannot follow the established format because the operands are too long to fit into their designated field. In that case, you enter the opcode followed by the first operand, followed by a comma and a hyphen (-). Keep in mind that the hyphen is not the same character as the underscore.) On the next line, begin entering the remaining operands starting in position 17; for example,

```
LABEL:  OPCODE    OPERAND_1,-        ;THIS EXAMPLE ILLUSTRATES
                  OPERAND_2,-        ;HOW AN INSTRUCTION CAN BE
                  OPERAND_3          ;ENTERED ON MULTIPLE LINES
```

If the remaining operands cannot fit on the second line, continue with as many lines as necessary. Each succeeding line follows the format of the second *continuation line*. Note that the last continuation line in the example does not have a hyphen. Hyphens within comments do not imply continuation; instead they are interpreted as part of the comment.

Blank Lines   5.6

Blank lines may be inserted freely anywhere in the source program to improve readability. Blank lines appear in the assembly listing but are otherwise ignored.

Methods of Expressing an Operand or an Argument   5.7

The executable instructions contain operands, and the nonexecutable instructions contain arguments. The operand in an executable instruction represents the data or the address to the data that is required to carry out the specified operation. The argument in a nonexecutable instruction can specify either the size of a memory block to be set aside or the constant that is to be stored; or the argument may specify some command to the assembler. The following methods can be used to represent an operand or an argument.

Operand representation	Argument representation
1. Register number	1. A term or an expression
2. A symbol (label)	2. Special assembly arguments
3. An alphanumeric value	
4. A term or an expression	
5. Current location counter	

Operands can be represented by any one of these methods, but the arguments must follow the format that is unique to the instruction. The following sections describe the methods for representing operands and arguments.

Register Number

You will recall that the VAX provides sixteen general-purpose registers that constitute the high-speed memory. The registers are very helpful when a data item has to be used repeatedly, because they reduce time required to access a data item. This data item may be an address or information needed by an opcode to perform the designated operation.

Registers R0 through R5 are used by some instructions during their execution to store intermediate results. Therefore, if these registers are to be used in a program, the programmer must verify that the instructions contained in the program are not using these registers. Otherwise, the expected values in these registers might be destroyed. Certain registers have specific uses and special names. Appendix F lists all registers, their special names, and their specific uses by the instructions and the system.

Symbol (Label)

A label is defined at assembly time and is placed into a symbol table along with its relative address. At link time, the relative address is converted to a virtual address; and at execution time, the virtual address is transformed into a physical address. The physical address is always represented by 32 bits (longword). A label being represented by either a relative, virtual, or physical address always addresses one byte of memory. This byte might contain data needed for manipulation or part of an address. Therefore the programmer must specify the purpose for which the byte is to be used.

Alphanumeric Values

An operand can be represented by a number or by a string of characters. It is convenient, however, to represent an operand by a character string that is not a label but rather is the required data. When this is the case, the assembler is informed by preceding the data with a *unary operator* (discussed below).

When a number represents an operand or an argument, the assembler assumes that the number is a decimal value. The VAX, however, supports other number systems; as a result, the assembler must be informed in which number system the numeric value is represented. The programmer informs the assembler of the different data types that represent operands or arguments by placing a unary operator (discussed below) in front of the operand or argument.

Term or Expression

The assembler assumes that each operand in an executable instruction represents an address. An operand can also be represented by a *term*.

However, a term is some form of information that the assembler re-places with its machine language version. A term can be represented by any one of the following:

1. A number
2. A symbol (see Section 5.9)
3. The current location counter (see Section 5.10)
4. A mask operator followed by text
5. An ASCII operator followed by text
6. Any of the above preceded by a unary operator

The assembler translates a term into a longword value. If an undefined symbol is used as a term, the linker determines the term's value. If the current location counter is used, the value obtained from it is the relative address of the first byte of the current operand. An operand represented by a term or an expression begins with a number sign (#).

When an operand is represented by a term or an expression, it is fre-quently called a *literal* or sometimes an *immediate addressing mode*. The word "immediate" applies because the data to be used in the operation are part of the instruction, and the CU does not therefore have to calcu-late the virtual address. The literal and the immediate addressing mode differ in the number of bytes used to represent a constant value. A literal is represented by 6 bits of a byte, while the immediate addressing mode is represented by a group of bytes. The assembler determines the num-ber of bytes to be used. Labels are referred to as immediate addressing modes; constants, however, are usually referred to as literals and not as immediate addressing modes.

A group of terms used to represent one operand is called an *expres-sion*. In an expression each term is separated from the other by a *binary operator*. The first operands of following instructions illustrate the use of a term and an expression, respectively.

```
MULL3   #7,HRS,PAY
MULL3   #2*3+1,HRS,PAY
```

When an expression is used to represent an operand, the assembler re-places the expression with the result obtained from its solution.

Expressions are combinations of terms joined together by binary op-erators (see Section 5.8). These expressions may in turn be joined by bi-nary operators to form new expressions. VAX MACRO evaluates ex-pressions from left to right with no operator precedence. However, angle brackets ($<$ $>$) can be used to change the order of evaluation. Any part of an expression that is enclosed in angle brackets is evaluated first; then the single value is used to evaluate the remainder of the expression. For example, the expressions $A*B+C$ and $A*<B+C>$ produce differ-ent results. If you assume that $A = 3$, $B = 2$ and $C = 5$, evaluating the expression $A*B+C$ produces a value of 11; and evaluating the expres-sion $A*<B+C>$ produces a value of 21.

Unary Operators

Unary operators are used to inform the assembler whether the constant value representing the operand is a numeric value, a character string, or a special value. When an operand is represented by a numeric value, it may be expressed by a number system other than the decimal. In that case, the unary operator indicates the radix of the number.

Unary operators can be divided into two general groups. The first group designates the sign of a numeric term or expression. The unary operators in this group are + (plus) and − (minus). In the second group each unary operator is preceded by a circumflex (^), which informs the assembler that the operand is to be converted to binary by methods other than decimal to binary. The unary operator immediately follows the circumflex and is represented by a letter. The letter informs the assembler which conversion procedure is to be used. The radix conversion unary operators are ^B, ^D, ^O, and ^X; binary, decimal, octal, and hexadecimal, respectively. The special data unary operators are ^A, ^M, ^F, and ^C; they correspond to ASCII (character), mask, floating-point, and complement, respectively. VAX MACRO supports ten unary operators, which are summarized in Appendix G.

Radix Conversion Operators

VAX MACRO accepts operands or arguments in four different radices: binary, decimal, octal, and hexadecimal. Their general formats and the legal digits that can be used in each are

Format	Radix name	Legal digits
^Bn	Binary	0 and 1
^Dn	Decimal	0 through 9
^On	Octal	0 through 7
^Xn	Hexadecimal	0 through 9 and A through F

The n represents a string of legal digits that must be used to define an operand or argument.

The assembler assumes that the terms contained in an expression are all decimal. If this is not the case, the assembler is informed of the differences by an appropriate unary operator. The unary operator indicates the radix of the terms used in the expression. The radix conversion unary operator applies only to one operand or argument; therefore, its use affects only the operand or argument that it immediately precedes. The following example illustrates the use of a hexadecimal conversion unary operator.

```
ADDL2    #^XAF,Y,X
```

The first operand begins with a number sign (#) because the operand represents a constant. The constant is represented in hexadecimal, therefore, the assembler was informed of it by the unary operator ^X. The following examples illustrate additional unary operators used in conjunction with storage directives.

```
.LONG     ^B00001101          ; BINARY RADIX
.LONG     ^D123               ; DECIMAL RADIX (DEFAULT)
.LONG     ^O47                ; OCTAL RADIX
.LONG     ^XAF34              ; AF34 IS IN HEX RADIX
```

Note that arguments do not begin with a number sign (#) because they are always represented by an expression or expressions.

Binary Operators   *5.8*

By definition a binary operator is an operator that operates on two terms, in contrast to a unary operator, which always operates on one term. Table 5.1 summarizes the binary operators.

Table 5.1

Binary Operator	Operator name	Example	Operation
+	Plus sign	A + B	Addition
−	Minus sign	A − B	Subtraction
*	Asterisk	A*B	Multiplication
/	Slash	A/B	Division
@	At sign	A@B	Arithmetic shift
&	Ampersand	A&B	Logical AND
!	Exclamation point	A!B	Logical inclusive OR
\	Backslash	A \ B	Logical exclusive OR

An expression is made up of terms, and is evaluated from left to right without any operator hierarchy. To force the evaluation of a certain part of the expression, that part must be enclosed by angle brackets (< >). The part of the expression enclosed in angle brackets is evaluated first; then the remaining expression is evaluated from left to right. For example,

```
CON_9:    .LONG     1+2*3               ; EQUALS 9
CON_7:    .LONG     1+<2*3>             ; EQUALS 7
```

The preceding data-storage directive instructions inform the assembler that the result obtained from solving each expression used for the arguments is to be stored in a longword of memory. The result is stored right justified in the longword. In these examples, the 9 and 7 are contained in the 0 byte of their respective longwords, as follows:

```
| 00 00 00 09 |        | 00 00 00 07 |
```

When the result does not entirely fill the longword memory location, the remaining high-order bytes are filled with zeroes. On the other hand, when the result obtained from solving an expression is too long to be contained in the specified memory location, the VAX MACRO assembler flags an overflow syntax error message.

When a radix unary operator precedes an expression, the expression is solved first; then the conversion is carried out according to the specified radix unary operator. An expression can contain radix terms other than the one preceding the expression. Any term in the expression that does not contain a radix unary operator is assumed to be of the same type as the radix conversion operator that precedes the entire expression. For example

```
.LONG   ^X<75D + 100 +^D16>
```

Here the values 75D and 100 are interpreted as hexadecimal values whereas 16 is interpreted as decimal because it is preceded by radix unary operator ^D.

5.9 *Direct Assignment Instructions*

In programming, various constants that represent known values are used in instructions. In assembly language a constant can be defined by a label. When a label representing a constant is used as an operand, the assembler translates the operand as an address to the constant. The address to a constant in an instruction can take up 2, 3, or 4 bytes of memory depending on the distance between where the constant is defined and where it is used. Therefore it is better to represent an operand by a constant because a constant usually will require fewer bytes. In addition, when a constant is used for an operand, the access time for the operand is shorter because the CU does not have to calculate a virtual address. For example,

```
MULL3   #7,HRS,PAY
```

Assuming that labels HRS and PAY require 2 bytes each, this instruction would occupy 6 bytes: one for the opcode, one for the constant value of 7, and 2 for each of the operands. The translation of the following instruction, however, would occupy 7 bytes: one for the opcode and 2 for each of the three operands.

```
MULL3   RATE,HRS,PAY
```

When many constants are used in a program, however, it is more difficult to remember what a constant represents. For this reason the MACRO language provides direct assignment instructions, which equate a constant to a label (symbol). When a direct assignment instruction defines a symbol for the first time, the symbol is entered into the user symbol table, and an assigned value is associated with it. The general format is as follows:

symbol = constant or expression
symbol = = constant or expression

The symbol is a user-defined label; the constant is a known value at assembly time. The expression is evaluated at assembly time and the result is equated with the symbol. The expression must not contain any undefined symbol. For example,

```
RATE = 7
        MULL3    #RATE,HRS,PAY
```

In this example, RATE is a symbol. When this instruction is translated, the symbol RATE is replaced by its equivalent constant and not by an address to the constant. Note that the symbol is preceded by a number sign (#) because the symbol is a constant.

The format with a single equal sign (=) defines a *local symbol,* and the format with a double equal sign (= =) defines a *global symbol.* The local symbol is only accessible in the program that defines the symbol. The global symbol is accessible by all modules that are linked together. The following syntactic rules apply to direct assignment instructions:

1. An equal sign (=) or double equal sign (= =) must separate the symbol from the expression defining the symbols's value. Spaces preceding and/or following the direct assignment operators have no significance in the resulting value.
2. Only one symbol can be defined in a single direct assignment instruction.
3. A direct assignment instruction can be followed by a comment field.

Following are additional examples of direct assignment instructions.

```
CLASS_SIZE = 20
LIST:    .BLKL    CLASS_SIZE
```

The symbol used for an argument in the preceding storage directive helps to identify what the argument represents. Another example of a direct-assignment instruction follows:

```
PI==3.1416    ;THE SYMBOL PI IS A GLOBAL SYMBOL
```

The symbol PI is defined in one module; it can, however, be used by all modules that are linked together. The symbol PI is associated with a real value that is discussed in Chapter 11.

A symbol may be redefined by assigning a new value to it. The newly assigned value will replace the previous value assigned to the symbol in the user symbol table. The use of direct assignment instructions provides identification for the constants and this improves the readability of the program. These instructions do not generate any machine code; therefore, the LC is not changed when the assembler encounters a direct assignment instruction.

5.10 *Current Location Counter (LC)*

The current value of the location counter can be used as an operand in an instruction. It can also be used as a value assigned to a symbol in a direct assignment instruction. When the current value of the LC is to be used in an instruction, it is represented by a period (.). A period that is used in place of an operand always has the value of the address of the byte being translated. For example,

```
CLASS_SIZE = 20
LIST:        .BLKL        CLASS_SIZE
UPDATE_CLASS_SIZE = (. - LIST)/4
```

In this example the expression uses the current contents of the LC to calculate the class size. Using the LC makes it easier to modify certain parts of a program, as this example illustrates. The preceding instructions make it possible to adjust the class size by changing only the direct assignment instruction.

The current location counter can be explicitly set by a special form of direct assignment instruction. The general format of the assignment instruction using the current location counter is as follows:

```
.=expression
```

The value obtained from evaluating the expression is placed into the location counter. The expression must not contain any undefined symbols; for example,

```
.=.+40          ;INCREMENTS THE VALUE IN THE
                ;LOCATION COUNTER BY 40
```

In a relocatable program section,[2] the expression must be relocatable; that is, the expression must be relative to an address in the current program section. It can be relative to the current location counter. When a program section previously defined in the current module is continued, the current location counter is set to the last value of the location counter in that program section.

When the current location counter is used in the operand field of an instruction, it has the value of the address of the first byte of that oper-

---

2. A program section is defined by the .PSECT assembler directive, which is discussed in Section 5.16.

and—it does not have the value of the address of the beginning of the instruction. For this reason, the current location counter is not normally
used as a part of the operand.

Assembly Listing Directives   *5.11*

MACRO assembly language provides a number of assembly directives
that alter the appearance of the program listing. Some of these assembly
listing directives enhance the documentation of the program, whereas
others are useful for debugging purposes. Some of the assembler directives that enhance the program listing are briefly described in this section.

The **.TITLE** directive is used to assign a name to a program. When
the program does not contain .TITLE directive, the assembler assigns
.MAIN as the name of the program. The general format for the .TITLE
assembly directive is as follows:

```
.TITLE name comment-string
```

Here *name* represents the title that will be assigned to the program module. This name will appear on each page of the listing and can contain
one to thirty-one non-blank characters. *Comment-string* represents a
comment that may be entered; however, it will not appear on each page
of the listing. The comment-string can consist of one to forty ASCII
characters. If a comment-string contains more than forty characters, the
excess characters will be truncated. An example of a .TITLE assembly
directive follows.

```
.TITLE HOMEWORK_ASSIGNMENT_#_1 THIS IS A COMMENT
```

In this example HOMEWORK__ASSIGNMENT__#__1 is the name
that will appear on each page of the listing. The comment
THIS IS A COMMENT will only appear in the .TITLE directive.

The assembly directive **.SBTTL** causes the character string that appears after the .SBTTL directive to be placed immediately before the assembly listing in the table of contents that the assembler produces. In addition, the assembler prints the character string as the subtitle on each
page of the assembly listing. The general format of the .SBTTL directive
is as follows:

```
.SBTTL comment-string
```

Here *comment-string* is a character string that is placed into the table of
contents and appears as a subtitle on each page. The comment-string is
made up of from one to forty ASCII characters. Any characters in excess
of forty will be truncated. The comment-string is used as a subtitle until
the assembler encounters another .SBTTL directive. When that occurs,

the assembler places the comment-string of the new .SBTTL directive into the table of contents and uses the new comment-string as the subtitle. The assembly directive .SBTTL cannot be used unless the assembly directive .TITLE is used.

The assembly directive **.PAGE** is used to force a new page for the listing, and the directive is not printed in the listing. This assembly directive is useful in forcing each program section to appear on a separate page.

The assembly directive **.IDENT** is used when the programmer needs to identify the object module. This is useful if the object module is to be placed into a library of object modules. The directive .IDENT provides a means of determining when a module was created or updated. The general format of the directive .IDENT is as follows:

```
.IDENT character-string
```

This *character-string* can contain one to thirty-one ASCII characters. This string must be enclosed by a set of delimiters, as in

```
.IDENT 'VERSION 1 10/15/85'
```

The character-string VERSION 1 10/15/85 in this example will be contained in the object module.

The assembly directive **.LIST** controls the lines that are to be included in the listing. The assembly directive **.NLIST** suppresses the printing of certain lines in a listing. When the assembler encounters the assembly directive .NLIST, it does not print the lines following the directive in the listing. To restart the printing of the listing, the assembler directive .LIST is used.

5.12   *Running a MACRO Program*

Running a VAX MACRO program is similar to running a program written in any language. The following DCL commands are necessary to run a MACRO program.

```
EDIT PROB1.MAR
```

This command is used to initiate an editing session which creates an assembly language source file. The type of file created is .MAR because the file name used in the command contains .MAR.

```
MACRO PROB1/LIS or MACRO/LIS PROB1
```

This command assembles the PROB1.MAR source file by searching the directory for the PROB1.MAR file and if it finds one takes the latest ver-

sion and translates it into machine language. The resulting file is
PROB1.OBJ. If the qualifier /LIS is used an additional file PROB1.LIS is
created.

LINK PROB1

This command makes the final adjustments on the latest version of the
PROB1.OBJ file and produces a PROB1.EXE file.

RUN PROB1

This command begins program execution of the latest version of
PROB1.EXE file.

Exhibit 5.2 summarizes the process of running an assembly language program including using the debugger for the execution of the
program. To obtain the results indicated by the dotted lines, the indicated
DCL command qualifiers must be used.

Exhibit 5.2

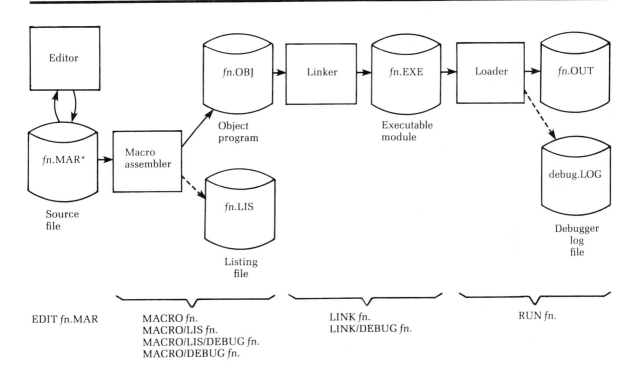

*In this diagram *fn.* denotes a user-generated file name.

5.13   *Function of the MACRO Command*

The assembly process for a program written in VAX MACRO language is initiated by the use of the DCL command MACRO. For example,

```
MACRO PROB1
```

This MACRO command uses a single parameter (PROB1). This parameter is a file name (or more formally, a file specification) indicating the source file to be assembled. The file type has been omitted. The DCL command MACRO searches the directory for the file PROB1.MAR. If the file PROB1.MAR is not found in the directory, an error message results. Successful execution of the MACRO command produces a file, PROB1.OBJ. The .OBJ type of file has the same name as the source file.

To provide flexibility during the assembly process, additional parameters and *qualifiers* are available for modifying this basic command. They are described in detail in Part 2 of the *VAX/VMS Command Language User's Guide*. The following qualifiers to the MACRO command can be very useful. Each qualifier must be preceded directly by a slash.

MACRO/LIST PROB1 or MACRO PROB1/LIST

In both cases the qualifier is /LIST, which can be abbreviated /LIS. This command produces files PROB1.OBJ and PROB1.LIS. The .OBJ file is the machine language version of the source program. The use of the qualifier /LIS produces a listing file, or module (listing is described in a later section). Note that the assembly listing is *not* automatically printed on the line printer or displayed on the interactive terminal; it must be explicitly spooled via the DCL PRINT command.

MACRO/NOOBJECT/LIS PROB1

The qualifiers are /NOOBJECT and /LIS. The qualifier /NOOBJECT suppresses generation of the object module. The presence of the qualifier /LIS produces only a listing file. These qualifiers are useful when making a preliminary syntax check.

MACRO/DEBUG PROB1

This qualifier informs the assembler to create a symbol table which is used by the debugger during a debugging session. Without this table labels defined in the program cannot be referred to during the debugging session. The debugging session begins when the command RUN PROB1 is issued. This is useful when there are logical errors, because it enables the user to examine intermediate results. The debugger was introduced in Chapter 3; for more information on it, see Appendix A.

MACRO PART1+PART2+PART3

This MACRO command has no qualifiers but it does however generate one object module from a group of source programs.

Diagnostic Messages

When the assembler encounters a syntax error during the assembly process, a *diagnostic message* for this error is displayed on a terminal (for interactive jobs), in a batchlog file (for batch jobs), and in a listing file. The general format of a diagnostic message is as follows:

%MACRO-*error-code*, *text*

In this message *error* indicates the level of severity of the error. There are two levels of severity: (1) *fatal* and (2) *warning*. A fatal error is indicated by the letter E, and a warning is indicated by the letter W. A fatal error indicates that if the instruction containing the error were to be translated into machine language, the CU would not be able to interpret parts of the instruction. A warning indicates that the instruction containing this error has been translated into machine language, but when the instruction is executed, it may produce an incorrect result.

In the preceding message, *code* is an abbreviation for an error message, and *text* is the explanation of the message. For example,

%MACRO-E-ARGTOOLONG

Here the %MACRO indicates that the MACRO assembler is used. The E indicates the severity of the error, and ARGTOOLONG is the abbreviation of the message text. Therefore this error message implies that no object module has been created and that an argument more than one thousand characters long caused the error.

The assembler summarizes the syntax error messages. This summary contains the total number of errors, warnings, and information messages with the line number and page number (enclosed in parentheses) of each error. The following example of a diagnostic summary could possibly have been produced by executing the command MACRO/LIST PROB1:

There were 6 errors, 1 warnings, and 0 information messages on lines:

    1 (1) 11 (1) 4 (2) 2 (3) 8 (3) 12 (3)
    4 (5)

The first error occurred in line 1, page 1; the second error in line 11, page 1; the third error in line 4, page 2; and so forth. Unfortunately, the list does not distinguish between fatal errors and warnings. At the end of the error summary, the assembler displays a list of the file specifications in the MACRO command.

5.14 *Function of the LINK Command*

The LINK command passes control to the linker. The object module produced by the MACRO command may be incomplete in itself. It may need to be joined, or linked, with other object modules or library files to form an executable program. An example of this process is the use of higher language procedures to perform the input/outout operation. The link operation performs the following tasks:

1. Joins the object modules that use symbols with the object modules that define them
2. Relocates individual object modules as necessary and assigns virtual memory addresses
3. Produces an executable image and an optional map

The linker joins separately assembled object modules into a single image. A *link map*, which designates the virtual addresses assigned to each module, may be generated optionally and has the file type .MAP. A cross-reference listing can be obtained as part of the link map.

The cross-reference listing provides all *global labels* in alphabetical order and indicates which modules refer to them as well as where the labels are defined. A *module* is a separately assembled source program (either a main program or subprogram). A global label (symbol) is a label that is defined in one module and may be referenced in modules other than the one that defines the label. A cross-reference listing is useful when trying to read or modify large programs consisting of many modules. This map informs the user which modules are going to be affected when a global label is changed.

The link operation, in addition to joining object modules, assigns virtual memory addresses to the relative addresses calculated by the VAX MACRO assembler. Because the memory addresses of one object module must be relocated to accommodate the addresses used in another object module, the link operation serves to resolve all address changes. The result of the link operation is an executable image with all module links resolved and all virtual memory addresses and storage information assigned. The most common uses of the LINK commands are

LINK PROB1

The LINK command searches the directory for a PROB1.OBJ file, and, if it finds one, takes the latest version and produces the PROB1.EXE file.

LINK PROB1,SUB

The LINK command searches the directory for PROB1.OBJ and SUB.OBJ[4] files, and, if it finds them, takes the latest versions of

---

4. The source file for SUB.OBJ could have been written in any language.

both and produces one file PROB1.EXE. When more than one object file is being linked, each file name must be separated from the others by a comma.

LINK PROB1,SUBA,SUBB,SUBC

Multiple files can be linked into one file. The process is the same as in LINK PROB1,SUB.

LINK/MAP PROB1

When the LINK command requests the generation of the link map, the map is not automatically printed; instead it must be printed by using the PRINT command. The command LINK/MAP = LP: PROB1 causes the map to be printed on the line printer (but not saved).

LINK/MAP/CROSS__REFERENCE PROB1

The LINK command produces the link map and a cross-reference listing.

LINK/DEBUG PROB1 or LINK/ENABLE = DEBUG PROB1

The LINK command produces the PROB1.EXE file in such a way that, when the RUN command is executed, control is passed to the debugger rather than to the program itself. The debugger was introduced in Chapter 3; for additional information on the debugger, see Appendix A.

An executable version of a program must be used in order to execute the program. If the program does not contain logical errors, the expected results are produced; however, if they are not, the program contains errors and the debugger should be engaged to help find these errors.

Assembly Listing   5.15

Assembly listing is a file created during an assembly process. It is only created when the DCL command MACRO contains the /LIS qualifier. For example, the MACRO/LIS PROB1 command generates the listing file where PROB1 is the name of the file that contains the program to be assembled. Figure 5.1 presents the assembly listing of the program that calculates a factorial. The assembly listing contains four major parts:

1. The machine language instruction (object code).
2. The location counter value.
3. The editor line numbers
4. The source instruction

The following sections explain each part.

Figure 5.1

Machine language instruction			Location counter value	Editor line number	Source instruction		
			0000	1	.TITLE FIG51		
			0000	2			
			0000	3	; THIS EXAMPLE SHOWS THE BASIC FORMAT OF A VAX MACRO		
			0000	4	; MAIN PROGRAM. THIS PROGRAM COMPUTES TEN FACTORIAL (10!)		
			0000	5			
			0000	6			
			0000	7	FACTORIAL:		
		00000004	0000	8	.BLKL 1		
			0004	9			
			0004	10	; MAIN PROGRAM		
			0004	11			
		0000	0004	12	.ENTRY START,0	; ENTRY MASK	
			0006	13			
F6 AF	0A	D0	0006	14	MOVL	#10,FACTORIAL	; N=10
50	09	D0	000A	15	MOVL	#9,R0	; I=9
EF AF	50	C5	000D	16	LOOP: MULL3	R0,FACTORIAL,-	; N=N*(N-1)
ED AF			0011	17		FACTORIAL	
F7 50		F5	0013	18	SOBGTR	R0,LOOP	; I=I-1
			0016	19			
			0016	20	$EXIT_S		
			001F	21			
			001F	22	.END	START	

The Machine Language Instructions

In the assembly listing in Figure 5.1 the machine language instructions are represented in hexadecimal. They must be interpreted from *right* to *left*. Therefore an address for an instruction addresses the byte on the far right of the instruction, which is always an opcode. Thus, in line 14 of Figure 5.1, the code F6 AF 0A D0 is interpreted as follows:

Machine code	Interpretation	Assemble mnemonic
D0	Opcode	MOVL
0A	Address mode of operand 1 (represented by constant)	#10
F6 AF	Address mode of operand 2 (represented by label)	FACTORIAL

The address of this instruction points to the byte containing D0.

When writing assembly language instructions, the programmer does not need to be concerned with the mode of expressing numeric values. The assembler assumes all numeric quantities are expressed in decimal, unless otherwise indicated. Therefore operand one, represented by the decimal number 10 when translated into machine language, is represented by 0A, which is its equivalent hexadecimal value.

When an instruction contains a label for an operand, its machine language version may require 2, 3, or 4 bytes of memory. One byte is required for the address specifier, and the remaining bytes are used for the offset. The number of bytes used to represent an offset depends upon how far away (in bytes) an operand is from where its label is defined. When a label is used as an operand, it is *not* replaced by its associated address from the symbol table; rather it is replaced by the distance (offset). In the instruction on line 17 in Figure 5.1 the label FACTORIAL is represented by two bytes. The first byte contains the address specifier, and the second byte contains the distance. The distance is expressed as a negative value when a label is used after its definition.

Relative Address

As the assembler translates each assembly instruction into its equivalent machine code, the instruction is assigned a relative address, which is the current contents of the location counter. For example, line 11 in Figure 5.1 has a location counter value of zero since it is the first instruction in the object program. Line 18 has a location counter value of 13_{16}, indicating that 13_{16} or 19_{10} bytes of generated code precede this instruction. These are not the true virtual addresses, they will be determined at link time. The location counter always specifies the relative position of the instructions; it will differ from the virtual address established at link time by a constant value.

Editor Line Numbers

As a convenience in correcting syntax errors, the editor usually provides line numbers for each instruction. Each line of source code is sequentially numbered by the editor. These line numbers are listed beside each source instruction. If an editor is used that does not produce line numbers, the sequence numbers of the lines are generated and printed by the assembler. When DCL command MACRO contains the /UPDATE qualifier, the listing numbers will be sequence numbers (even if the original file has editor-generated line numbers). Inserted lines will be indicated by line numbers containing decimal points.

Source Instructions

This section contains all instructions in the source program. If any syntax errors are detected, the line number of each instruction containing a syntax error(s) along with the description of the error is displayed on the screen. If the /LIS qualifier is used in the MACRO command, the assembler also inserts the error message right below each instruction containing an error.

5.16 .PSECT Assembler Directive

A program written in assembly language has the capability to alter the contents of all memory locations. These memory locations contain answers obtained from a program's execution and also contain the instructions that make up the program. Therefore, during assembly language program execution, the instructions that make up the program can be changed. They should not be changed during program execution, however, because if program instructions could be changed during program execution, the results produced by the program would be unpredictable. In addition, a program cannot be tested during the debugging process to determine if it is working correctly. To prevent an accidental change, the assembler provides an assembler directive instruction, **.PSECT**, one of whose functions is to protect a section of the program from being changed. The following is the general format for the .PSECT instruction:

.PSECT:	SECTION_NAME	,ARGUMENTS	;COMMENT

In this instruction SECTION__NAME is a name developed by the user that identifies a section. It is created in the same manner as a variable name. ARGUMENTS represents a list of attributes assigned to this section. The following is a partial list of the attributes:

1. **NOEXE** (Not executable) This program section contains data and not instructions.
2. **EXE** (Executable) This program section contains executable instructions.
3. **NOWRT** (Nonwritable) This program section's contents cannot be altered (written into) at execution time. This attribute helps protect constants and instructions from being accidentally destroyed.
4. **WRT** (Write) This program section's contents can be altered (written into) at execution time.
5. **LONG** Entering LONG in the argument list informs the assembler that the program section is to begin on a longword *boundary*.

The longword boundary means that the first byte of the section must be stored in the zero byte of a longword. In Chapter 1 it was explained that memory is a continuous linear array of bytes, as in the following example on the top of page 131. When storage directives are defined by the word, longword, or quadword data type, each may start at any byte in memory. Working with these data types would be more efficient, if, for example, the word data type began on a word boundary, meaning that its address would be divisible by 2. Similarly, if a longword began on a longword boundary, its address would be divisible by 4, and so forth. This condition is called *boundary alignment*. During the assembly process

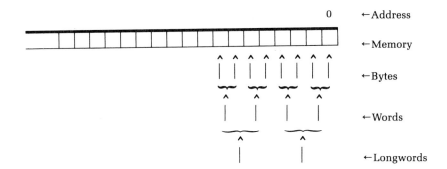

there is no boundary alignment. Therefore the assembler will allocate or store data in the next available byte, the one whose location is given in the location counter. If an assembly instruction requests alignment, the assembler increases the location counter by a necessary value so that the next instruction begins on a boundary of the requested type. The LONG attribute used in the .PSECT assembler directive forces the first storage directive or an executable instruction to begin on a longword boundary as in the following example:

```
            .PSECT    DATA,NOEXE,LONG

ARRAYA:     .BLKL     20
COUNT:      .WORD     0
ARRAYB:     .BLKL     20
```

The second array (ARRAYB) does not begin on longword boundary because the .WORD storage directive precedes it. The assembler directive **.ALIGN** LONG must be used in order to force the second array onto a longword boundary; for example,

```
            .PSECT    DATA,NOEXE,LONG
ARRAYA:     .BLKL     20
COUNT:      .WORD     0
            .ALIGN    LONG
ARRAYB:     .BLKL     20
```

A program can be partitioned into as many as 254 sections by using the .PSECT instruction. The assembler initializes the LC to a zero when a new .PSECT instruction is encountered; therefore, each section begins with a relative address of 0. The assembler, however, saves the old value contained in the LC in case it encounters the same .PSECT name in another .PSECT instruction. Therefore, in this case the section will start off with the value contained in the LC from which the previous section left off.

When a program does not contain any .PSECT assembler directives, the assembler assumes the following attributes:

1. The complete program is executable
2. The complete program can be written over.

Summary

Assembly instructions are represented in alphanumeric symbols that, when submitted to the assembler, are translated into machine language instructions. The program represented in machine language is referred to as an object program. In order for the translation to be correct, each assembly instruction must be coded according to a specific format. There are four types of assembly language instructions, and each instruction is coded according to its own format.

The operands used in executable instruction are labels that are defined by storage directives. The operands can also be represented by constants of any type. If this is the case, the constant is preceded by the number sign (#). This sign informs the assembler that the constant is a value to be used in the operation rather than a physical address. In addition, if the constant is not decimal, the number sign must be followed by a unary operator, which indicates to the assembler the type of constant used for the operand. The operand can also be represented by an expression, which is evaluated by the assembler; the result is used as the constant.

The programmer may direct the assembler as to the format of the listing. This can be done by using the assembler directive. These instructions can be used to provide a title to the listing, force a new page for the remaining part of the listing, suppress part of the listing, restart the listing again, or include the data from the last modification of the program.

An assembly program is translated into machine language and executed by means of DCL commands. These commands may have qualifiers, which, when used, inform the operating system of additional tasks to be done in conjunction with a DCL command.

New Instructions

.ALIGN	.NLIST	.SBTTL
.IDENT	.PAGE	.TITLE
.LIST	.PSECT	

New Terms

assembly listing	free format
binary operator	global label
boundary alignment	global symbol
comment-string	immediate addressing mode
continuation line	link map
cross reference listing	literal
diagnostic message	local symbol
directive table	module
executable module	object file
expression	object module
fatal error	opcode table

operator hierarchy
qualifier
radix conversion unary operator
relative address
symbol table
syntax error

table lookup
term
transfer of control instructions
unary operator
warning error

Exercises

1.   What function does the assembler perform other than translating assembly language instructions into machine language?

2.   What is the difference between an executable and a storage directive instruction?

3.   What is an object file?

4.   Why shouldn't assembly instructions represented in free format be used?

5.   Why should integer arithmetic instructions have at least two operands?

6.   Why should unique labels be used to define constants and used to reference them in place of one label and offsets?

7.   What is a global label?

8.   Why wouldn't you include a storage directive instruction among the executable instructions?

9.   What are the functions of assembler directive instructions?

10.   What are the functions of storage directive instructions?

11.   Within the limits of a program, where should the assembler directive instructions be placed?

12.   List the information an opcode provides to the CU.

13.   What does the argument represent in a storage directive instruction?

14.   List the ways in which an operand can be represented.

15.   The machine language format of any executable instruction contains the opcode in its first byte. Why?

16.   How is each field of an executable instruction translated?

17.   When is the location counter used? How?

18. What are the differences between the location counter (LC) and the program counter (PC)?

19. What is mnemonic?

20. Give three reasons why a syntax error can occur.

21. What is contained in the symbol table?

22. What will be the contents of the LC after the following group of instructions are translated? To answer this question assume that the LC contains a 12 at the start of the translation of the instruction ARRAY: .BLKL 10.

```
ARRAY:     .BLKL 10
COUNT:     .LONG 5
MAX:       .BLKL 1
POS:       .BLKL 1
```

23. Why do assembly instructions not require the address of the next instruction to be executed except when the instruction in a branch instruction?

24. How does the CU know where to find the first executable instruction of a program?

The questions 25 through 40 are to be answered true and false. In each case give the reason for you answer.

25. An assembly language instruction can be represented on more than one line.

26. Blank lines inserted in a program will cause a syntax error.

27. Any one of the fifteen registers can be used to represent an operand.

28. Each label in the symbol table is associated with its physical address.

29. Each operand represents an address.

30. Literal and immediate addressing mode represent the same.

31. Binary operator can perform any one of four basic arithmetic operations.

32. Unary operator performs an operation of one data item.

33. All numeric constant values used in expressing an operand are decimal values.

34. Direct assignment instruction are used to store constants in memory.

35. Only the assembler has access to the contents of the LC.

36. The assembler directive is just another name for a data-storage directive.

37. If there are syntax errors in a program they are automatically included in a listing when a request for a listing is made.

38. The LINK command is only necessary when more than one module are to be executed as one program.

39. The debugger is used by the assembler to help it find syntax errors.

40. Assembly listing displays machine language instruction in hexadecimal rather than in binary.

41. What operations are carried out by unary operator?

42. Why would a direct assignment instructions be used in place of a data-storage directive?

43. How does the assembler translate a label into machine language code?

44. What are the four items of information that an assembly listing contains? Explain how each can be used by a programmer.

45. What function does the assembler perform when a .PSECT assembler directive is encountered?

46. Why is it desirable to have certain instructions begin on certain boundaries?

47. How many bytes does each of the following storage directives reserve? What are the contents of each byte for each storage directive?

```
a.   A:    .LONG    5,-16,24
b.   B:    .BLKL    5
c.   C:    .LONG    20,-1
d.   D:    .LONG    0
```

48. Given that the contents of the LC equals 784 at the beginning of an assembly process for the following group of instructions, what are the contents of the LC after the instructions are assembled?

```
RESULT:   .LONG    0

          MOVL     #5,R5
          MOVL     #6,R6
          ADDL3    R5,R6,RESULT
```

49. Assume that the instructions in question 48 are being executed; and that, when the instruction MOVL #5,R5 is obtained from memory, the contents of the PC is 2000_{16}. What will the contents of the PC be when the execution of the ADDL3 instruction is completed?

50. How many memory locations are required to store each of the following instructions? Assume that the offset for each label is represented by a byte.

```
a.   ADDL3    (R8)[R7],SUM
b.   ADDL3    (R8)[R7],R6
c.   ADDL2    #286,SUM
d.   MULL3    LB,PRICE,TOTAL
e.   MULL3    LB,#3,TOTAL
f.   PRICE=3
     MULL3    LB,#PRICE,TOTAL
```

51. In the given source code, indicate whether there are errors in the executable instructions. If an error exists, indicate what it is.

```
VAL1:    .LONG    5
VAL2=10
VAL3:    .LONG    0
OUT1:    .LONG    0
OUT1:    .LONG    0

         MOVL     VAL1,OUT
         MOVL     5,OUT1
         MOVL     VAL2,OUT2
         ADDL3    VAL1,VAL2,VAL2
         ADDL     VAL1,VAL2
         ALLL     ^XA5FF,OUT1
         ADDL     ^X(03+08),OUT2
```

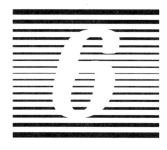

C H A P T E R

Stacks, Subroutines, Subprograms or Procedures

Outline

Part 1. Core Topics

A programmer must consider the organization of the program and write the program in such a way that it is easy to understand and maintain. Program maintenance includes improving and modifying the program to accommodate the changing needs of users. One effective way to achieve this goal is to divide a problem into a number of subproblems and then write a program for each subproblem. The program for each subproblem can be thought of as a *subprogram*. Each subprogram is simpler than the original program; therefore it is easier to develop its algorithm and to debug its assembly language program. Because each subprogram solves one well-defined portion of the original problem, it is easier for people to follow the solution of the entire problem. The use of subprograms is a building block in the construction of almost any size program.

Another reason why a problem should be subdivided is that real-world programs tend to be very large and written by a group of people, rather than by one person. This group approach to a solution of a problem decreases the time required to write a program. Rather than dealing with the entire program, a programmer working on one subprogram needs to know only the description of the subprogram, what kinds of data it will be given to work with, and what results it must produce.

After programming in assembly language for a short time, you will become aware that assembly language instructions tend to be repetitive in nature. For example, consider a problem where the management of a chain store requires a list of sale items that remain unsold in each store after a big sale in order to determine how successful the sale was. Therefore the program would require a set of instructions to arrange (sort) each list in numerical order. Repeating these instructions several times within the same program is boring; in addition, because so many instructions must be repeated, the chance of incorrectly writing an instruction is very high. Therefore the sorting process should be written as one subprogram and then used (called) whenever the sorting has to be done.

A subprogram is arranged so that it can be called from any point in a program or another subprogram. At the conclusion of the execution of the subprogram, the control flows back to the program or subprogram that called the subprogram.

Another advantage of using a group of subprograms in place of one large program is the reduction in testing, debugging, and maintenance time. To a large extent, testing and debugging can be done as each of the various subprograms is written. In the case of maintenance work, changes need to be made only to the subprogram involved. Before discussing subprograms in detail, however, the concept of a stack must be examined because this construct plays an important role when subprograms are called.

6.1   Stack

The **stack** is one of the most important data structures in both systems and applications programming. A stack is a storage device from which data can be accessed in a last-in, first-out manner. To better visualize a stack, imagine you are wearing seven rings on a finger. You wish to remove the farthest ring on your finger, but to remove this ring, you must first remove the preceding six rings. The last ring placed on the finger is removed first; the next-to-the-last ring is removed next; and, in this order, all six rings are removed. The placing of rings onto a finger simulates the placing of data onto a stack, and removing rings simulates the removal of data from a stack. Figure 6.1 illustrates a sample stack.

Figure 6.1

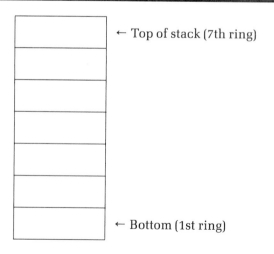

← Top of stack (7th ring)

← Bottom (1st ring)

Building a **hardware stack** is expensive; for this reason stacks are usually simulated through programming as a data type in the primary memory. This type of stack can be thought of as a group of contiguous memory cells. At the start of program execution, the operating system allocates a block of memory, which is to be used as a stack. This block of memory is partitioned into longwords. The address of the block is placed into R14, which is reserved for use as the *Stack Pointer* (SP). The address contained in the SP points to the bottom of the stack. As data items are added onto the stack, the stack "grows" toward lower addresses. Eventually, if enough data are added and none is removed, the stack's memory allotment becomes filled, and the limit of the stack is reached. This problem is not the concern of the programmer; it is resolved by the operating system, which will extend the stack size.

The stack is used to store data temporarily as well as to store subprogram invocation information. Data items are dynamically added to or removed from a stack in *last-in, first-out* (LIFO) fashion. Any item that is removed from the stack is always the last item that was placed onto the stack. The process of placing data onto the stack is called *pushing*. The process of removing data from the stack is called *popping*. The push operation is accomplished by decrementing the stack address, and the pop operation is accomplished by incrementing the stack address. Figure 6.2 illustrates this graphically.

The address contained in the SP is the address of the last data item placed onto the stack. Therefore, before data can be pushed onto the stack, the contents of the SP must be decreased by a value of 4. Likewise, in popping (removing) data from the stack, the contents of SP are increased by a value of 4 after the data item has been removed. VAX pro-

Figure 6.2

General purpose registers

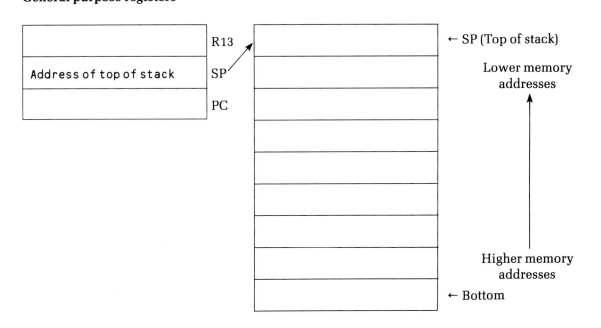

vides instructions that will perform the operations of pushing and popping. These operations can be summarized as

```
PUSH data = decrease SP; then move data onto stack
POP data = remove data from stack; increase SP
```

To understand how these operations are used, consider a problem where the number directly below the top number on the stack must be removed. For example, in the following stack, the value of 75 must be removed, and the value of 88 must be placed into its position.

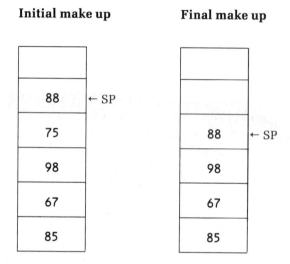

The first step in this process is to move 88 to a temporary memory location. This is accomplished by the following group of instructions:

```
MOVL    (SP),R8      ;MOVE TOP VALUE FROM STACK INTO TEMPORARY STORAGE
ADDL    #4,SP        ;ADJUST P   SO THAT IT POINTS
                     ;TO THE NEXT ELEMENT ON THE STACK
```

The MOVL and ADDL instructions are used because a stack consists of longwords.

The second step is to replace the value 75 with 88. You do not need to save the value of 75, because it is not required for any further use. Therefore the value of 88 can be placed into 75's old memory location by the following instruction:

```
MOVL    R8,(SP)      ;88 IS MOVED TO THE TOP OF THE STACK
```

Since a stack on the VAX is implemented by using memory rather than a separate hardware unit, accessibility to the stack is the same as to any memory cell. Whenever you use a stack, however, you should assume that it is a separate hardware unit. This will help make a transition to a hardware stack much easier.

Stack Instructions 6.2

Not only does a subprogram make use of a stack, but the operating system also uses a stack for many of its own operations. For this reason the VAX has a special set of instructions that are specifically used when working with a stack. These instructions operate on a longword data type because the system's stack consists of longwords. The reason the stack is partitioned into longwords is that it is heavily used to store addresses and contents of registers. The following sections discuss the stack instructions that can be used *only* in conjunction with a system stack.

Push and Pop Register Instructions: PUSHR and POPR

Some instructions make use of registers to store intermediate results that are required by the instruction as it is being executed. Therefore, if these registers contain data that must be retained for further use, this data must be stored somewhere else prior to the instruction's execution. The stack is a convenient place to store the contents of registers. When the execution of the instruction is completed, the data stored on the stack can be moved back into the registers; therefore, the registers will contain the data that was there prior to the instruction's execution. In this way, the contents of registers are safe from being altered by some instructions. To save the contents of the registers, the instruction **PUSHR** (push register) is used; and to restore the registers, the instruction **POPR** (pop register) is used. The instruction PUSHR places the contents of a register onto a stack, and the instruction POPR takes the top value from a stack and places it into a register. The general format for both instructions is as follows:

LABEL:	OPCODE	MASK	;COMMENT

Both of these instructions have only one operand, which is called the *mask*. The mask is used to specify the number(s) of the register(s) to be pushed (saved) or popped (restored).

Mask   The mask is used to list the registers that are to be stored or restored. In an instruction, a mask is always represented by a word data type. The word data type consists of 16 bits that are numbered 0 through 15. This numbering directly corresponds to the register number. That is, bit position 0 would indicate whether the contents of R0 are to be saved or restored; bit position 1 would indicate whether or not the contents of R1 are to be saved or restored, and so forth. This is indicated by the presence or absence of binary digit 1. For example, if bit 0 contains 0, R0 *is not saved or restored;* however, if it contains 1, it *is saved or restored.* Figure 6.3 illustrates two masks, where mask (a) can be used to store or restore R3 and (b) can be used to store or restore R5.

Figure 6.3

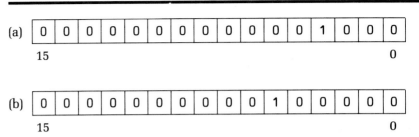

One way to represent a mask in the instruction PUSHR or POPR is to define the mask as a constant and then use its label as the operand. Figure 6.4 illustrates the definition of two masks and the use of their labels as operands.

Figure 6.4

```
MASK1:   .WORD   ^B0000000000001000   ;BIT 3 IS SET FOR R3
MASK2:   .WORD   ^B0000000000100000   ;BIT 5 IS SET FOR R5

         PUSHR   MASK1                ;SAVES R3
         PUSHR   MASK2                ;SAVES R5
```

The mask may have more than one bit set; in that case more than one register can be saved or restored. The two PUSHR instructions used in Figure 6.4 can be replaced by one instruction as follows:

```
MASK:    .WORD   ^B0000000000110000   ;BIT 3 AND 5 ARE SET

         PUSHR   MASK                 ;SAVES R3 AND R5
```

The operand representing a mask, like most other types of operands, can be represented by a constant. For example,

```
PUSHR    #^B0000000000101000   ;BIT 3 AND 5 ARE SET
```

or

```
PUSHR    #^X0028               ;BIT 3 AND 5 ARE SET
```

The operand in the second PUSHR instruction represents the same constant as the operand in the first instruction, except that it is represented by a hexadecimal value. An easier way to represent a mask is by listing the registers that are to be stored or restored. In order to include the list in the mask, the following format must be used.

```
#^M<list of registers in the form of Rn>
```

For example,

```
PUSHR    #^M<R5,R3>
```

This instruction saves the contents of R5 and R3 on the stack. The order of register entries in the list is not important. The mask could have been represented as #^M<R3,R5>. The assembler knows how to build a mask by encountering the #^M, and the list contained in the angular brackets informs the assembler which corresponding bits should be set as the list is being processed.

When the instruction PUSHR is executed, the processor scans the mask starting at bit 14 and continuing through bit 0. During this scanning, whenever a bit is set to 1, the contents of the register whose number is equal to the bit position are pushed onto the top of the stack. For the instruction POPR, the processor scans the mask in the opposite direction. The mask is scanned, starting at bit 0 and continuing through bit 14. In this way the register contents will be restored to the correct register when the PUSH and POP instructions use the same mask. Bit 15 is not scanned because it corresponds to the PC. Manipulation of the PC contents could lead to serious programming errors; hence, this is a safety feature.

Push and Pop Longword Instructions: PUSHL and POPL

The **PUSHL** and **POPL** instructions work with a longword of memory rather than a register like PUSHR and POPR. The general format of both instructions is as follows:

LABEL:	OPCODE	ADDRESS	;COMMENT

The only operand used by both instructions represents an address. In the case of PUSHL, the address indicates the longword whose contents are to be copied onto the stack. In the case of POPL, the address indicates the longword that will receive the contents from the top of the stack. For example, when the contents of memory locations A and B have to be swapped, the stack can be used to store the value temporarily. For example,

```
A:       .LONG   0
B:       .LONG   0

         PUSHL   A
         MOVL    B,A
         POPL    B
```

After executing the preceding instructions, memory location A will contain what was in memory location B and vice versa.

Push Address Instruction: PUSHAt

The **PUSHA*t*** instruction pushes the address of a data type that is indicated by the *t* onto the stack. The *t* is replaced by a letter indicating the type of data whose address is pushed onto the stack. Each permissible data type has its own unique PUSHAt instruction. Figure 6.5 illustrates how the stack can be used to sum twenty test scores contained in the array GRADE. The PUSHAt instructions are useful when organizing an argument list to be used in conjunction with the **CALLS** instruction.

Figure 6.5

```
GRADE:    .BLKL     20

          PUSHAL    GRADE           ;ADDRESS TO THE FIRST GRADE IS ON TOP OF STACK
          CLRL      R10             ;SET INDEX REGISTER TO 0
          CLRL      R9              ;SET REGISTER USED AS ACCUMULATOR TO 0
LOOP:     ADDL2     (SP)[R10],R9    ;ADD A TEST SCORE TO R9
          AOBLSS    #20,R10,LOOP    ;IF R10 IS < THAN 20 CONTINUE WITH LOOP
                                    ;   ELSE CONTINUE WITH NEXT INSTRUCTION
```

In Figure 6.5 the instructions CLRL R10 and CLRL R9 could have been replaced by the following single instruction

```
          CLRQ      R9
```

The CLRQ instruction always clears a quadword of memory, therefore the above instruction CLRQ R9 clears R9 and R10. This instruction may be used to clear any contiguous pair of registers by entering the lower numbered register as its operand.

6.3   Designing a User Stack

The programmer can define a user stack and use it rather than the stack provided by the system. A user-defined stack could grow from a lower address to a higher address and it can be made up of any data type. The disadvantage, however, in using a user-defined stack is that the instructions PUSH and POP cannot be used. The following steps can be used as a guideline when defining and using a user-defined stack.

1. Allocate a contiguous block of memory cells.
2. Store the address of the bottom of the stack in a register.
3. Increase the address each time an element is pushed onto the stack, and decrease the address each time an element is popped from the stack.

Figure 6.6 illustrates the creation and use of a programmer's stack.

Figure 6.6

```
                .TITLE   FIG66

; THIS PROGRAM SEGMENT ILLUSTRATES THE USE OF A 100 ELEMENT
; USER DEFINED STACK WHERE EACH ELEMENT IS 1 BYTE LONG

STACK_SIZE=100

        STACK:   .BLKB    STACK_SIZE  ; ALLOCATES 100 BYTES

        BOTTOM:  .BYTE                ; ONE EXTRA MEMORY CELL
        ITEM:    .BYTE    0

; THE FOLLOWING GROUP OF INSTRUCTIONS ILLUSTRATES
; THE USE OF THE-USER DEFINED STACK.


        MOVAB    BOTTOM,R2

; PUSHES ONE VALUE FROM THE BYTE ITEM ONTO STACK

        SUBL2    #1,R2
        MOVB     ITEM,(R2)   ; PUSHES ITEM ONTO THE STACK [1]
```

In Figure 6.6 the STACK is a user-defined stack of one hundred bytes. A user-defined stack does not need to grow to lower addresses. It can grow to a "higher" address.

Subprograms   *6.4*

A *subprogram* is a group of instructions that perform a specified task. In assembly language there are two types of subprograms: *subroutine*[2] and *procedure*[3]. A subroutine consists of a group of instructions that are contained within the boundaries of a program. In contrast, a procedure consists of a group of instructions that do not have to be within the boundaries of a program.

Referencing a subroutine is accomplished by a set of branch instructions. Referencing a procedure is accomplished by a set of *call instructions*. Both the branch instructions and the call instructions are types of transfer-of-control instructions. Both sets are discussed in a later section.

---

1. If Section 4.8 was covered, replace the instructions SUBL2 and MOVB by the MOVB ITEM,-(R2) instruction.
2. This type of subroutine is sometimes called *open subroutine*.
3. Sometimes a procedure is called a *closed subroutine*.

A subprogram is executed by transferring the control to its entry point. A subprogram performs the task for which it was written and then returns the control to the instruction that immediately follows the instruction that originally transferred the control. A subprogram may be completely self-contained, or it may need to refer to another subprogram.

When a problem is represented by a main program and a number of subprograms, it is called a *system of programs*. Both the main program and subprograms may be called *routines*. Whenever a subprogram is invoked, two routines are involved: the *calling routine* and the *called routine*.

One of the most important aspects when developing a subprogram is to define the standards to be followed when transferring the control. A good set of standards must include the following properties:

1. A subprogram should be able to be called from many different places in the calling routine.
2. A subprogram must be able to return control to the routine calling it regardless of the point from which it was called.
3. A simple and unambiguous mechanism must exist for transmitting information (arguments) between the calling routine and the called routine.
4. The subprogram must be able to operate without knowledge of the environment in which it is called or the state of the variables in the outside program, except for the information passed explicitly in the calling sequence.

If a subprogram is designed in such a way that it receives its input information only through the argument list, then this subprogram can be debugged independently. For the debugging processes, a special test program may be written that passes arguments to the subprogram and examines the results. Both the input data and the results are passed between the called and calling routines via the calling process. Neither party has any global knowledge as to what the other is doing. Subprograms written in this manner can be used without change as parts of other programs that need the same operations performed. The use of a subprogram by many programs tremendously reduces work because commonplace functions need to be written only once.

The calling of subprograms and the passing of arguments to them is so important that the VAX provides a group of instructions that only deal with calling and passing arguments to subprograms. These instructions can be divided into two groups: one dealing with the subroutines, and the other with the procedures. The significant difference between these two groups is in the *linkage mechanism*. The procedure call, which is discussed later, is much more powerful but is slower in handling arguments than the subroutine call. When a procedure is called, several of the registers are used, and the stack is heavily used to automate the transfer of control and the passing of arguments; in contrast, a subroutine call is simpler and faster because it uses fewer registers and less of the stack.

Subroutine Call: JSB (BSBB, BSBW)/RSB   *6.5*

The subroutines that are part of a program are called by the Jump to Subroutine (**JSB**) and Branch to Subroutine (**BSBB, BSBW**) instructions. These instructions push the return address onto the stack, after which the control is transferred to the called subroutine. The address that is pushed onto the stack is the address of the instruction that immediately follows the JSB, BSBB or BSBW instruction. The JSB instruction is the most flexible, because any addressing mode (except register mode) can be used to specify the *destination address*. In the BSBB and BSBW instructions, however, the destination address can be only represented by a label; and, as a result, these instructions are shorter than the JSB. The general format for the instructions JSB, BSBB, and BSBW is as follows:

LABEL:	OPCODE	DESTINATION	;COMMENT

All three instructions contain one operand that represents the destination address. This operand is the address of the subroutine to which the control is to be passed. The JSB instruction has no restrictions on memory space as to where the subroutine resides, because the destination address (offset) is contained in a longword. The BSBB and BSBW instructions, however, do have restrictions. The BSBB instruction can be used only when the subroutine is located within $+127$ bytes, and the BSBW can be used only when the subroutine is located within $+32767$ bytes.[4] These restrictions are due to the fact that the instruction BSBB contains its offset value in a byte, and the instruction BSBW contains it in a word. When the subroutine call instructions are used, the information required by a called subroutine is passed in one of the following ways:

1. The information is in the calling program, but the called subroutine is provided with the starting address of the required information.
2. The information is in general-purpose registers.
3. The information is on the stack.

Returning the control from the subroutine is accomplished by executing the **RSB** (Return from Subroutine) instruction. The general format is as follows:

LABEL:	RSB	;COMMENT

The RSB instruction returns control to the instruction immediately following the jump or branch instruction. The return address is obtained

---

4. The BSBB instruction may jump to within -127 bytes, and the BSBW instruction to within -32767 bytes. This use is not recommended, however, because it does not follow the top-down programming approach.

Figure 6.7

```
1                .TITLE    FIG67
2
3      ; PASSING ARGUMENTS WITH EITHER JSB, BSBB, OR BSBW
4
5      ARGS:     .LONG     5,2              ;ARGUMENTS TO BE USED BY SUBROUTINES
6                .LONG     0                ;ARGUMENT RETURNED FROM SUBROUTINES
7
8      ; MAIN PROGRAM
9
10               .ENTRY    START,0
11
12     FIRST:    MOVL      #5,R7
13               MOVL      #2,R8
14               JSB       SUBA             ;RESULT WILL BE CONTAINED IN R9
15
16     SECOND:   MOVAL     ARGS,R6
17               JSB       SUBB             ;RESULT WILL BE CONTAINED IN ARGS+8
18
19     THIRD:    PUSHL     #5
20               PUSHL     #2
21               BSBB      SUBC             ;RESULT WILL BE CONTAINED IN R8
22               ADDL2     #8,SP            ;POPS TWO ELEMENTS FROM THE STACK
23
24     ; DO NOT PROCEED IF SECTION  4.7  WAS NOT COVERED
25
26     FOURTH:   MOVAL     ARGS,R6
27               JSB       SUBD             ;RESULT WILL BE CONTAINED IN ARGS+8
28
29     FIFTH:    PUSHAL    ARGS             ;ADDRESS OF THE ARGUMENT LIST IS PUSHED ONTO THE STACK
30               BSBW      SUBE             ;RESULT WILL BE CONTAINED IN R1
31               ADDL2     #4,SP            ;POP ONE ELEMENT FROM STACK
32
33               $EXIT_S
34
35     ; SUBROUTINES
36
37     SUBA:     ADDL3     R7,R8,R9
38               RSB
39
40     SUBB:     CLRL      R10              ;SET R10 TO ZERO
41               ADDL2     (R6),R10         ;FIRST VALUE IS ADDED TO R10 (R10=5)
42               ADDL2     #4,R6            ;R6 POINTS TO THE SECOND VALUE
43               ADDL2     (R6),R10         ;SECOND VALUE IS ADDED TO R10 (R10=7)
44               ADDL2     #4,R6            ;R6 POINTS TO WHERE THE RESULT IS TO BE PLACED
45               MOVL      R10,(R6)         ;RESULT IS MOVED TO ARG+8
46               RSB
47
48     SUBC:     ADDL3     4(SP),8(SP),R8   ;BOTH VALUES ARE ADDED AND THE SUM IS PLACED INTO R8
49               RSB
50
51     ; DO NOT PROCEED IF SECTION  4.7 WAS NOT COVERED
52
53     SUBD:     ADDL3     (R6)+,(R6)+,(R6) ;BOTH VALUES ARE ADDED AND THE RESULT PLACED INTO ARGS+8
54               RSB
55
56     SUBE:     MOVL      4(SP),R1         ;ADDRESS OF ARGUMENT LIST IS MOVED INTO R1
57               ADDL3     (R1)+,(R1)+,R1   ;RESULT IS CONTAINED IN R1
58               RSB
59
60               .END      START
```

from the top of the stack. The RSB instruction causes the POPL process to occur, and the contents obtained from the top of the stack are placed into the PC, which is the address of the next instruction to be executed. Figure 6.7 presents four variations of passing the information to a subroutine. The job performed by each subroutine is to add two numbers (passed to it) and return the sum (result).

Case 1. In lines 12–14 the two arguments are passed in the two registers, R7 and R8, and the result is received in a third register, R9.

Case 2. Lines 16–17 pass the address of an argument list in register R6. The result is received in the third longword reserved within the argument list.

Case 3. In lines 19–22 the two arguments are pushed onto the stack, and the result is returned in register R8. The instruction on line 22 decreases the stack pointer by 8. This operation is equivalent to popping two elements from the stack. It is necessary in order to control the growth of the stack.

This operation is also necessary when a subroutine calls another subroutine. For example, assume that lines 19–22 make up a subroutine called SUBX. Note that this subroutine contains a branch instruction to subroutine SUBC. Exhibit 6.1 presents these instructions and shows the path that the computer takes during the execution of the subroutines. The exhibit also illustrates the contents of the stack during the processing of the subroutine SUBX. The solid lines indicate the progress of the calling subroutines, and the broken lines indicate the progress of returning from the subroutines.

When the control is returned from SUBC to SUBX, the top of the stack contains the value that was placed there before going to SUBC. In order to obtain the correct return address from SUBX, the two values must be removed from the stack. If the stack was not cleared, the PC would receive a value of 2 as the return address. This address would cause the system to display an error message because the physical address 2 is not accessible to applications programs.

In line 48 the displacement addressing mode is used in conjunction with the stack pointer to obtain the arguments. Note that the value on top of the stack when entering SUBC is not the first argument, but is instead the return address that was placed there by the BSBB instruction. In order to obtain the first argument, 4 must be added to the SP. Although it does not matter here, you should keep in mind that line 48 retrieves the arguments in the opposite order than they were pushed on the stack (the value at address 4(SP) is a 2).

Case 4. In lines 26–27 the address of the argument list is passed in register R6. The result is received in the third longword of the argument list.

Case 5. In lines 29–31 the address of the argument list is pushed onto the stack, and the result is returned in register R1.

Exhibit 6.1

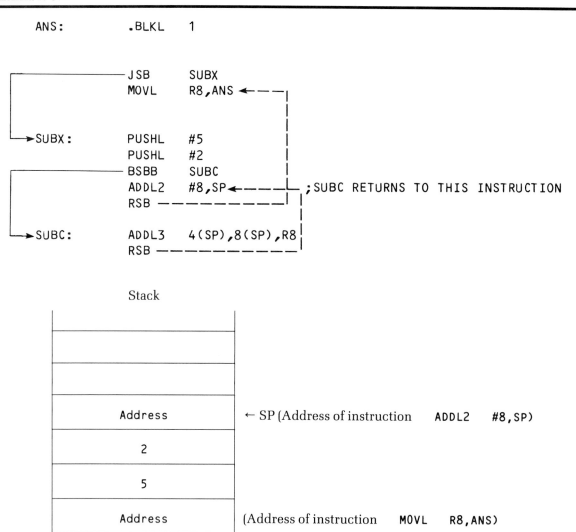

```
ANS:            .BLKL    1


                JSB      SUBX
                MOVL     R8,ANS  ◄ ─ ─┐
                                      │
                                      │
                                      │
 SUBX:          PUSHL    #5           │
                PUSHL    #2           │
                BSBB     SUBC         │
                ADDL2    #8,SP◄─ ─ ─ ─┴─ ;SUBC RETURNS TO THIS INSTRUCTION
                RSB ─ ─ ─ ─ ─ ─ ─ ─┘ │
                                     │
 SUBC:          ADDL3    4(SP),8(SP),R8│
                RSB ─ ─ ─ ─ ─ ─ ─ ─ ─┘
```

Stack

Address	← SP (Address of instruction ADDL2 #8,SP)
2	
5	
Address	(Address of instruction MOVL R8,ANS)

In Cases 3 and 5, you should take care in both the calling and called routines to handle properly the arguments passed on the stack. Programming errors are easy to make, particularly if you have several nested levels of subroutine calls, and the routines at each level use the stack. The
stack must be absolutely correct before the RSB instruction is executed,
or an *execution error* will result. For this reason the most practical method
for passing arguments with JSB, BSBB or BSBW would be Case 1 or 2.

6.6   *Procedure Call: CALLG/CALLS/RET*

The set of instructions that are used for transferring control to a procedure are known as the Call Procedure with General Argument List

(**CALLG**) and the Call Procedure with Stack Argument List (**CALLS**). The instruction for returning to the program that called a procedure is the **RET** (Return from Procedure) instruction. The CALLG and CALLS instructions differ from the JSB (BSBB,BSBW)/RSB in the following ways:

1. An *entry mask* is required as the first word in the called procedure. An entry mask is defined by the second operand of the .ENTRY instruction. This mask indicates to the operating system which registers are to be saved and restored before and after execution of the called procedure, respectively. The entry mask is developed in the same manner as the mask operand for the PUSH and POP instructions.

2. The execution of either instruction CALLG or CALLS creates a *call frame* (a special data structure) on the stack. The contents of the call frame can be addressed by a pointer called the *frame pointer* (FP). The call frame is removed from the stack when the RET instruction is executed.

3. When a procedure is called by the CALLS instruction, the arguments are found on the stack. The called routine receives the number of arguments in the list that is placed onto the stack and the addresses to the argument list is obtained from the register AP (*argument pointer*).

4. When a procedure is called by the CALLG instruction, the address to the argument list is placed into the AP. The argument list remains in contact within the calling procedure.

5. If a called procedure uses the stack for temporary storage, it does not need to clean up the stack. This chore is performed by the RET instruction.

6. Although it will not be discussed in detail in this text, a special routine, called an *exception handler,* can be established when entering a procedure via CALLS or CALLG. The exception handler provides a method for detecting certain kinds of errors, such as *integer overflow* or *floating underflow,* without explicitly checking for them. Therefore this detection provides an opportunity to recover from these types of errors.

The following sections describe procedure calls.

Argument List

To access a procedure, a calling routine calls a procedure by using CALLG or CALLS instruction. In addition, the calling routine must communicate with the called procedure in order to supply the whereabouts of the information needed for its execution. This communication is accomplished through an *argument list.* An argument list is a *data structure* that may contain any one or any combination of the following: (1) addresses or (2) constant; or (3) character strings, or (4) arrays. The most common type of information contained in an argument list is addresses. One reason for this is that if the needed information is an array or a long character string, then every element of the array would have to be entered into the argument list; the same is true for a character string where each character has to be entered. It is simpler if only the address for the array or the character string is entered into the argument list. When the argument list contains an address, the mode of communications is referred to as *call by reference* or *call by address*. When values are entered into the argument list, the mode of communications is referred to as *call by value*.

The standard argument list format used by VAX when calling a procedure consists of a sequence of consecutive longwords at an arbitrarily selected memory location. The low-order byte of the first longword in the argument list contains the number of arguments in the list. The remaining bytes of the first longword are set to 0. Because 1 byte is used to store the length of an argument list, the maximum number of arguments that can be contained in an argument list cannot exceed 255. The format for a standard VAX argument list appears in Figure 6.8.

Figure 6.8

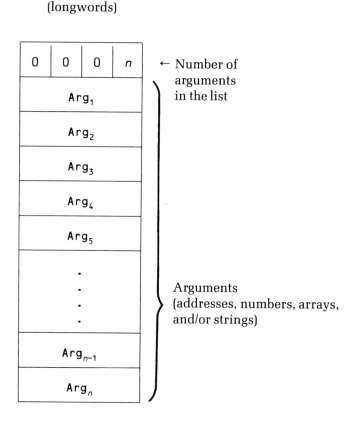

Argument list
(longwords)

Arg_1

Arg_2

Arg_3

Arg_4

Arg_5

Arg_{n-1}

Arg_n

← Number of arguments in the list

Arguments (addresses, numbers, arrays, and/or strings)

Figure 6.9

```
RESULT:      .LONG     0

ARGLIST:     .LONG     4          ; NUMBER OF ARGUMENTS
             .LONG     5          ; 1ST VALUE
             .LONG     7          ; 2ND VALUE
             .LONG     6          ; 3RD VALUE
             .ADDRESS  RESULT     ; ADDRESS WHERE THE SUM IS TO BE STORED
```

To understand how an argument list is set up, consider a problem where the procedure SUM adds three numbers: 5, 7, and 6. The information that the procedure SUM requires is the location of the values and the location of where to place the sum. This information can be passed to the procedure in a number of ways: (1) as values, (2) as an address for each value, or (3) as an address to a list of the values. The procedure must also know where to place the result. Figure 6.9 presents an argument list for this problem.

In Figure 6.9 ARGLIST is the *symbolic address* that points to the top of the argument list. This address points to a longword whose low-order byte contains the number 4. The second, third, and fourth longwords contain the numbers whose sum is to be calculated, and the fifth contains the address of memory location where to store the result.

The second version of the argument list could be an address to each value. Figure 6.10 illustrates an argument list consisting of addresses. Note that the symbolic address ARGLIST is again an address to the longword containing the length of the argument list. The next three longwords contain the addresses of the numbers, and the fourth longword contains the address to the memory location where their sum is to be stored.

The argument list could have been represented by two arguments as in the example on page 156. The first argument is the address of the list

Figure 6.10

```
FIRST:       .LONG     5
SECOND:      .LONG     7
THIRD:       .LONG     6
RESULT:      .LONG     0

ARGLIST:     .LONG     4          ; NUMBER OF ARGUMENTS
             .ADDRESS  FIRST      ; ADDRESS OF THE FIRST VALUE
             .ADDRESS  SECOND     ; ADDRESS OF THE SECOND VALUE
             .ADDRESS  THIRD      ; ADDRESS OF THE THIRD VALUE
             .ADDRESS  RESULT     ; ADDRESS WHERE THE SUM IS TO BE STORED
```

of numbers, and the second argument is the address of the memory location where the result is to be stored.

```
LIST:       .LONG      5,7,6            ; ARRAY OF NUMBERS
RESULT:     .LONG      0

ARGLIST:    .LONG      2                ; NUMBER OF ARGUMENTS
            .ADDRESS   LIST             ; ADDRESS OF THE LIST OF VALUES
            .ADDRESS   RESULT           ; ADDRESS WHERE THE SUM IS TO BE STORED
```

The preceding method is possible because each number is stored in a longword. This method is employed when an array is an argument. Given the address to the first element of an array, the procedure can access any element in the array. To process the array correctly, the procedure must also know the data type of the elements in the array.

The called procedure has access to the argument list in two ways: (1) the list resides on the stack or (2) remains in the calling procedure. In both cases, the AP will contain the address to the first longword of the argument list.

When the argument list resides on the stack, the system stack, which was described in Section 6.1, is used. The system stack makes it very convenient to push addresses onto the stack because each address is represented by a longword, and the system stack is made up of longwords. Figure 6.11 presents the contents of the stack for the argument list in Figure 6.9.

In order for the called procedure to obtain the arguments, it must have access to the address of the argument list. By convention, when the procedure is called, this address is placed into the AP. The address in AP points to the top of the argument list, which contains the *size of the argument list*. In order to obtain the arguments, the contents of AP are always offset by a value of 4, 8, or 12, and so forth. This is because each argument in the list is a longword. The displacement addressing mode can be used to obtain the argument.

Figure 6.11

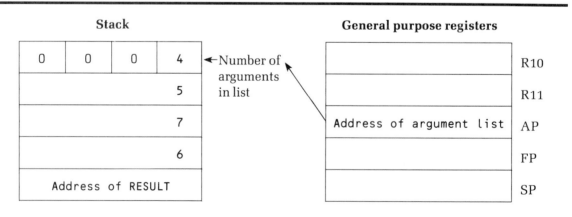

Call Frame—Data Structure

When a procedure is called by a CALLG or CALLS instruction, a special data structure *call frame* is created; this call frame is placed onto the stack. The information contained in the call frame is the current state of the procedure that is currently executing the CALLG or CALLS. It is necessary to retain information about the current state of the calling procedure to ensure that, when control returns to the calling procedure, it can resume its execution as if it had never left. When one procedure relinquishes control of the computer to another procedure, the called procedure has access to all the CPU facilities. For example, it can alter the contents of a register or the PSW. Therefore, the information placed in the call frame is the contents of the registers that might be altered, the current PSW, entry mask, and other information, shown in Figure 6.12.

The left-hand side of Figure 6.12 illustrates a possible call frame data structure that would be created when either a CALLS or a CALLG instruction is executed. Whenever the argument list is on the stack, the call frame occupies the portion of the stack that is just above the argument list.

Figure 6.12

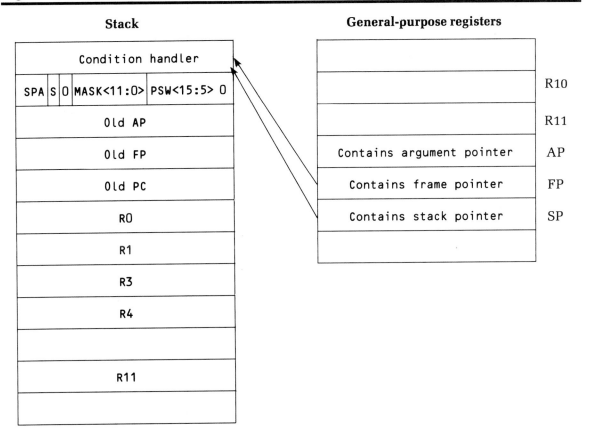

You will recall that each program must begin with an .ENTRY instruction. This is also true for a procedure; however, the second operand in the .ENTRY instruction must be a mask rather than a 0. For example,

```
.ENTRY    PROC,^M<R6,R7>
```

In this example PROC is the symbolic address used by the calling routine to enter the procedure PROC. The mask represents the list of registers that are to be stored at the beginning of the procedure's execution and restored at the end of its execution. The mask is necessary to prevent the procedure from destroying information placed into the registers by the calling routine. Registers R12, R13, and R15 are not to be included in the mask because they are automatically saved on the stack in such a way that R15 (PC) is pushed onto the stack first, followed by R13 (FP), and finally by R12 (AP). Directly above the longword containing the contents of the old AP is the longword that contains many items of information about the calling procedure. Interpreting this longword from right to left is as follows:

1. The first five bits are set to zero.
2. The next eleven bits contain the contents of current PSW bits 5 to 15.
3. The next twelve bits contain the entry mask.
4. The next bit (28th bit) is set to zero.
5. The next bit (29th bit), if set to zero indicates that CALLG is used and, if it is set to one, indicates that CALLS is used.
6. The last two bits are the SPA (Stack Pointer Alignment).

The call frame is accessed by using the *frame pointer* (FP). The FP contains the address to the top of the frame. The FP, which is the register 13 (R13), will always receive the address of the top of the frame as a result of executing either CALLG or CALLS instructions.

Upon completing the CALLG or CALLS instructions, the contents of the PSW, AP, FP, and PC reflect the current status of the called procedure. Therefore the contents saved on the stack of the PSW, AP, FP, and PC reflect the status of the calling procedure. This ensures that, when execution of the procedure is terminated, the calling routine can resume its execution with the same program status.

The CALLG Instruction

The CALLG instruction has two operands. The first operand is the address of the argument list, and the second operand is the address of the procedure being called. Both of the operands can be represented by most VAX addressing modes. The general format of the CALLG instruction is as follows:

		First Operand		Second Operand	
LABEL:	CALLG	ARGADDRESS,		SUBNAME	;COMMENT

Here ARGADDRESS is the address of the first longword of the argument list. Arguments are said to be *passed* from the calling routine to the called procedure. This means that the called procedure can operate on the data provided in the argument list. In addition, values may be *returned*, or transferred back from the called procedure to the calling routine, via the same argument list.

The procedure called by the CALLG instruction obtains the arguments by using the address contained in the AP. This address points to the argument list that is located in the calling routine. Figure 6.13 presents a *main program* that calls the procedure SUM, which calculates the sum of a list of test scores.

Figure 6.13

```
            .TITLE      FIG613

; MAIN PROGRAM CALLS PROCEDURE SUM WHICH ADDS 20 TEST SCORES

GRADE_ARRAY_SIZE=20

GRADE:      .BLKL       GRADE_ARRAY_SIZE
COUNT:      .LONG       GRADE_ARRAY_SIZE
RESULT:     .LONG       0
ARG_LIST:   .LONG       3
            .ADDRESS    GRADE
            .ADDRESS    COUNT
            .ADDRESS    RESULT

            .ENTRY      START,0

; ASSUME THAT THE TEST SCORES ARE READ HERE

; CALL THE PROCEDURE SUM

            CALLG       ARG_LIST,SUM

; THE SUM OF 20 TEST SCORES IS FOUND IN MEMORY LOCATION RESULT

            $EXIT_S

; BEGINNING OF THE PROCEDURE SUM

ARRAY_GRADE=4
S_COUNT=8
S_RESULT=12

            .ENTRY      SUM,^M<R6,R7,R8,R9>
            MOVL        ARRAY_GRADE(AP),R6      ; R6 CONTAINS THE ADDRESS OF ARRAY GRADES
            MOVL        S_COUNT(AP),R7          ; R7 CONTAINS THE ADDRESS OF COUNT
            MOVL        S_RESULT(AP),R8         ; R8 CONTAINS THE ADDRESS OF RESULT
            CLRL        (R8)                    ; INITIALIZE RESULT TO 0
            CLRL        R9                      ; SET TO ZERO THE INDEX REGISTER
LOOP:       ADDL2       (R6)[R9],(R8)           ; ADD A VALUE TO RESULT
            AOBLSS      (R7),R9,LOOP            ; IF INDEX < COUNT THEN CONTINUE THE LOOP
            RET                                 ;     ELSE EXIT PROCEDURE
            .END        START
```

Executing the program in Figure 6.13 produces a stack with the contents shown in Exhibit 6.2. Here the procedure SUM has access to the addresses COUNT, RESULT, and array GRADE by using the offset (displacement address mode) to the AP. To obtain the address of the array GRADE, an offset of 4 must be used because the first longword of the argument list contains the size of the list. The offset of 8 is used to obtain the address of COUNT, and an offset of 12 is used to obtain the address of RESULT. You will note that the argument list is in the calling routine and not on the stack.

The addressing mode used to access the needed information for the solution of a procedure will depend on the setup of the argument list. Therefore, during the development of a system of programs, one type of argument list should be agreed upon and adhered to by every procedure that is part of the system.

The execution of the instruction CALLG can be summarized as follows:

1. The contents of the registers denoted in the entry mask are pushed onto the stack.
2. The contents of the PC, FP, and AP, respectively, are pushed onto the stack.
3. The calling procedure status information is organized in a longword and then pushed onto the stack.

Exhibit 6.2

Format of argument list

Condition handler	← FP and SP
Status information	(During execution of
Old AP	the procedure SUM)
Old FP	
Old PC	
R6	
R7	
R8	
R9	
	← SP (Before and after
	execution of
	the instruction
	`CALLG   ARGLIST,SUM`)

3	← (AP)
Address of array GRADE	← 4(AP)
Address of COUNT	← 8(AP)
Address of RESULT	← 12(AP)

4. A longword equaling 0 is pushed onto the stack (condition handler).
5. The contents of the FP are replaced by the contents of the SP.
6. The contents of the AP are replaced by the address represented by the first operand of CALLG.
7. The contents of the PC are replaced by the sum of the address represented by the second operand and 2. The procedure's address is increased by 2 because the first two bytes (word) contain the mask. Therefore, the first executable instruction is two bytes beyond the entry point.

The CALLS Instruction

The CALLS instruction has two operands. The first operand is a numeric value representing the number of arguments in an argument list. The second operand is the address of the procedure being called. The second operand can be represented by most VAX addressing modes. The general format of the CALLS instruction is as follows:

		First Operand	Second Operand	
LABEL:	CALLS	NUMBER	,SUBNAME	;COMMENT

The CALLS instruction differs from the CALLG in that the CALLS instruction assumes that the arguments are on the stack. The arguments on the stack must be arranged according to some predefined order.

The arguments can be placed onto the stack in several ways. The most common way is by using the instructions PUSHL and PUSHAt. The PUSHL instruction pushes a longword data type onto the top of the stack. This longword may contain either data or an address. The PUSHAt instruction pushes an address of the data type denoted by t onto the top of the stack. The arguments are pushed in the reverse order to the predefined order. Thus, the argument that is to be on top of the list is the last one to be pushed. As an illustration, consider a main program that calls the procedure SUM, which calculates the sum of a list of test scores. The length of the test score list is not a constant. The argument list for this procedure must consist of the address of the list of test scores, the number of test scores in the list, and the address of where to place the sum. Figure 6.14 presents the main program and the procedure SUM.

Exhibit 6.3 presents the contents of the stack after the instruction CALLS is executed and during the execution of the procedure SUM. Compare Exhibit 6.3 with Exhibit 6.2 to note the difference in the contents of the stacks when the CALLG and CALLS instructions are used. When CALLG is used, the stack does not contain the arguments, but when CALLS is used, the arguments must be on the stack. This difference is transparent to the procedure, but not to the user. The user must arrange the argument list on the stack rather then define it by using stor-

Figure 6.14

```
                .TITLE      FIG614

; MAIN PROGRAM CALLS PROCEDURE SUM WHICH ADDS 20 TEST SCORES

GRADE_ARRAY_SIZE=20

GRADE:      .BLKL       GRADE_ARRAY_SIZE
COUNT:      .LONG       GRADE_ARRAY_SIZE
RESULT:     .LONG       0

            .ENTRY      START,0

; ASSUME THAT THE TEST SCORES ARE READ HERE

; CALL THE PROCEDURE SUM

            PUSHAL      RESULT          ; FIRST ADDRESS TO BE PLACED ONTO THE STACK
            PUSHAL      COUNT           ; SECOND ADDRESS TO BE PLACED ONTO THE STACK
            PUSHAL      GRADE           ; THIRD ADDRESS TO BE PLACED ONTO THE STACK
            CALLS       #3,SUM          ; CALL PROCEDURE SUM

; THE SUM OF 20 TEST SCORES IS STORED IN MEMORY LOCATION RESULT

            $EXIT_S

; BEGINNING OF THE PROCEDURE SUM

ARRAY_GRADE=4
S_COUNT=8
S_RESULT=12

            .ENTRY      SUM,^M<R6,R7,R8,R9>
            MOVL        ARRAY_GRADE(AP),R6      ; R6 CONTAINS THE ADDRESS OF ARRAY GRADES
            MOVL        S_COUNT(AP),R7          ; R7 CONTAINS THE ADDRESS OF COUNT
            MOVL        S_RESULT(AP),R8         ; R8 CONTAINS THE ADDRESS OF RESULT
            CLRL        (R8)                    ; INITIALIZE RESULT TO 0
            CLRL        R9                      ; SET TO ZERO THE INDEX REGISTER
LOOP:       ADDL2       (R6)[R9],(R8)           ; ADD A VALUE TO RESULT
            AOBLSS      (R7),R9,LOOP            ; IF INDEX < COUNT THEN CONTINUE THE LOOP
            RET                                 ;     ELSE EXIT PROCEDURE
            .END        START
```

age directive instructions. The remaining operations performed by the CALLS instruction are identical to the operations performed by the CALLG instruction.

The RET Instruction

The **RET** instruction resets the state of the calling procedure to the condition prior to the execution of the CALLG or CALLS instructions. The RET instruction has *no* operands. Its general format is as follows:

| LABEL: | RET | ;COMMENT |

Exhibit 6.3

Condition handler	← FP and SP (During the execution of the procedure SUM)
Status information	
Old AP	
Old FP	
Old PC	
R6	
R7	
R8	
R9	
3	← AP
Address of array GRADE	
Address of COUNT	
Address of RESULT	
	← SP (Before and after the execution of the instruction CALLS #3,SUM)

RET instruction obtains the old contents of the PC from the stack and places it into the PC. You will recall that the old contents of the PC is the address of the instruction that immediately follows CALLG or CALLS. Therefore the PC contains the address where execution in the calling routine is to resume. In addition, the RET instruction restores the SP to the address it contained prior to executing CALLG or CALLS. If the stack was used to store data during the procedure's execution, execution of the RET instruction causes the stack to be cleared of that data.

Summary of Procedure-Calling Standards   *6.7*

Invocation

a. Procedures are called by the transfer of control instruction CALLG or CALLS, and the procedures are exited by the RET instruction.

b. A register mask is required as the first word of the called procedure. This is supplied by ^M< > as an operand of the first executable instruction.

Register Usage

a. It is the responsibility of the called procedure to save, via the register mask, any registers, other than R0 and R1, that are used. This is accomplished by a mask in the .ENTRY instruction which is the first executable instruction.

b. The FP must not be altered.

c. R0 and R1 are used to return a function value, if appropriate. Otherwise, they can be used as temporary registers.

Passing Arguments

a. The argument list must consist of longwords. The first longword contains the argument count, and the successive longwords are the arguments.

b. The arguments may be passed by value, by reference, or by descriptor.

c. The arguments should be treated as read-only data.

d. Interpretation of the arguments depends on the agreement between the calling and called routines.

Part 2.   Enrichment Topics

6.8   Displacement Deferred Addressing Mode

The *displacement deferred addressing mode* is used primarily in conjunction with MACRO assembly language procedures. When a procedure is called, the address to the argument list is placed into the AP. The address within the AP usually points to a list of addresses. Therefore a procedure has access to an address that points to a list of addresses. Using the displacement deferred addressing mode in a procedure eliminates one instruction. For example, in Figure 6.13 the instruction MOVL ARRAY__GRADE(AP),R6 would not be necessary if the procedure used the displacement deferred addressing mode. The general format of an instruction using the displacement deferred addressing mode is as follows:

		First Operand		Second Operand	
LABEL:	OPCODE	@DISPLACEMENT (R*n*)	, ...	;COMMENT

Note that the displacement is preceded by an at (@) sign and is immediately followed by the (Rn). The CU calculates the virtual address for the displacement deferred addressing mode according to the following steps:

1. If the displacement is contained in a byte or word, the displacement value is sign-extended to a 32-bit value.
2. The CU adds the displacement value and the value obtained from the Rn.
3. It retrieves the contents of memory specified by the virtual address.
4. It uses the value just retrieved as the new virtual address to access the needed data.

To illustrate the use of the displacement addressing mode, Figure 6.15 presents the same problem as Figure 6.13. The procedure adds the test scores in the array GRADE. You will note that the MOVL instructions are not included in this procedure because the address does not have to be copied into a register before the data is accessed. The displacement deferred addressing mode allows direct access to the data.

Figure 6.15

```
            .TITLE      FIG615

; MAIN PROGRAM CALLS PROCEDURE SUM WHICH ADDS 20 TEST SCORES

GRADE_ARRAY_SIZE=3

GRADE:      .BLKL       GRADE_ARRAY_SIZE
COUNT:      .LONG       GRADE_ARRAY_SIZE
RESULT:     .LONG       0

ARG_LIST:   .LONG       3
            .ADDRESS    GRADE
            .ADDRESS    COUNT
            .ADDRESS    RESULT

            .ENTRY      START,0

; ASSUME THAT THE TEST SCORES ARE READ HERE

; CALL THE PROCEDURE SUM

            CALLG       ARG_LIST,SUM                        ; CALL IS ISSUED TO PROCEDURE SUM

; THE SUM OF 20 TEST SCORES IS STORED IN MEMORY LOCATION RESULT

            $EXIT_S

; BEGINNING OF THE PROCEDURE SUM

ARRAY_GRADE=4
S_COUNT=8
S_RESULT=12

            .ENTRY      SUM,^M<R6,R7,R8,R9>
            CLRL        @S_RESULT(AP)                       ; INITIALIZE RESULT TO 0
            CLRL        R9                                  ; SET TO ZERO THE INDEX REGISTER
LOOP:       ADDL2       @ARRAY_GRADE(AP)[R9],@S_RESULT(AP)  ; ADD A VALUE TO RESULT
            AOBLSS      @S_COUNT(AP),R9,LOOP                ; IF INDEX < COUNT CONTINUE THE LOOP
            RET                                             ;     ELSE EXIT THE PROCEDURE
            .END        START
```

6.9 *Calling a Procedure Written in a Different Language*

The language in which the called procedure is written is transparent to the calling procedure. As a result, a system of programs may have procedures written in many different languages. This is often true in large application programs where coding certain parts of the problem in the primary language would be very difficult or, if possible, very inefficient in that it would take up too much CPU time. The calling procedure and the called procedures need only be in agreement on the argument list; that is, on the data type of each argument and its relative position within the argument list.

When a problem is coded by a group of procedures, quite often each procedure is assembled or compiled as a separate program. To execute this system of programs as one problem, all of the required procedures must be linked together to form one executable image. The use of higher-level language procedures to perform input and output operations, which was used in Chapter 3, illustrates this process.

6.10 *Higher-Level Language Programs Calling MACRO Procedures*

In previous chapters it was shown that a MACRO program can reference a procedure written in FORTRAN or Pascal. A program written in FORTRAN or Pascal can also reference a procedure written in MACRO. To illustrate, consider a problem that reads in two values, interchanges them, and prints the interchanged values. Figure 6.16 presents a FORTRAN program that reads in two values, and then calls a MACRO procedure that interchanges the two values; after that the same FORTRAN program prints the interchanged values.

The FORTRAN program in Figure 6.16 stops its execution when the *end-of-file* (*EOF*) mark has been read. The test for the EOF mark is carried out when END= is contained in the READ statement. The READ statement in Figure 6.16 contains END=95, which causes the computer to test for the EOF mark every time a record is read. When the EOF mark is encountered, the control is passed to the line whose *statement number* is the same as the one found after the equal sign in the END= portion of the READ instruction; therefore, in Figure 6.16 control is passed to the *STOP statement* when the EOF mark is encountered. Figure 6.17 presents the MACRO program that is called by the FORTRAN program in Figure 6.16.

The MACRO procedure can be written so that it expects arguments to be passed in the manner required by FORTRAN language. The procedure must also adhere to the conventions of the procedure-calling standards. If the MACRO procedure does not expect arguments in the form that FORTRAN would normally pass them, three intrinsic functions are available that allow an argument to be passed in the appropriate fashion:

%VAL (arg)

Entry is the actual 32-bit value of the argument arg, as defined by the language.

%REF (arg)

Entry is a pointer to the value of the argument arg, as defined by the language.

%DESCR (arg)

Entry is a pointer to a VAX descriptor of the argument.

These operations are often required when you call VAX system services from FORTRAN. These intrinsic functions are necessary to enable any procedure to be called by programs written in any higher-level language.

Figure 6.16

```
                PROGRAM FIG616
                INTEGER I,J

    C READ VALUE I AND J

    10          READ(5,*,END=95)I,J

    C CALL PROCEDURE CHANGE

                CALL CHANGE(I,J)

    C PRINT THE RESULT

                WRITE(6,20)I,J
    20          FORMAT(9X,I10,10X,I10)

    C REPEAT PROGRAM UNTIL EOF MARK IS READ

                GO TO 10
    95          STOP
                END
```

Figure 6.17

```
                .TITLE     FIG617

                .ENTRY     CHANGE,^M<>
                MOVL       a4(AP),(SP)
                MOVL       a8(AP),a4(AP)
                MOVL       (SP),a8(AP)
                RET
                .END
```

Careful design of procedure packages will minimize the actual need to use these escape mechanisms.

Figure 6.18 provides an example of these escape mechanisms in a MACRO procedure that determines the larger value of two given values. Note that the entry point of each procedure is not the customary .ENTRY instruction. Instead the .WORD data-storage directive is used. The label used in the first field of this instruction ends with a double colon (::), which informs the assembler that the label is defined as a global label.

Figure 6.18

```
1                 .TITLE     FIG618
2
3       ;  THE FOLLOWING ARE THREE MACRO PROCEDURES THAT DETERMINE
4       ;  THE LARGEST VALUE OF GIVEN TWO VALUES
5
6       ;  EACH PROCEDURE IS CALLED BY THE CALL STATEMENT THAT IS SHOWN
7       ;  IN THE COMMENT INSTRUCTION PRECEDING THE PROCEDURE
8
9       ;  THE LAST EXAMPLE IS A FUNCTION IN WHICH CASE
10      ;  THE ANSWER IS RETURNED IN R0
11
12      ;  CALL   MAXREF(VAL1,VAL2,MAX)
13
14      MAXREF:: .WORD      ^M<>
15               CMPL       @4(AP),@8(AP)
16               BGTR       CONT
17               MOVL       @8(AP),@12(AP)
18               RET
19      CONT:    MOVL       @4(AP),@12(AP)
20               RET
21               .END
22
23      ;  CALL   MAXVAL(%VAL(VAL1),%VAL(VAL2),MAX)
24
25      MAXVAL:: .WORD      ^M<>
26               CMPL       4(AP),8(AP)
27               BGTR       CONT
28               MOVL       8(AP),@12(AP)
29               RET
30      CONT:    MOVL       4(AP),@12(AP)
31               RET
32               .END
33
34      ;  MAS = MAXFUN(VAL1,VAL2)
35
36      MAXFUN:: .WORD      0
37               CMPL       @4(AP),@8(AP)
38               BGTR       CONT
39               MOVL       @8(AP),R0
40               RET
41      CONT:    MOVL       @4(AP),R0
42               RET                              ; THE MAX VALUE IS RETURNED IN R0
43               .END
```

This method of defining the entry point is equivalent to using .ENTRY instruction.

Figure 6.18 illustrates three such procedures that could be called from FORTRAN:

1. Procedure MAXREF (lines 14–21) expects the arguments to be passed by reference. A typical FORTRAN subroutine call is shown in line 12.

2. Procedure MAXVAL (lines 25–32) expects the first two arguments to be passed by value. The destination is still passed by reference. The appropriate FORTRAN subroutine call is in line 23.

3. Procedure MAXFUN (lines 36–43) expects the arguments to be passed by reference, but the result is returned in a register. By convention the result obtained from a FORTRAN function subprogram is returned in register R0. If the result is a *double precision* value, it will be returned in registers R0 and R1. Line 34 gives the appropriate FORTRAN function call.

Figure 6.16 presented a FORTRAN program calling a MACRO procedure, this part presents a Pascal program calling a MACRO procedure. To illustrate this, Figure 6.19 presents a Pascal program that reads two numbers and prints the larger of the two. The Pascal program processes an input file until an end-of-file mark is encountered. It also calls a MACRO procedure that determines the larger of two values and passes the larger value back to the Pascal program. When the control is returned to the Pascal program, the program prints this value. The MACRO procedure that the Pascal program calls is written in the same manner as if a MACRO program were to call it. This is because the procedure is developed so that the language used to write the calling routine is transparent to the procedure.

Referencing External Routines   *6.11*

Large application programs may consist of many procedures that have been edited in separate source files and assembled separately. These are then linked together to form a single executable program. To enable one routine to call another that has been separately assembled, the assembler must be informed that the labels being referenced by the call instruction are external to the caller (that is, not defined by it). If this information is not provided, at link time the linker will display an error message indicating that there are undefined labels. Furthermore, the procedure being called must define its name as a *global name*. To illustrate this, consider a procedure that searches a list of test scores for the maximum score and its position in the list. This procedure is called by

Figure 6.19

```
(* THE PASCAL PROCEDURE WILL CALL THE MACRO PROCEDURE WHICH   *)
(* DETERMINES THE LARGEST VALUE FROM THE TWO GIVEN VALUES     *)

PROGRAM CALC (INPUT,OUTPUT);
VAR I,J,VAL : INTEGER;
PROCEDURE MAX (VAR I,J,VAL : INTEGER); EXTERNAL;
BEGIN { PROGRAM }
      WHILE NOT EOF(INPUT) DO
            BEGIN { CALC }
                  READLN (I,J);
                  MAX (I,J,VAL);
                  WRITELN ('THE LARGEST VALUE IS ',VAL)
            END; { CALC }
END. {PROGRAM}




FIRST_VAL = 4
SECOND_VAL = 8
LARGEST = 12

          .ENTRY    MAX,^M<R7,R8,R9>
          MOVL      FIRST_VAL(AP),R7        ; R7 = ADDRESS OF THE 1ST VALUE
          MOVL      SECOND_VAL(AP),R8       ; R8 = ADDRESS OF THE 2ND VALUE
          MOVL      LARGEST(AP),R9          ; R9 = ADDRESS OF THE LARGEST VALUE

          CMPL      (R7),(R8)               ; IF 1ST VALUE > 2ND VALUE
          BGTR      CONT                    ;     THAN GO TO STORE 1ST VALUE IN LARGEST
          MOVL      (R8),(R9)               ;     ELSE STORE 2ND VALUE IN LARGEST
          RET
CONT:     MOVL      (R7),(R9)
          RET
          .END
```

another procedure that reads the grades into a list and counts the number of grades that were read. Figure 6.20 presents the main program and the procedure. Note that the procedure in Figure 6.20 uses the .WORD storage directive as its entry point instead of the customary .ENTRY instruction.

The first procedure in Figure 6.20, called the main program, contains the .END instruction with an operand. When a problem is solved by a system of programs that were assembled separately, the main program must contain the .END instruction with an operand. This is necessary to inform the operating system of the first executable instruction in the system of programs.

.EXTERNAL Assembler Directive

A procedure name defined as a global name makes the procedure accessible to every procedure linked together to form a system of programs.

Figure 6.20

```
          .TITLE   FIG620
          .PSECT   DATA,NOEXE,WRT

; THIS PROGRAM READS GRADES INTO AN ARRAY
; AND COUNTS THE NUMBER OF GRADES READ

ARRAY_SIZE=100

GRADE:    .BLKL    ARRAY_SIZE
MAXGR:    .BLKL    1
POS:      .BLKL    1
COUNT:    .BLKL    1
ARGLIST:  .LONG    4
          .ADDRESS GRADE
          .ADDRESS COUNT
          .ADDRESS MAXGR
          .ADDRESS POS

          .PSECT   CODE,NOWRT,EXE
          .ENTRY   START,0

; INSERT INSTRUCTIONS TO READ AND COUNT THE GRADES

          CALLG    ARGLIST,SEARCH

; INSERT INSTRUCTIONS TO PRINT RESULTS

          $EXIT_S
          .END     START




          .TITLE   FIG620A

; THIS PROCEDURE SEARCHES THE ARRAY FOR THE LARGEST GRADE
; AND DETERMINES ITS POSITION IN THE ARRAY


LARGE:    .BLKL    1
POS1:     .BLKL    1
COUNT1:   .BLKL    1

SEARCH::  .WORD    ^M<R6,R7>        ; PROCEDURE NAME IS DEFINED GLOBALLY
          MOVL     4(AP),R4
          MOVL     @8(AP),COUNT1
          CLRL     R7               ; CLEAR INDEX REGISTER
          MOVL     (R4),LARGE       ; INITIALIZE LARGE TO THE FIRST GRADE
          MOVL     #1,POS1          ; SET POSITION TO ONE
AGAIN:    CMPL     LARGE,(R4)[R7]   ; COMPARE TWO GRADES
          BGTR     OK               ; LARGE CONTAINS THE LARGEST GRADE
          MOVL     (R4)[R7],LARGE   ; STORE THE CURRENT LARGEST GRADE
          MOVL     R7,POS1          ; STORE ITS POSITION
          ADDL     #1,POS1          ; ADJUST POSITION VALUE BY ONE BECAUSE THE
                                    ; FIRST VALUE WAS ASSUMED TO BE AT POSITION ZERO
OK:       AOBLSS   COUNT1,R7,AGAIN  ; IF INDEX < COUNT THEN CONTINUE THE LOOP
          MOVL     LARGE,@12(AP)    ;    ELSE PASS THE LARGEST GRADE AND
          MOVL     POS1,@16(AP)     ;    ITS POSITION TO THE CALLING PROCEDURE
          RET
          .END
```

This accessability is also made possible by the use of the assembly directive **.EXTERNAL** (.EXTRN). Its general format is as follows:

The .EXTERNAL assembler directive can be abbreviated to .EXTRN. The LABEL__LIST consists of labels that are *not* defined in the main program or procedure in which the .EXTERNAL instruction appears. Each label is separated by a comma. The labels entered in the directive .EXTERNAL are defined at link time; therefore, at the time of execution all labels are defined. Figure 6.21 illustrates the use of the assembler directive .EXTERNAL that defines two labels (procedure names), which were assembled as separate modules.

Figure 6.21

```
            .TITLE   FIG621

;  THIS PROGRAM READS IN AN ARRAY OF TWENTY GRADES, CALCULATES THE AVERAGE,
;  AND COUNTS THE NUMBER OF GRADES THAT ARE ABOVE THE AVERAGE.

            .EXTERNAL ADDITION,COMPARE
            .PSECT    DATA,NOEXE,WRT

TABLE_SIZE=20

GRADE:      .BLKL  0
TABLE:      .BLKL  TABLE_SIZE
NUMBER:     .BLKL  1
SUM:        .BLKL  1                     ;RESERVES A LONGWD FOR SUM OF NUMBERS
AVERAGE:    .BLKL  1                     ;RESERVES A LONGWD FOR AVERAGE OF NUMBERS
COUNT:      .BLKL  1                     ;RESERVES A LONGWD FOR COUNT OF NUM

MES1:       .ASCIZ /THE AVERAGE IS:                        /
MES2:       .ASCIZ /THE NUMBER OF GRADES ABOVE THE AVERAGE: /
MES3:       .ASCIZ /THE SUM IS:                            /

ARGLST1:    .LONG 2                      ;ARGUMENT LIST FOR ADDITION PROCEDURE
            .ADDRESS TABLE
            .ADDRESS SUM

ARGLST2:    .LONG 3                      ;ARGUMENT LIST FOR COMPARE PROCEDURE
            .ADDRESS TABLE
            .ADDRESS AVERAGE
            .ADDRESS COUNT

IN_ARG_LIS:
            .LONG    1
            .ADDRESS GRADE
```

Figure 6.21 (*continued*)

```
ADD_MES1:  .ADDRESS MES1
ADD_MES2:  .ADDRESS MES2
ADD_MES3:  .ADDRESS MES3
MESX:      .LONG    0                       ;RECEIVES ADDRESS OF THE MESSAGE
           .LONG    0                       ;          TO BE PRINTED

;ARGUMENTS USED IN THE OUTPUT PROCEDURE

OUT_ARG_LIS:
           .LONG    2
           .ADDRESS MESX                    ;CONTAINS THE ADDRESS OF THE MESSAGE
                                            ;          DESCRIPTOR
           .LONG    0                       ;CONTAINS THE ADDRESS OF THE VALUE


           .ENTRY   START,^M<>              ;BEGINNING OF EXECUTABLE CODE
BEGIN:     CLRL     R7                      ;CLEARS OUT R7 REGISTER
           CLRL     R8                      ;CLEARS OUT R8 REGISTER
           MOVAL    TABLE,R8                ;MOVES THE ADDRESS OF TABLE TO R8
TABLE_LOOP:
           CALLG    IN_ARG_LIS,INPUT        ;CALLS INPUT PROCEDURE
           MOVL     GRADE,(R8)[R7]          ;MOVE CONVERTED NUMBER TO ARRAY
           AOBLSS   #TABLE_SIZE,R7,TABLE_LOOP   ;DOES THIS 20 TIMES
CALC_SUM:
           CALLG    ARGLST1,ADDITION        ;CALLS ADDITION PROCEDURE
CALC_AVERAGE:
           DIVL3    #TABLE_SIZE,SUM,AVERAGE      ;CALCULATES THE AVERAGE
COMPARISON:
           CALLG    ARGLST2,COMPARE         ;CALLS COMPARE PROCEDURE
WRITE:     MOVL     ADD_MES3,MESX+4
           MOVAL    SUM,OUT_ARG_LIS+8
           CALLG    OUT_ARG_LIS,OUTPUT
           MOVL     ADD_MES2,MESX+4
           MOVAL    AVERAGE,OUT_ARG_LIS+8
           CALLG    OUT_ARG_LIS,OUTPUT
           MOVL     ADD_MES1,MESX+4
           MOVAL    COUNT,OUT_ARG_LIS+8
           CALLG    OUT_ARG_LIS,OUTPUT
           $EXIT_S
           .END     START


           .PSECT        ADDITION


;THIS PROCEDURE ADDS ALL THE GRADES IN THE GIVEN TABLE

           .ENTRY        ADDITION,^M<R6,R7>
           CLRL          R7
           CLRL          @8(AP)
           MOVL          4(AP),R6
LOOP:      ADDL2         (R6)+,@8(AP)
           AOBLSS        #20,R7,LOOP
           RET
           .END
```

Figure 6.21 (*continued*)

```
        .PSECT          COMPARE

;THIS PROCEDURE COMPARES EACH GRADE IN THE ARRAY OF 20 GRADES
;TO THE AVERAGE OF THE GRADES AND COUNTS HOW MANY ARE GREATER
;THAN THE AVERAGE GRADE

        .ENTRY          COMPARE,^M<R6,R7>
        MOVL            4(AP),R6
        CLRL            R7
LOOP:   CMPL            (R6)+,@8(AP)
        BLSS            JUMP
        INCL            @12(AP)
JUMP:   AOBLSS          #20,R7,LOOP
        RET
        .END
```

6.12   More on the RET Instruction

Section 6.6 introduced the RET instruction. This instruction not only restores the PC with the return address, but also performs the following tasks.

1. Replaces SP by FP + 4.
2. Pops the longword containing status information from the stack and saves it in a temporary register in the ALU.
3. Replaces the PC, FP, and AP with longwords popped from the stack.
4. Forms a register-restore mask from bits 27 through 16 of the temporary register.
5. Scans the mask from bit 0 through 11 and restores the contents of the registers, the number of which corresponds to set bits in the mask with the longwords popped from the stack.
6. Replaces bits 1 and 0 of the SP with bits 31 and 30 of the status information longword.
7. Replaces the PSW with bits 15 through 0 of the status information longword.
8. Checks bit 29 of this longword. If the bit is set to 1 (indicating CALLS), the RET instruction pops the longword containing the number of arguments from the stack. This number is multiplied by 4 and added to the SP contents to clear the argument list from the stack.

The SP has now been restored to its value before the procedure is called and before any stack argument list has been created. In addition, the PC, FP, AP, PSW, and the registers contained in the mask of the .ENTRY instruction have now been restored to their original state (just prior to the execution of CALLG or CALLS). After the RET instruction has been executed, the SP contains an address that points to the long-word that was pointed to just before the execution of either the CALLG or CALLS instructions. This ensures that the stack has been cleared of information that was placed onto the stack during the execution of a procedure. The condition codes in the PSW, however, are *not* restored to their original state, because they were not saved. In addition, the called procedure may possibly have modified the low-order four bits of the longword containing the procedure status information within the call frame; these bits are relevant to calling FORTRAN and Pascal subroutines from within a MACRO program, and vice versa.

Additional Uses of the Stack   *6.13*

Traditionally, in mathematics, an operator is placed between operands as shown in $x + y$. This form of expressing an algebraic formula is called *infix notation*. However, Polish mathematician Lukasiewicz showed that operators also can be placed either before or after the operands. The form when operators precede the operands is called *prefix notation* or *Polish notation*, and when they follow the operands it is called *postfix notation* or *reverse Polish notation*. The following examples illustrate the three notations;

$$x + y \quad \text{Infix notation}$$

$$+ xy \quad \text{Prefix or Polish notation}$$

$$xy + \quad \text{Postfix or reverse Polish notation}$$

An algebraic equation expressed in postfix notation can be solved by the use of the stack. However, before it is shown how the stack can be used to solve the equation expressed in reverse Polish notation it would be advantageous to solve an equation by longhand. For example the equation to be solved is; $(x + y)/(z - v)$ when expressed in postfix notation it is; $xy + zv - /$. The solution of such an equation begins at the left and moves to the right performing the encountered operations. In the equation $xy + zv - /$ at the left is an operand x, as the move continues to the right the operand y is encountered, another move to the right encounters the addition operator. At this time addition is performed on the two operands which preceded the addition operator and the result replaces the two operands and the operator (x, y and $+$). The solution of the equation continues by moving to the right from the point where the result was placed. Operand z is then encountered, and again moving to the right the operand v is encountered, and again moving to the right the operator minus is encountered. At this time the subtraction operation is performed on the preceding two operands (z and v). The result of the subtraction replaces the two operands and the operator (z, v, and $-$). Continuing to move to the right the division operator is encountered. Division is performed on the two operands that are the results obtained from the addition and subtraction. The division is performed and the result replaces the two operands and the operator. Because there are no more operands or operators left this last result is the answer to the solution to the equation.

The solution to this same equation is now illustrated by the use of the stack. It is easier to follow a solution of an equation if its variables are replaced by values. Therefore, in the equation $xy + zv - /$ replacing its variables with constants is 5 7 + 8 2 - /. The solution proceeds from left to right. In the above equation the value 5 is pushed onto the stack, moving to right again the value 7 is encountered which also is pushed onto the stack, continue moving to the right the operator addition is encountered. At this point the two values are popped from the stack (5 and 7) and the encountered operation is performed. The result obtained from the addition is pushed onto the stack and again the move begins to the right. The value of 8 is pushed onto the stack, followed by the value of 2, then the minus operator is encountered at which time the subtraction is performed on the two values which were popped from the stack (8 and 2). The result obtained from this subtraction is pushed onto the stack and the move continues to the right. At this point the operator division is encountered and division is performed on the two values popped from the stack which are the results obtained from the addition and subtraction. The result of the division is pushed onto the stack and because there are no more operands or operators the value on top of the stack is the answer to the solution of the equation. Figure 6.22 presents the contents of the stack as the solution progresses from left to right.

Figure 6.22

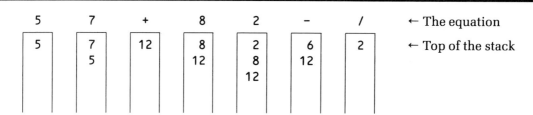

The stack is used to hold intermediate results as the solution progresses from left to right. At the end of the solution the value left on top of the stack is the answer to the equation.

Summary

Procedures are a necessary ingredient in programming. When programmers work on large problems, they subdivided them into smaller problems, each of which is called a procedure or module. Designing a problem in this fashion makes it possible to implement each module as it is finished. Thus part of the program can be productive while the other parts are still in their development stage. VAX recognizes this need by providing a special group of instructions that deal only with the procedure calls. These instructions are CALLG, CALLS, and RET. Use of these instructions makes it easier to link (connect) with the procedures. In addition, the procedures could be written in any language because this set of instructions does not distinguish the language used to write the procedure.

In summary, CALLG and CALLS provide a powerful and generalized way to transfer control to a procedure. Registers may be automatically saved and restored, proper stack alignment is guaranteed, and exceptional conditions occurring within the procedure may be detected. Furthermore, the CALLG/CALLS instructions are used to implement the VAX/VMS Procedure Calling Standard, which allows the programmer to

1. access Common Run-time Library routines from any VAX/VMS native-mode language
2. call routines written in one VAX/VMS native-mode language from programs written in a different native-mode language.

New Instructions

BSBB	POPL	RET
BSBW	POPR	RSB
CALLG	PUSHA*t*	.EXTERNAL
CALLS	PUSHL	
JSB	PUSHR	

New Terms

argument list
argument pointer
call by address
call by reference
call by value
call instruction
call frame
calling routine
called routine
closed subroutine
data structure
destination address
displacement deferred addressing
  mode
double precision
entry mask
EOF (end-of-file)
execution error
exception handler
floating underflow

frame pointer
global name
hardware stack
infix notation
integer overflow
LIFO (last in, first out)
linkage mechanism
mask
main program
main procedure
open subroutine
Polish notation
popping
postfix notation
prefix notation
procedure
pushing
reverse Polish notation
routine
size of the argument list

stack   subroutine
stack pointer   symbolic address
statement number   system of programs
STOP statement   user stack
subprogram

Exercises

1. Why should a large problem be subdivided into smaller ones when the problem is to be implemented on a computer?

2. What is the difference between an open subroutine and a closed subroutine or procedure?

3. How is the system's stack implemented on most computers and why?

4. How is the system's stack accessed?

5. What does the MASK indicate when used in the PUSHR or the POPR instruction?

6. How does the instruction POPR work when its operand is a MASK?

7. Distinguish between the terms calling a procedure and the called procedure.

8. Is the stack used by the JSB(BSBB,BSBW)/RET instruction? If your answer is yes, explain how.

9. Why should you use a BSBB instruction, if a BSBW instruction will always do the job of the BSBB instruction? Why use either BSBB or BSBW instructions when the JSB instruction will always do their job?

10. How do you identify the beginning and the end of a procedure?

11. What is the function of the RET instruction in a procedure?

12. What is the function of the argument list?

13. What can be contained in an argument list?

14. What should be contained in an argument list? Why?

15. What three general-purpose registers are used by the procedure call instructions CALLG and CALLS? Why are these registers used?

16. What does the MASK represent in the .ENTRY instruction? Why is it necessary?

17. Is there any difference between the CALLG and the CALLS instructions? If your answer is yes, what is the difference?

18. Can higher-level languages call a procedure written in MACRO language? If they can, why?

19. Why would it be awkward for procedure A to save all of its own registers contents before calling to procedure B and then restore the registers after its return from B? Is this possible? If so, how? If not, why not?

20. What is the difference between "call by value" and "call by reference"?

21. Assume an input record contains the following values: 5, 8, 3, 7, and 9. What results are produced after executing the following system of programs?

```
LIST:       .BLKB     5
NLIST:      .BLKB     5
INARG:      .LONG     1
            .ADDRESS  LIST
X:          .LONG     0
OUTARG:     .LONG     1
            .ADDRESS  X
CONS:       .BYTE     8
SARG:       .LONG     4
            .ADDRESS  LIST
            .ADDRESS  NLIST
            .ADDRESS  X
            .ADDRESS  CONS
            .ENTRY    BEGIN,0


; INSERTED HERE ARE THE INSTRUCTIONS THAT WOULD READ THE ABOVE
; STATED INPUT RECORD INTO THE ARRAY LIST


            CALLG     SARG,SUB


; INSERTED HERE ARE THE INSTRUCTIONS THAT WOULD PRINT THE ANSWER(S)


            $EXIT_S

            .ENTRY    SUB, ^M<R7,R8,R9,R10,R11>
            MOVL      4(AP),R7
            MOVL      8(AP),R8
            CLRL      R9
            CLRL      R11
LOOP:       MULB3     (R7)[R9],@16(AP),(R8)[R9]
            MOVL      #1,R10
            MULB2     (R8)[R9],R10
            ADDL2     R10,R11
            AOBLEQ    #4,R9,LOOP
            MOVB      R11,@12(AP)
            RET
            .END      BEGIN
```

22.   The following MACRO procedure NARRAY is called by the procedure INPUT. Procedure NARRAY received from the procedure INPUT the address of a five element array as the only argument. Assuming that the five elements in the array are 5, 9, 6, 2, and 8, what are the contents of the array after the procedure NARRAY finishes its execution?

```
LIMIT:    .LONG      5
X:        .LONG      0
          .ENTRY     NARRY,^M<R2>
          PUSHAL     X
          PUSHL      4(AP)
          PUSHL      LIMIT
          CALLS      #3,CHANGE
          MOVL       4(AP),R2
LOOP:     SUBL2      X,(R2)+
          SOBGTR     LIMIT,LOOP
          RET
          .END


INDEX:    .LONG      0
          .ENTRY     CHANGE,^M<R2,R3,R4>
          CLRL       R2
          MOVL       8(AP),R3
          MOVL       4(AP)R4
ALOOP:    ADDL2      (R3)+,R2
          AOBLSS     R4,INDEX,ALOOP
          DIVL2      R4,R2
          MOVL       R2,@12(AP)
          RET
          .END
```

23.   Upon executing the following system of programs, what would be the contents of the array ARRAYB? Write the answer as a sentence, rather than showing the actual numeric value.

```
ARRAYA:  .BLKL      20
ARRAYB:  .LONG      0[20]
N:       .LONG
OUT:     .LONG
INARG:   .LONG      1
         .ADDRESS   N
OUTARG:  .LONG      1
         .ADDRESS   ARRAYB
ARGSUB:  .LONG      3
         .ADDRESS   ARRAYA
         .ADDRESS   ARRAYB
         .ADDRESS   N
         .ENTRY     START,0
         MOVAL      ARRAYA,R5
         CLRL       R6
```

```
READ:   CALLG    INARG,INPUT
        MOVL     N,(R5)[R6]
        AOBLSS   #20,R6,READ
        CALLG    INARG,INPUT
        CALLG    ARGSUB,SUBA
        CALLG    OUTARG,OUTPUT
        $EXIT_S

        .ENTRY   SUBA,^M<R6,R7>
        CLRL     R6
        CLRL     R7
LOOP:   CMPL     @4(AP)[R6],@12(AP)
        BNEQ     TEST
        ADDL3    #1,R6,@8(AP)[R7]
        INCL     R7
TEST:   AOBLSS   #20,R6,LOOP
        RET
        .END     START
```

24. What is produced as a result of executing the following main program and the procedure? Also, where is the result stored after the main program and the procedure are executed?

```
LIST:     .BYTE     5,6,13,25,7,13,27,45,9,32
VAL:      .BYTE     0
ARGLIST:  .LONG     2
          .ADDRESS  LIST
          .ADDRESS  VAL
          .ENTRY    START,0
          CALLG     ARGLIST,PROC

; INSTRUCTIONS TO DISPLAY THE ANSWER ARE INSERTED HERE

          $EXIT_S

          .ENTRY    PROC,^M<R7,R8,R9>
          MOVL      4(AP),R7
          MOVL      8(AP),R8
          SUBL3     R7,R8,R9
          SUBL2     #1,R9
LOOP1:    ADDB2     (R7)+,(R8)
          SOBGEQ    R9,LOOP1
          RET
          .END      START
```

Problems

1. Write a procedure that receives an address to a list of grades and the number of grades in the list. Each grade is represented by a longword data type. The procedure calculates the average for the given list and counts the number of grades above the average. The information returned from the procedure is the average and the count (number of grades above the average).

2. Write a procedure that sorts in ascending order an array of word elements. The procedure receives an address to the array and the number of elements in the array. The result is the sorted array, which replaces the unsorted array.

3. Write an assembly language program that reads morning and evening temperature readings for the month of January. Each input record contains both readings. The first is morning and the second is evening.

  a. Call a procedure that you write, which calculates the average temperature for each day in the month of January.
  b. Call a procedure that you write, which lists the date of each day when the daily temperature, either morning or evening, was above the average for the month of January.
  c. Call a procedure that you write, which calculates the highest daily average temperature for the month of January.
  d. Output the results obtained in b and c.

4. You are to write a main program and several procedures that will simulate a grade book. The grade book contains for each student a record of the student's input which is used to calculate his or her final course grade. The main program does the following:

  a. Calls a higher-level language procedure that reads a roster of students listed by their ID#s. Each ID# is composed of up to seven digits.
  b. Calls a MACRO procedure that sorts the roster of ID#s into numerical order.
  c. Calls a higher-level language procedure that reads n records. Each record contains an ID# and three quiz grades. The input file is not sorted. In addition, this input file does not have to contain all the ID#s read in part a. For example, a student drops the course: therefore that student did not participate in the course. DO NOT SORT THIS LIST.
  d. Calls a MACRO procedure that will update the class roster with the quiz grades. The update consists of matching the ID#s sorted in b with the ID#s read in c, after which the quiz grades are stored along with the ID#s.
  e. Completes the steps described in parts c and d, except that it reads the ID# and a final exam grade.
  f. Calls another MACRO procedure that calculates a course grade for each student. The course grade is based on the average of the

two best quiz grades and the final exam. The final exam counts 60 percent and the quizzes 40 percent.

   g. Calls a higher-level language procedure that prints the list of ID#s along with each course grade.

All the procedures that the main program calls are to be written by the student.

When using FORTRAN input procedure, label the three input data files: IN1.DAT for part a, IN2.DAT for part c, and IN3.DAT for part d. In order for a FORTRAN procedure to read a specific input file, the READ statement must contain information indicating which file the READ statement will read. In order for a READ statement to read a different input file, the DCL command ASSIGN must be used to match the READ statement to the input file. The following are the DCL ASSIGN commands and their respective FORTRAN READ statements.

DCL ASSIGN Commands   FORTRAN READ Statements

```
ASSIGN IN1.DAT FOR005        READ(5,*)
ASSIGN IN2.DAT FOR006        READ(6,*)
ASSIGN IN3.DAT FOR007        READ(7,*)
```

When you use a Pascal input procedure, the input file should be as follows:
Every student ID#

                                  First input file

999
Student ID# along with 3 quiz grades

                                  Second input file

888
Student ID# along with final exam grade

                                  Third input file

End of file mark <CTRL> <Z>

5. Write an assembly language system of programs that will build a chained list by adding links at the end, at the beginning, and in the middle. Write a main program that does the following:

   a. Calls a higher-level language procedure that reads a link and a code. The link is the data item that is added to the list. The data items should be longword data type. The code represents whether the link is to be added at the beginning, the end, or the middle. When the code equals 1, add a link at the beginning; when it equals 2, add a link at the end; and when it equals 3, in the middle. The read operation should be interactive; therefore you do not need to assign an input file. The interactive process will end when the code equals 9.

   b. Calls a MACRO procedure to insert a link at the beginning of the list.

   c. Calls a MACRO procedure to insert a link at the end of the list.

d. Calls a MACRO procedure to insert a link anywhere but at the beginning or the end.

e. Calls a higher-level language procedure to output the linked list.

6. Write a procedure that uses the stack to solve a given equation expressed in reverse Polish notation. The argument list to the procedure consists of the address of the equation and the address where to place the solution of the equation.

7. Write a program that uses the procedure described in Question 6. The program reads equations expressed in reverse Polish notation. Each line of output must contain the equation and its solution. Use the following equations to test the procedure and the program.

Algebraic	Reverse Polish notation
3 + 5*2	3 5 2* +
(8 + 2*5)/(1 + 3*2 − 4)	8 2 5* + 1 3 2* + 4 −/
((1 + 4)*2 + 8)/(5 + 3 + 1)	1 4 + 2*8 + 5 3 + 1 +/

8. Write a procedure that converts an algebraic equation to its equivalent reverse Polish notation. The argument list should contain the address of the algebraic equation and an address where to store the resulting equation.

9. Write a program that uses the procedures described in Questions 6 and 8. This program reads equations in algebraic form. Each input record contains an algebraic equation followed by a number indicating the number of variables contained in the equation. The end of the portion of the input file containing the equations is indicated by a 999. The remaining input file contains the values for the variables in the equations. The first line in this portion of the input file contains the values for the variables in the first equation, the second line contains the values for the variables in the second equation, etc.

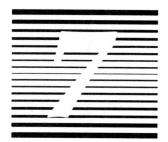

CHAPTER

More on Integer Type Instructions

Outline

Part 1. Core Topics

Partial integer instruction set was introduced in Chapter 3. This partial set contained instructions that performed the basic arithmetic operations on integer values. In addition, Chapter 3 presented the compare and branch instructions. In order to be able to solve all types of problems by using integer instructions, additional instructions are required. These are the move, convert, test, extended divide, and extended multiply instructions.

Integer Instructions   7.1

Most arithmetic integer instructions are represented by one, two, or three operands. In all cases the result is placed in the operand on the far right of the instruction. The data type with which these instructions may operate is either byte, word, or longword. Because some operations require longer integer data types, the VAX provides two additional integer data types: Q (quadword) and O (octaword). Each integer data type is supported by a unique set of instructions.

A number of integer instructions were covered in Chapter 3, however all of which operated on the longword data type. The longword data type was chosen to eliminate an overflow error that could occur during an integer instruction execution. An overflow error is caused by a value that is too large to be represented by the given data type of the instruction; for example,

Figure 7.1

```
VAL1:   .BYTE    91
VAL2:   .BYTE    55
SUM:    .BYTE    0


        MULB3    VAL1,VAL2,SUM
```

In Figure 7.1 the MULB3 instruction informs the CU that the resulting product is to be represented by one byte because the third letter in MUL**B**3 is **B**. If this instruction were to be executed, the product obtained from its execution would be 5005. The 5005 cannot be represented by the 8 binary bits (one byte) reserved for this data type because the largest possible value that can be represented by the byte data type is +127. As a result, an overflow error would occur in this example. The problem with this type of error is that the execution of the program continues, and the incorrect value contained in memory location SUM is used in subsequent calculations that reference that memory location. The only record of the error's occurrence is the setting of the overflow condition code in the PSW.

One way to eliminate this type of an error is to redefine VAL1, VAL2, and SUM by using word data storage directives. Another way is to include a move instruction that would move each value into a word data type and then operate on that word data type. Just redefining or moving SUM would not be correct, because the CU acts according to the information found in the opcode and not in the operands. In the example in Figure 7.1, the opcode MUL**B**3 is interpreted by the CU as a multiplication of two 1-byte data type values. Their product cannot exceed a value that can be represented by the byte data type. The third operand provides the CU with the address of the first byte where the result from the operation is to be placed. It does not indicate the possible size of the result. Therefore the memory location defined for the result is not important; what is important is the data type specified by the opcode. As a matter of fact, every operand can be defined by any integer data type because the operation performed will be on the data type indicated in the opcode of the instruction.

The complete integer instruction set expects each of the operands used in calculations to be integer data or an address to a location that contains integer data. Therefore the programmer must make sure that each operand abides by these rules. The instructions themselves *do not* test each operand to determine whether it is in correct format; the instruction obtains the data designated by the operand and carries out the specified operation. If the data obtained were not in the correct format, the result produced by the operation will be incorrect.

Move Instructions   *7.2*

The move instructions move (copy) the contents of one group of bytes into another group of bytes. The first group of bytes, or *source operand*, can be represented by any addressing mode, register, or literal. The second group of bytes, or *destination operand*, can be represented by any addressing mode or register. All move instructions follow the two-operand arithmetic instruction format. The first operand specifies the data or an address to the data that is to be copied. The second operand specifies the address of where to place a copy of the data.

Move Instruction: MOVt

The **MOV***t* instructions copy the contents of the memory location addressed by the first operand (source field) into the second operand (destination field). The *t* of the MOV*t* instruction indicates the integer data type that is to be copied. Because each data type is associated with a constant number of bytes, the *t* designates the number of bytes to be copied. The *t* can be replaced by either B, W, L, Q, or O.

To understand the use of a MOV*t* instruction, consider a problem where a list of grades must be read. The input file consists of *n* records with each record containing one grade. The last record in the input file contains −1, which is used as an EOF mark. This program can handle up to one hundred grades. The grades are read and are then placed sequentially into an array. Repeatedly executing the instruction MOVL GRADE,GR_LIST[R5] causes each of the grades to be placed sequentially into the array GR_LIST.

In the program in Figure 7.2 both the source and destination of the MOVB GRADE,GR_LIST[R5] instruction are the same integer data type. Data can also be moved when the source and the destination are different integer data types. In that case, keep in mind that the number of bytes copied is indicated by the move opcode. In Figure 7.2 the move instruction copied a byte not because the first and second operands were defined as byte data type, but because the opcode is MOV**B**, where B indicates byte data type. For example, assume the following:

```
SOURCE:       .LONG    ^X7583A543
DESTINATION:  .WORD    ^X0000
DUMMY:        .LONG    0


        MOVW     SOURCE,DUMMY
```

Figure 7.2

```
          .TITLE    FIG72

; THIS PROGRAM READS ONE GRADE AT A TIME AND SEQUENTIALLY BUILDS
; AN ARRAY OF GRADES. THE END—OF—FILE IS INDICATED BY —1.
; THE MAXIMUM NUMBER OF GRADES THAT CAN BE READ IS 100.

          .PSECT    DATA,NOEXE,WRT

GR_LIST_SIZE=100

GR_LIST:  .BLKL     GR_LIST_SIZE          ; DEFINE THE ARRAY
GRADE:    .LONG     0
ARG:      .LONG     1
          .ADDRESS  GRADE

          .PSECT    CODE,EXE,NOWRT
          .ENTRY    START,0
          CLRL      R5                    ; SET INDEX REGISTER TO ZERO
READ:     CALLG     ARG,INPUT

; READ A GRADE INTO MEMORY LOCATION GRADE

          CMPL      GRADE,#-1             ; IF GRADE = —1 THEN
          BEQL      PROCESS              ;    STOP READING
          MOVL      GRADE,GR_LIST[R5]    ; ELSE MOVE GRADE INTO LIST
          INCL      R5                   ; INCREASE INDEX REGISTER BY ONE
          CMPL      R5,#GR_LIST_SIZE     ; IF INDEX REGISTER < 99 THEN
          BLSS      READ                 ;    CONTINUE WITH READING
                                         ; ELSE STOP READING
PROCESS:

          $EXIT_S
          .END      START
```

The contents of memory before and after execution of the preceding MOVL instruction would be

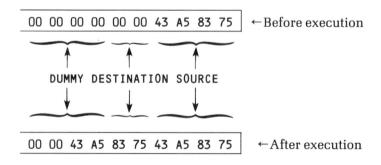

The L of the MOVL instruction indicates that a longword is to be copied starting from SOURCE to DESTINATION. Note that DESTINATION was defined as a word data type. Therefore, in this example, the first two bytes copied will be placed into DESTINATION and DESTINATION + 1; bytes numbered 2 and 3 of the source operand, however, are copied into the first two bytes of the field defined by the label DUMMY.

Another possibility using different data types for the two operands is to copy a word into a longword. To understand this, use the preceding definition of the labels SOURCE and DESTINATION. The instruction and the result produced by executing it would be

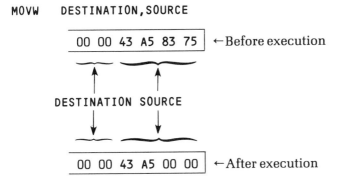

```
MOVW    DESTINATION,SOURCE
```

In this example, bytes number 0 and 1 of SOURCE were replaced with the contents of DESTINATION, and bytes 2 and 3 remain unchanged.

Move Negated Instruction: MNEGt

Another type of integer move instruction is the *move negated*. This move instruction provides the means to change the sign of an integer value. For example, if the source operand contains + 77, the destination operand will receive − 77; and, if the source operand contains − 77, the destination operand will receive + 77. The *t* of the **MNEG*t*** instruction represents the integer data type to be copied, which can be B, W, or L.

To understand the use of a MNEG*t* instruction, consider a problem where a set of temperature readings must be placed into an array. All of the temperatures placed into the array must be positive. Therefore, after each temperature has been read, and before it is placed into the array, the temperature must be tested to determine whether it is negative or positive. If the temperature is negative, it must be converted to positive and then placed into the array. Assume that the input file consists of one hundred records and that each record contains one temperature reading. The end of the input file is indicated by the system EOF mark.

The program in Figure 7.3 uses a procedure to read the temperatures. This procedure tests for the EOF mark and sets a *flag* if it encounters it. A flag is implemented by a memory location that uses one value to indicate that the flag is on and a different value to indicate that the flag is

Figure 7.3

```
                .TITLE    FIG73

; THE MAIN PROGRAM READS TEMPERATURE VALUES INTO AN ARRAY IN WHICH
; THEY ARE STORED AS ABSOLUTE VALUES. THE READING IS PERFORMED
; BY A FORTRAN PROCEDURE. THE FORTRAN PROCEDURE SETS A FLAG
; WHEN THE EOF IS ENCOUNTERED.  THE MAIN PROGRAM TESTS
; THE FLAG TO DETERMINE WHETHER TO CONTINUE WITH READING OR NOT.

                .PSECT    DATA,NOEXE,WRT

ARRAY_SIZE=100

TEMP_LIST:   .BLKL     ARRAY_SIZE
TEMP:        .LONG     0
FLAG:        .LONG     0
ARG:         .LONG     2
             .ADDRESS  TEMP
             .ADDRESS  FLAG

             .PSECT    CODE,EXE,NOWRT
             .ENTRY    START,0
             CLRL      R5
READ:        CALLG     ARG,INPUTEOF       ; PERFORM INPUT
             CMPL      FLAG,#1            ; IF EOF THEN
             BEQL      PROCESS            ;    STOP PROGRAM EXECUTION
             CMPL      TEMP,#0            ; IF TEMP < 0 THEN
             BLSS      CONT               ;    GO TO CONVERT
             MOVL      TEMP,TEMP_LIST[R5] ; ELSE MOVE TEMP INTO LIST
             JMP       INC_REG
CONT:        MNEGL     TEMP,TEMP_LIST[R5] ; MOVE ABSOLUTE TEMP INTO LIST
INC_REG:     INCL      R5                 ; INCREASE INDEX REGISTER
             JMP       READ

PROCESS:
             $EXIT_S
             .END      START
```

off. The MACRO program tests for the flag to determine whether there are any more temperature readings to be read. The sample FORTRAN and Pascal procedures found in Appendix C can be modified so that the flag is set when EOF is read.

Move Zero-Extended Instruction: MOVZt

The move zero-extended instruction is used when an integer value must be lengthened. The lengthening is done by copying the lesser number byte data type into a longer data type and filling the remaining high order bytes of the longer data type with zeroes. For example, the word data type AWORD is to be copying into the longword data type ALONG. The following two instructions define the two constants:

```
AWORD:  .WORD    ^X9999
ALONG:  .LONG    ^X11111111
```

The following is the contents of AWORD and ALONG after the operation of move zero-extended is performed.

| 99 99 | ←Word data type (AWORD)

| 00 00 99 99 | ←Longword data type (ALONG)

One possible use for this type of operation is if during the execution of the multiplication instruction the result produced is too long to be represented by the data type used in the multiplication operation. To prevent this type of problem both of the operands are moved into a larger data type after which the multiply operation is performed on the larger data type. Keep in mind that a different opcode must be used to reflect the changed data type.

In the **MOVZ***t* instruction, the *t* represents two items of information: (1) the integer data type of the source field and (2) the integer data type of the destination field. Each of these items is represented by a letter. Therefore, *t* is replaced by two letters: **BW, BL,** and **WL** (byte to word, byte to longword, and word to longword, respectively). To understand the use of the MOVZ*t* instruction, refer to Figure 7.1. It shows that this program segment, when executed, would produce an overflow error. One way to correct this error would be to copy each operand into a larger (more bytes) data type; for example,

```
VAL1:    .BYTE    91
VAL2:    .BYTE    55
TEMP1:   .WORD    0
TEMP2:   .WORD    0
TEMP3:   .WORD    0

         MOVZBW   VAL1,TEMP1
         MOVZBW   VAL2,TEMP2
         MULW3    TEMP1,TEMP2,TEMP3
```

Note that the multiply instruction used is the MUL**W**3 not the MUL**B**3 which is used in Figure 7.1. This change is necessary because the values that are to be multiplied are represented by word data type rather than byte data type.

An easier way to correct the overflow error would be to redefine the three operands; for example,

```
VAL1:     .WORD     91
VAL2:     .WORD     55
SUM:      .WORD     0


          MULW3     VAL1,VAL2,SUM
```

There are, however, situations when it is not possible to redefine the operands. This occurs when the values used in multiplication arrive from a procedure as a byte data type. In this case the MOVZ*t* instruction must be used.

The MOVZ*t* instruction should not be used to lengthen a negative value, because the sign of the longer data type is always plus. Recall that negative values are represented in two's complement in which case the high order bit is always one. Because of this the use of MOVZ*t* instruction to lengthen a negative value will produce an incorrect value in the longer data type. This error is not flagged, therefore it is up to the user to prevent it. The occurrence of this type of an error is illustrated in the following example.

```
VAL1:     .BYTE     -91
VAL2:     .WORD     55
SUM:      .WORD     0
TEMP1:    .WORD     0


          MOVZBW    VAL1,TEMP1
          MULW3     TEMP1,VAL2,SUM
```

Execution of the preceding instructions produces the incorrect result + 9075 instead of the correct result − 5005. The reason is that the value of − 91 is represented as byte integer data type as follows:

$$1010 \quad 0101$$
$$\uparrow$$

The high-order bit (pointed to by the arrow) indicates the sign of the value. When this value is copied by use of the MOVZBW instruction, byte 1 of the word data type is zero-filled not sign-filled. The contents of TEMP, represented in binary, after the preceding MOVZBW instruction is executed, is as follows:

$$0000 \quad 0000 \quad 1010 \quad 0101 \leftarrow \text{TEMP}$$

Because the sign is not propagated into byte 1 of the word data type, the value used in the multiplication is + 165 instead of − 91. To overcome this problem, a convert instruction must be used in place of the move instruction. Convert instructions are discussed in Section 7.3.

Move Address Instruction: MOVAt

The move address instruction accomplishes the same operation as the .ADDRESS storage directive. The two differ in that the .ADDRESS instruction is a storage directive instruction and is therefore not an executable instruction. This type of instruction is interpreted and translated at the time of assembly. On the other hand, **MOVAt** instructions are executable instructions and can therefore be interleaved among the executable instructions. Because of this, the move address operation is carried out whenever it is necessary to store an address in a memory location.

Move address instructions differ from the rest of the move instructions in that they copy an address rather than the data found at an address. Move address instructions are always represented by the two-operand format. The first operand is an address to be copied. It can be expressed by any addressing mode, but not by a literal or a register. The second operand, the destination operand, must *always* be represented by an address to a longword or a register. The reason is that an address is *always* represented by a longword data type. The t of the MOVAt instruction indicates the data type whose address is to be copied into a longword. The t can be replaced by B, W, L, Q, or O. The following example illustrates how the MOVAt instruction works:

```
A:            .BYTE    78
B:            .WORD    32
C:            .LONG    12
ADDRESS_A:    .LONG    0
ADDRESS_B:    .LONG    0
ADDRESS_C:    .LONG    0


              MOVAB    A,ADDRESS_A
              MOVAW    B,ADDRESS_B
              MOVAL    C,ADDRESS_C
```

To understand what the contents of the longwords addressed by ADDRESS__A, ADDRESS__B, and ADDRESS__C would be, assume that the address for label A is 2000_{16}.

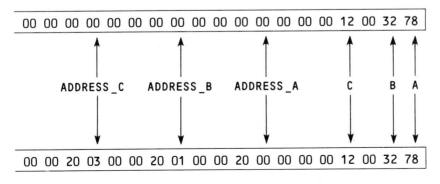

00 00 00 00 00 00 00 00 00 00 00 00 00 00 00 12 00 32 78   ←Memory before execution

ADDRESS_C   ADDRESS_B   ADDRESS_A   C   B   A

00 00 20 03 00 00 20 01 00 00 20 00 00 00 00 12 00 32 78   ←Memory after execution

Note that the contents of the longword addressed by ADDRESS__A contain 2000_{16} and not 78. The 2000_{16} is the address with which label A is associated, and 78 is the value found at the address 2000_{16}.

7.3 *Convert Instruction: CVTt*

The convert integer instruction converts one integer data type into another integer data type. The convert instruction contains two operands: the first operand represents the data or the location of the data to be converted; the second operand represents the location where the converted data is to be stored. The type of data to be converted is indicated by the fourth letter of the opcode, and the type to which it is converted is indicated by the fifth letter. For example, the instruction CVT**BW**, converts a byte to a word data type.

The CVT*t* instructions differ from both MOV*t* (move) and MOVZ*t* (move with zero-extended). The MOV*t* instructions copy the contents of an integer data type into the same length integer data type. The MOVZ*t* instructions copy and extend the contents of a shorter integer data type into a longer integer data type. The CVT*t* instructions copy one integer data type into another; if the destination data type is longer than the source data type, the high-order bytes become sign-filled. When the destination is shorter than the source, the high-order bytes of the source are truncated.

In Chapter 2 it was shown that the negative decimal quantities in memory are stored in two's complement. For example, -3 as represented by the integer byte data type would be

$$\boxed{1\ 1\ 1\ 1\ 1\ 1\ 0\ 1}$$

(Sign bit for the byte data type)

When the instruction MOVZBW is executed using this byte data type as its first operand, the contents of the receiving word would be

$$\boxed{0\ 0\ 0\ 0\ 0\ 0\ 0\ 0\ 1\ 1\ 1\ 1\ 1\ 1\ 0\ 1}$$

(Sign bit for the word data type)

which, when used in another integer instruction as a word data type, would be interpreted as a positive value of 253. If the CVT**BW** (convert byte to word) instruction is used, the contents of the receiving word would be

(Sign bit for the word data type)

which, when used by another integer instruction as a word data type, would be interpreted as a − 3. The extension of the sign bit is necessary to ensure that the high-order bits of the destination data type reflect the correct sign of the value.

In cases when the conversion is from a larger field to a smaller, the high-order bytes are truncated as in Exhibit 7.1.

Exhibit 7.1

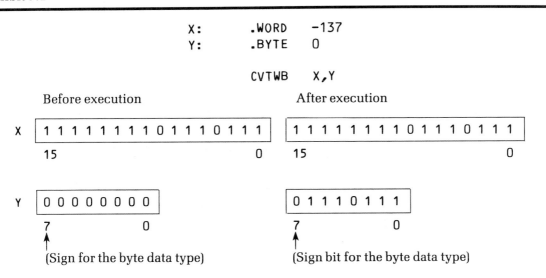

Note that the contents of Y is an incorrect value because the high-order bit is zero (0), which indicates that the value in Y is + 119. The reason the value in Y is incorrect is that − 137 cannot be represented by the byte data type. The largest negative value that can be represented by the byte data type is − 127. Therefore care must be taken when converting from a larger data type to a smaller. Also, note that the computer does *not* stop program execution when this error occurs; it does, however, set the overflow condition code in the PSW.

Condition Codes   *7.4*

All branch instructions make a decision whether to branch or to continue with the execution of the next sequential instruction. The decision to branch or not is based upon the condition code found in the PSW. The majority of VAX MACRO instructions record information about the result obtained from the execution of an instruction. The information that is recorded indicates whether the result was positive, negative, or zero. It also records whether an overflow, underflow, carry, or borrow condition occurred. All of this information is recorded in the PSW (Program Status Word). The PSW is the low-order 16 bits of a hardware register that is the part of the CPU called the PSL (Program Status Longword). Four of the *condition codes* are contained in the low-order 4 bits of the

PSW. The following diagram shows the names and positions of the four condition codes discussed in the following four sections.

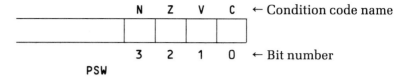

Condition Code: C

The zero bit of the PSW is called the C bit or Carry bit. It is set to 1 when a carry or borrow has been performed. Otherwise it is set to zero. Figure 7.4 illustrates the C bit in PSW. In Figure 7.4(a) the carry bit is set, and in Figure 7.4(b) it is cleared

Figure 7.4

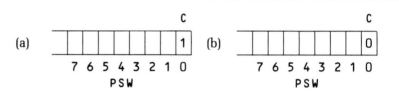

The *carry condition* occurs when an operation causes a carry out of the highest-order bit of a result. For example, consider the following binary addition of bytes:

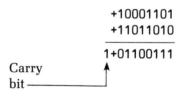

Addition of the high-order bits produces 1 plus 1, which is 0 with a carry of 1.

A *borrow condition* occurs when an operation requires a borrow from beyond the highest-order bit of the minuend. For example:

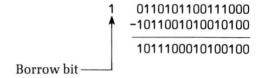

Condition Code: V

The one bit of the PSW is called the V bit or overflow. It is set to 1 when an overflow occurs during the operation of an instruction. Otherwise it is set to zero (0). Figure 7.5 illustrates the V bit in the PSW. In Figure 7.5(a) the overflow bit is set, and in Figure 7.5(b) it is cleared.

Figure 7.5

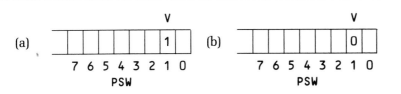

The *overflow condition* occurs when a result becomes too large to be represented by the data type indicated in the opcode. For example,

```
OPER1:    .BYTE    113
OPER2:    .WORD    76


          ADDB     OPER1,OPER2
```

The result obtained by executing this instruction is − 62, because the sum of 113 + 76 = 189, a result that is too large to be contained in the byte data type. The largest possible value that can be contained in a byte is 127. The value − 62 is the overflow value obtained from the subtraction of 127 − 189.

Condition Code: Z

The two bit of PSW is called the Z bit. It is set if the result of an operation is zero (0). If the result is non-zero, the Z bit will be cleared. Figure 7.6 illustrates the Z bit in the PSW. In Figure 7.6(a) the Z bit is set, and in Figure 7.6(b) it is cleared.

Figure 7.6

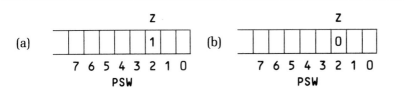

Condition Code: N

The three bit of the PSW is called the N bit. It is set if the result of the operation is a negative value. If the result is zero or a positive value, the N bit will be cleared. Because a value cannot be both negative and zero, the N and Z bits are not normally set at the same time. Figure 7.7 illustrates the N bit in the PSW.

Figure 7.7

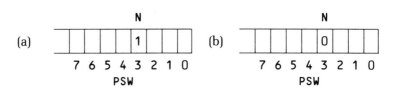

At certain levels of assembly programming, the physical arrangement of the condition codes in the PSW are transparent to the programmer. The reason is that VAX provides a set of branch instructions that are designed to test specific condition codes. For example, the BLSS (branch on less than) tests the N bit in the PSW. The BLSS instruction tests whether the result obtained from a previous instruction is less than zero, because if it is, the execution of the program continues with an instruction other than the next sequential instruction. In such cases we are not concerned with which condition codes to use, but with the fact that the BLSS instruction will test for the correct condition code.

7.5   *Add Compare and Branch Instructions: ACBt*

The add compare and branch instructions provide more freedom when implementing a loop. Loops are usually implemented by initially setting a counter to 0 or 1 and increasing the counter by 1 for each execution of the loop. When the counter has reached a specified value, the loop is aborted. In some applications, after each execution of a loop, the counter should be increased by a value other than 1. The ACB instructions make it possible to step through a loop at increments other than 1. Most higher-level languages such as FORTRAN, PL/1, ALGOL and Pascal have loop control statements that can step through a loop at various increment values. The ACB instructions allow implementation of these more flexible higher-level language loop control statements. The general format of the ACB set of instructions is as follows:

LABEL:	ABCt	LIMIT	,INCREMENT_VALUE	,COUNTER	,DESTINATION_ADDRESS	;COMMENT

Here the *t* represents the data type for the first, second, and third operands. It is replaced by B, W, or L.

You will recall that the opcode of an instruction informs the CU of how many bytes are to be used for each operand during the execution of the instruction. Therefore, to avoid unnecessary errors, the first three operands in the instruction **ACBt** should be defined as the data used for *t* in the instruction. For example, if LIMIT is defined as byte data type, the INCREMENT__VALUE and COUNTER operands should also be defined as byte data type. The big difference between this set of instructions and the SOBGEQ/SOBGTR and AOBLSS/AOBLEQ instructions is the value used to increment the COUNTER. In the SOBGEQ/SOBGTR instructions the value is always −1 and in the AOBLSS/AOBLEQ instructions, the value is *always* 1. In the ACB instructions, the incremental value varies. The computer executes the ACB instructions in the following manner:

```
COUNTER = COUNTER + INCREMENT VALUE
if INCREMENT_VALUE ≥ 0 and COUNTER ≤ LIMIT, then branch
or
if INCREMENT_VALUE < 0 and COUNTER > LIMIT, then branch
```

The ACB*t* instructions allow the incremental value to be a negative value. For example, if you want to start processing a 20 element array with the last value in that array, LIMIT will be assigned a 0, the INCREMENTAL__VALUE will be − 1, and the COUNT will be set to 19. For example:

```
ACBL    #0,#-1,#19,LOOP
```

The LIMIT, INCREMENT__VALUE and COUNTER operands can be represented by a constant, a register, or an address. The fourth operand, DESTINATION__ADDRESS, is an offset. You will recall that an offset is the distance in bytes from the instruction ACB*t* to the instruction to which a branch is to be made. The offset in ACB*t* instructions is contained in a word. As a result, it is possible to branch as far as ± 32767 bytes away. In comparison with the AOB*t* and SOB*t* instructions, the ACB*t* instructions make it possible to branch farther away than the AOB*t* and SOB*t*. This is because the offset in AOB*t* and SOB*t* is contained in 1 byte, which can only contain a value up to ± 127.

To understand the use of an ACB*t* instruction, consider a problem where a variance for a set of test scores is required. The variance is a statistical measure of how the test scores are dispersed. Although the set contains ten thousand test scores, it is not necessary to use every test score in the calculation. Every second test score will be sufficient. The following formula is used to calculate the variance:

$$V = \sum \frac{(x_i - \bar{x})^2}{n - 1} \, i = 1, \dots, n$$

The program in Figure 7.8 calculates the variance. This program calls two procedures: the first procedure calculates the average, and the second calculates the variance. The two procedures were assembled separately.

The SOB/AOB and ACB instructions implement a *post-test loop.* A post-test loop is one in which the loop completion test is done at the end of the instructions that make up a loop. This means that the test for loop completion is done after the loop has been executed at least once. To implement the more common loop, in which the loop completion test is done before the loop execution (*pre-test loop*), an additional test must be

Figure 7.8

```
          .TITLE    FIG78

; THE MAIN PROGRAM CALLS A PROCEDURE WHICH CALCULATES
; THE AVERAGE OF EVERY OTHER GRADE IN THE ARRAY GRADES
; THIS SAME MAIN PROGRAM CALLS ANOTHER PROCEDURE WHICH
; CALCULATES THE VARIANCE OF THE ARRAY GRADES

          .PSECT    DATA,NOEXE,WRT

ARRAY_SIZE=10000

GRADES:   .BLKL     ARRAY_SIZE
VAR:      .LONG     0
COUNT:    .LONG     0
AVE:      .LONG     0
ARG_AVE:  .LONG     3                   ;ARGUMENT LIST TO CALCULATE AVERAGE
          .ADDRESS  GRADES
          .ADDRESS  COUNT
          .ADDRESS  AVE
ARG_VAR:  .LONG     4                   ;ARGUMENT LIST TO CALCULATE VARIANCE
          .ADDRESS  GRADES
          .ADDRESS  COUNT
          .ADDRESS  AVE
          .ADDRESS  VAR

          .PSECT    CODE,EXE,NOWRT

          .ENTRY    START,0

; ASSUME THAT THE LIST OF GRADES IS READ AND COUNTED AT THIS POINT

          CALLG     ARG_AVE,AVERAGE     ;GO TO THE PROCEDURE THAT CALCULATES THE AVERAGE

          CALLG     ARG_VAR,VARIANCE    ;GO TO THE PROCEDURE TO CALCULATE THE VARIANCE

; PRINT THE VARIANCE OBTAINED FROM THE PROCEDURE

          $EXIT_S
          .END      START
$
```

made at the start of the loop. This test will not be part of the loop. To include the pre-test loop in the procedures in Figure 7.8, the following instructions must be added to the two procedures.

```
          CMPL      (R7),#0
          BEQL      END
```

```
END:      RET
```

The first two of the preceding instructions should be inserted right after the .ENTRY instruction. In addition, the instruction RET in its first field must include the label END. This pre-test prevents execution of the loop when there are no test scores.

Figure 7.8 (*continued*)

```
          .TITLE    FIG78A

; BEGINNING OF THE PROCEDURE WHICH CALCULATES THE AVERAGE
; OF N NUMBER OF DATA POINTS.

          .PSECT    DATA,NOEXE,WRT
SUM:      .LONG     0
ADJUSTED_COUNT:
          .LONG     0

GRADES=4
COUNT=8
AVE=12
          .PSECT    CODE,EXE,NOWRT
          .ENTRY    AVERAGE,^M<R5,R6,R7,R8,R9>
          CLRL      R9                      ;CLEAR INDEX REGISTER
          MOVL      GRADES(AP),R6           ;R6 CONTAINS THE ADDRESS OF ARRAY GRADES
          MOVL      COUNT(AP),R7            ;R7 CONTAINS THE ADDRESS OF COUNT
          MOVL      AVE(AP),R8              ;R8 CONTAINS THE ADDRESS OF AVE
          SUBL3     #2,(R7),R5
LOOP:     ADDL      (R6)[R9],SUM            ;ADD A VALUE TO SUM
          ACBL      R5,#2,R9,LOOP
          DIVL3     #2,(R7),ADJUSTED_COUNT

; THE ABOVE INSTRUCTION IN NECESSARY
; BECAUSE EVERY OTHER POINT IS USED IN SUMMATION

          DIVL3     ADJUSTED_COUNT,SUM,(R8)
          RET
          .END
```

Test Instruction: TSTt   *7.6*

The **TSTt** instruction tests its only operand for 0. The result of this operation is the setting of an appropriate condition code. The *t* indicates the data type to be tested, which can be byte (B), word (W), or longword (L). For example, in Figure 7.3 the instruction

```
          CMPL    TEMP,#0
```

could be replaced by the

```
          TSTL    TEMP
```

instruction. The CMPt and TSTt instructions differ in the speed of executing the instruction. The TSTt instructions are executed faster than the CMPt instructions.

Figure 7.8 (*continued*)

```
         .TITLE    FIG78B

; BEGINNING OF THE PROCEDURE WHICH CALCULATES THE VARIAI

SUM:     .LONG     0
ADJUSTED_COUNT:
         .LONG     0


GRADES=4
COUNT=8
AVE=12
VAR=16


         .PSECT    CODE,EXE,NOWRT
         .ENTRY    VARIANCE,^M<R6,R7,R8,R9,R10,R5,R4>
         CLRL      R10                      ;CLEAR INDEX REGISTER
         CLRL      SUM                      ;INITIALIZE SUM
         MOVL      GRADES(AP),R6            ;R6 CONTAINS THE ADDRESS TO ARRAY GRADES
         MOVL      COUNT(AP),R7             ;R7 CONTAINS THE ADDRESS TO COUNT
         MOVL      AVE(AP),R8               ;R8 CONTAINS THE ADDRESS TO AVERAGE
         MOVL      VAR(AP),R9               ;R9 CONTAINS THE ADDRESS OF VARIANCE
         SUBL3     #2,(R7),R4

; THE ABOVE INSTRUCTION IS NECESSARY IN ORDER FOR THE LOOP TO BE
; REPEATED THE CORRECT NUMBER OF TIMES. THIS IS BECAUSE THE COUNT STARTS
; AT ZERO AND NOT AT TWO

LOOP:    SUBL3     (R8),(R6)[R10],R5        ;DATA POINT - AVERAGE OF DATA POINTS
         MULL      R5,R5                    ;SQUARE THE DIFFERENCE
         ADDL      R5,SUM                   ;ACCUMULATE THE SQUARED DIFFERENCE
         ACBL      R4,#2,R10,LOOP           ;IF INDEX < ADJUSTED COUNT THEN
                                            ;   GO BACK TO LOOP
         DIVL3     #2,(R7),ADJUSTED_COUNT   ;   ELSE FINISH CALCULATING THE FORMULA
         SUBL      #1,ADJUSTED_COUNT        ;N - 1
         DIVL3     ADJUSTED_COUNT,SUM,(R9)
         RET
         .END
```

7.7 *Extended Multiply and Extended Divide:*
EMUL and EDIV

The **EMUL** instruction is needed to develop a product that is more precise than is possible with the **MUL*t*** instruction. The **EDIV** instruction is
used when the remainder is to be retained, because the **DIV*t*** instruction
truncates the remainder.

The extended-multiply instruction multiplies first and second operands that are represented by 32 bits; therefore, the possible product of

this multiplication is 64 bits. This instruction, in addition to multiplying the two 32-bit quantities, adds the third operand to the product and stores the result in the fourth operand. For example,

```
A:         .LONG
B:         .LONG
TEMP:      .QUAD
           .ENTRY  START,0

           EMUL    A,B,#0,TEMP      ;A*B+0-->TEMP
```

Operands one, two, and three must be integer longword data type. The product obtained by executing EMUL is a 64-bit quantity; therefore, the fourth operand should be defined as a quadword data type. The execution of the EMUL instruction performs the following list of operations.

1. Oper1 is multiplied by oper2.
2. The result of Step 1 is a quadword data type.
3. Oper3 is converted to a quadword data type with the sign propagated through bits 32–63 of the quadword.
4. The result of the multiplication in Step 1 is added to the new version of oper3.
5. The result (sum) is placed into oper4.

The integer DIVt instructions does not produce a remainder; instead the remainder is truncated. For example, when 17 is divided by 2, the answer is 8 not 8.5. It is sometimes necessary, however, to retain the remainder of the answer. The extended-divide instruction retains the remainder as well as the quotient.

The EDIV (extended-divide) instruction contains four operands as does EMUL. This instruction requires that operands one, three, and four are longword data type while operand two is a quadword data type. This instruction is useful when solving a sequence of operations such as (A*B)/C, which may cause an integer overflow if A and B contain very large numbers. The overflow condition may be avoided by the following sequence of instructions:

```
           EMUL    A,B, #0,TEMP
           EDIV    C,TEMP,ANS,REMAIN
```

To understand the use of the EMUL instruction in a program, consider a problem where the greatest common divisor (GCD) is to be calculated. The program in Figure 7.9 calculates GCD using Euclid's algorithm.

Figure 7.9

```
          .TITLE    FIG79     GREATEST COMMON DIVISOR

; MAIN PROGRAM COMPUTES GREATEST COMMON DIVISOR OF TWO
; INTEGERS (M,N) USING EUCLID'S ALGORITHM;
;         1. REM = REMAINDER (M/N)
;         2. M = N, N = REM
;         3. IF N IS NOT ZERO, RETURN TO STEP 1
; INITIAL DATA IS STORED IN {MO, NO}. ANSWER WILL BE STORED
; IN {RESULT}.  NOTE: NO EXTERNAL ROUTINE OR DATA AREAS ARE USED.

; REGISTER ASSIGNMENTS:
;      {RO, R1} HOLDS M IN QUADWORD FORM
;      R2        HOLDS N
;      R3        REMAINDER FROM DIVISION M/N
;      R4        QUOTIENT FROM DIVISION M/N

        .PSECT    DATA,QUAD,NOEXE,WRT
MO:     .LONG     544                     ; FIRST INPUT VALUE
NO:     .LONG     119                     ; SECOND INPUT VALUE
RESULT: .BLKL     0                       ; RESULT

; MAIN PROGRAM

        .PSECT    CODE,WORD,EXE,NOWRT
        .ENTRY    GCD,0

; INSERT HERE INPUT INSTRUCTIONS IN ORDER TO CALCULATE OTHER GCD

; INITIALIZE REGISTERS

        MOVL      MO,RO                   ; MOVE FIRST VALUE
        MOVL      NO,R2                   ; MOVE SECOND VALUE
        CLRL      R1

; LOOP WHICH COMPUTES THE GCD BETWEEN VALUE IN RO AND R2

LOOP:   EDIV      R2,RO,R4,R3             ; R3 = REMAINDER[M/N]
        MOVL      R2,RO                   ; M = N
        MOVL      R3,R2                   ; N = R3 (REMAINDER)
        BNEQ      LOOP                    ; CONTINUE WITH LOOP UNTIL R3 = 0

; STORE ANSWER

        MOVL      RO,RESULT

; INSERT OUTPUT INSTRUCTION

        $EXIT_S
        .END      GCD
```

Part 2. Enrichment Topics

Use of Integer Instructions in Character Manipulation   *7.8*

In assembly language every character in memory is represented by its
ASCII binary code. Every ASCII binary code is represented by 8 bits in
such a way that its binary representation contains a 0 in the high-order
bit position. By this design all ASCII characters can be treated as positive integer numbers. As a result, integer instructions can be used to perform a limited number of operations on character data. For example,
consider a problem where a line of text is to be edited so that the first letter of each sentence is capitalized and the subsequent letters are lower-
case. Assume that punctuation remains unchanged. The program in Figure 7.10 translates the following lines of text that are defined by the label
SRC.

The output produced from execution of the program in Figure 7.10
is as follows:

```
A TEXT EXAMPLE. a text example. A Text ExamplE.
Special characTER TEST, ***,((((>> 7& ###$.222.
```

This type of operation is possible because each character, number, special character, and so forth occupies 1 byte. In addition, each code represented in a byte is interpreted by the integer instructions as a positive integer number. Therefore, comparisons on these bytes will set the correct
condition code.

Move Complement Instructions: MCOMt   *7.9*

The move complement instruction takes the source operand, converts it
into one's complement, and places the converted data into the destination operand. The *t* in the **MCOM*t*** instruction is to be replaced by B, W,
or L. Figure 7.11 illustrates the use of the MCOM*t* instruction. In the
first instruction in the figure, the contents of the memory location designated by the first operand (00 07) is converted to one's complement
(FF F8) and stored in C, the second operand. The same type of conversion happens in the second instruction, the one's complement of the value (FF F9) is converted and stored in the second operand as (00 06).

Figure 7.10

```
            .TITLE      FIG710

; THE MAIN PROGRAM TRANSLATES A LINE OF TEXT INTO SENTENCES WITH THE
; WITH THE FIRST LETTER CAPITALIZED AND SUBSEQUENT LETTERS LOWER CASE.
; PUNCTUATION IS UNCHANGED.

; THIS PROGRAM USES TWO LOOPS, THE FIRST SCANS FOR THE FIRST LETTER OF
; A SENTENCE AND THE SECOND SCANS FOR A PERIOD ENDING A SENTENCE.

; THE SOURCE TEXT IS DEFINED WITHIN THE PROGRAM. IT BEGINS AT {SRC}
; AND ENDS WITH "$". THE TRANSLATED TEXT IS FOUND AT {DEST}.

            .PSECT      DATA,NOEXE,WRT
SRC:        .ASCII      'A TEXT EXAMPLE. a text example. A Text ExamplE.'
            .ASCII      'Special characTER TEST, ***,((((>> 7& ###$.222.'

DEST:       .ASCII      '**********************************************'
            .ASCII      '**********************************************'

            .PSECT      CODE,EXE,NOWRT
            .ENTRY      START,0
            CLRL        R0                  ; INDEX REGISTER SET TO ZERO

; BEGINNING OF THE LOOP THAT SCANS FOR THE BEGINNING OF A SENTENCE

FIRST_LOOP:
            MOVB        SRC[R0],R1          ; OBTAIN FIRST CHARACTER FROM TEXT
            CMPB        R1,#^A'$'           ; IF TRAILER CHARACTER IS FOUND
            BEQL        DONE                ;      STOP

            CMPB        R1,#^A' '           ; IF CHARACTER IS NOT A BLANK
            BNEQ        NONBLK              ;     CONTINUE WITH NONBLK
            MOVB        R1,DEST[R0]         ;     ELSE MOVE CHARACTER TO DESTINATION
            INCL        R0                  ; INCREASE INDEX REGISTER
            BRB         FIRST_LOOP          ; CONTINUE SEARCH FOR BLANK

NONBLK:     CMPB        R1,#^A'a'           ; IF CHARACTER < 'a' PROCEED TO LEAVE
            BLSS        LEAVE               ;     ELSE CONTINUE
            CMPB        R1,#^A'z'           ; IF CHARACTER > 'z' PROCEED TO LEAVE
            BGTR        LEAVE               ;     ELSE CONTINUE
            SUBB        #^X20,R1            ; CONVERT LOWER CASE TO UPPER CASE

LEAVE:      MOVB        R1,DEST[R0]         ; MOVE CHARACTER TO DESTINATION
            INCL        R0                  ; INCREASE INDEX REGISTER

; SECOND LOOP SCANS FOR THE END OF A SENTENCE

SECOND_LOOP:
            MOVB        SRC[R0],R1          ; MOVE A CHARACTER
            CMPB        R1,#^A'$'           ; IF TRAILER CHARACTER IS FOUND
            BEQL        DONE                ;     STOP PROGRAM EXECUTION
                                           ;     ELSE CONTINUE PROGRAM EXECUTION
            CMPB        R1,#^A'A'           ; IF CHARACTER < 'A'
                                           ;     CONTINUE BECAUSE IT IS PUNCTUATION
            BLSS        CONT                ;     ELSE GO TO CONT
            CMPB        R1,#^A'Z'           ; IF CHARACTER > 'Z'
                                           ;     CONTINUE BECAUSE IT IS LOWER CASE CHARACTER
            BGTR        CONT                ;     ELSE GO TO CONT
            ADDB        #^X20,R1            ; CONVERT TO LOWER CASE
```